PRISONS
AND
PUNISHMENT
IN
SCOTLAND

PRISONS
AND
PUNISHMENT
IN
SCOTLAND

from the Middle Ages
to the Present

JOY CAMERON

Edinburgh
CANONGATE
1983

First published in 1983
by Canongate Publishing Ltd
17 Jeffrey Street
Edinburgh EH1 1DR

ISBN 0 86241 031 2

The publishers acknowledge
the financial assistance of
the Scottish Arts Council
in the publication of this
volume

Printed by Butler and Tanner
The Selwood Printing Works
Frome, Somerset

Contents

To my husband, sons
and grandchildren
with love

Foreword

Dr Cameron has written a book which is topical in the best sense, for it presents material highly relevant to the continuing debate about crime and punishment. Far too often those who are most vocal about present-day problems are singularly ill-informed about the historical background. The truth is that – simply because human nature does not change much from generation to generation – few problems are new; most of those familiar today were live issues in the past as well. Assessment of the merits of different methods of dealing with offenders should therefore take account of the information about the theories and practice of previous generations which Dr Cameron's researches have made available.

Discussion of the prison system is usually based on the assumption that it is something that has always been with us, but Dr Cameron shows that this is not so. There were indeed always prisons, but for long they were places not primarily of punishment but mainly of mere detention, pending trial, conviction and sentence – sentence in the form usually of the capital penalty or transportation. It was not until we ceased to use territories overseas as dumping grounds for undesirables that we turned our minds seriously to providing accommodation for them on a large scale in this country. It is no accident that so many of Scotland's notable prisons were built in the early nineteenth century in the 'baronial' style characteristic of the romantic revival. It was only after 1800 that a prison sentence in the modern sense of the term became the regular penalty for crime, and one of the most interesting parts of Dr Cameron's book is the explanation she gives of the process by which imprisonment came to be a punishment and not merely a stage on the way to punishment.

Dr Cameron covers the factual history of imprisonment in Scotland from medieval times, with ample quotations from the sources and shrewd comments on the social and psychological consequences of prolonged confinement. For those whose interest lies in social history there is ample illustration of the cruelties of earlier times, and there is a chapter on the ever-fascinating subject of the French prisoners of war before and after 1800. To those whose interest lies in current affairs rather than in history the most valuable parts of the book will be her account of recent developments in opinion about the prison system and her description of conditions in prisons today. Those who think our present system barbarous may acquire a sense of proportion when they read of conditions even in fairly recent times, let alone the middle ages, and see the enormous changes which have been made.

The urge to relieve public funds of the cost of maintaining prisoners still has its appeal today, but those who seek economies would hardly share the medieval (and post-medieval) determination that criminals must by some means be got rid of, if only by moving them to the next parish or to another country. Equally, the notion that imprisonment should not be a punishment is one that appeals to modern reformers, but they are not likely to concur with the older view that prison should be a step to the gallows or deportation.

Gordon Donaldson
Historiographer Royal for Scotland

Acknowledgements

In the course of a family discussion some years ago one of our sons observed that while there seemed to be no lack of literature on English prisons little had been written on the history of Scottish ones. Why such neglect, I wondered, especially when prisons and their inmates are of such absorbing interest? Hardly a day passes without their receiving some mention in the media. Surely it was time this gap in our knowledge of Scottish history was filled. In trying to fill it, it became clear to me that the dramatic nature of the subject would have an appeal beyond a specialist readership. This book is therefore written with the general reader also in mind.

Throughout the writing of *Prisons and Punishment in Scotland* I have received the support of many people. My warmest thanks are due to Professor Gordon Donaldson. Without his wise and unfailing encouragement my work would never have seen the light of day.

I would also like to acknowledge the willing assistance of Mr Easterbrook of the Signet Library, Edinburgh, the staffs of West Register House, the Central Library, Edinburgh, the National Library of Scotland, the Royal Scottish Museum, the Royal Commission on the Ancient and Historical Monuments of Scotland, the National Portrait Gallery, London, the Sandeman Library, Perth, the Prison Service College, Polmont, the State Hospital, Carstairs, the Royal Edinburgh Hospital, the Scottish United Services Museum, Edinburgh Castle, and the Lexington Public Library, Massachusetts. The governors and staffs of those Scottish prisons I visited could not have been more helpful.

For the front jacket illustration I thank the Edinburgh City Libraries and for that on the reverse the Prison Service College, Polmont. Those institutions who kindly made available other illustrations are acknowledged in the relevant captions.

The publishers and I are indebted to the Carnegie Trust for the Universities of Scotland for financial aid towards the cost of publication.

Finally I shall always be grateful to my family for their enthusiasm, tolerance, and help.

Joy Cameron
April 1983

1
Medieval Scotland

*The Scots are a bold and hardy race, and much
inured to war.*

Froissart★

*They spend all their time in wars and when
there is no war they fight with one another.*

Ayala†

1

The concept of prison as a form of punishment was virtually unknown in early and medieval Europe. The function of such prisons as existed was purely custodial. The wrongdoer was held in them until he could be disposed of by execution, banishment or mutilation, or until some other solution such as compensation in cash to the victim could be decided upon.[1] Before the reign of David I (1125-53) little is known about the structure of Scottish society, the life of its people, or about 'government' and the maintenance of law and order. The only existing 'laws' that possibly belong to this period are to be found in a code known as 'the laws in use among the "Bretts and Scots"', although that code is in fact little more than a society valuation roll.[2] These local laws certainly persisted until the end of the 14th century; the law of the Gallovidians, for example, survived until at least 1384.

In those early times, everywhere in Scotland, compensation was a matter of course for murder, theft, assault, and all other crimes, the injured person or his kin receiving the awards. The code of Bretts and Scots gives a scale of fines according to the rank of the injured person and the nature of the crime. Thus the 'cro' or blood money for killing the King was given as 1,000 cows, for the King's son 150 cows, for killing a thane 100 cows. In the lower ranks, the fine for slaying an earl was 16 cows. Penalties for lesser crimes were stated in equal detail - if anyone drew blood from the head of a king's son or earl's son the fine was 9 cows, and so on down the line.[3]

With the steady growth of records and charters in the reign of David I we learn much more. Brought up at the court of Henry I he had married an English wife, and returned to his kingdom bursting with English ideas. One of these was the Anglo-Norman feudal system, and David seized the opportunity presented by revolts of the baronial families to deprive them of their lands and bestow these under feudal tenure on Norman friends of his youth. The result was a hierarchy in which many of the great nobles and landlords were of a different race from the common people. Many of them, including at a later date Robert the Bruce, held lands in England as well as in Scotland, their sympathies thereby divided, their patriotism suspect.

David I granted with land the rights and privileges of justice, and this meant jurisdiction over all the inhabitants of the land in a charter. It was granted with the right to hold courts, fine, imprison, and hang vassals, and to fine thieves taken within or without the boundary of one's own jurisdiction. These heritable jurisdictions were to last until 1747.

Gradually the authority of the barons became practically absolute in civil and criminal matters. The weaker successors of David I, notably Robert II and Robert III, allowed the nobles much more power and by the end of the 14th century they were virtually independent. Gradually royal charters granted more and more of the King's rights of justice, including in certain cases the Four Pleas of the Crown – murder, rape, robbery and fire-raising.[4] Not granted was jurisdiction in the crime of treason (crimen majestatis).

Apart from baronial rights, almost the only reference to imprisonment during this period is found in an Assize attributed to David I which states that if a man was accused of theft and had no 'plegius' (surety) he was to be kept in prison until the next court, unless he had been taken 'red-hand.'[5] But the domination of baronial justice emerges in a later Act (attributed to Malcolm II though clearly not earlier than the 12th century) which states that a thief was to be 'led to the presoun of the baron in quhais barony he beis takin.'[6] Scotland came to be divided into royalties and regalities, that is into those lands in which the King's writ ran, and those in which it did not.[7] There were also baronies within the regalities, held from earls, not from the King. Their rights of public justice were also held directly of the earl, although almost always with the proviso that the trial by ordeal was to be held in the earl's court and the executions were to be carried out on the earl's gallows.

The baron led his men in time of war, and the central government relied on the barony as an integral part of the maintenance

of law and order, particularly in outlying districts. This may have
been excellent in theory, but human frailty ensured that it was
very different in practice. For feudalism, although at first a power
for good, eventually degenerated into an instrument of petty
tyranny and greed.[8] This is clearly seen in the record of the Baron
Courts, where everything was arranged to serve the interest of the
strong against the weak.[9]

It is not possible to say when the baron courts began to keep
record of their proceedings. The court of the regality of Aberdeen
was keeping record as early as 1382. The earliest existing record of
a baron court is that of Longforgan, held 1385–1386, but records
were probably kept from a much earlier date for the larger hold-
ings, particularly those of the church.[10] But even after our records
begin, the entries for criminal actions before the baronial courts
'are so brief that they afford no clue as to the procedure which was
followed . . . All the enactments bespeak summary justice, and the
meagre entries in the court books tell the same tale.'[11]

Although the struggle for independence from England created
a fragmentary national consciousness, its effect on the social and
economic life of the country was disastrous. In England the mon-
archs were not too pre-occupied with the Scottish wars to curb
the overweening ambitions of their barons, and the feudal system
itself rapidly withered. But in Scotland the disruptive effect of the
war was much greater. The danger from England was no mere
nuisance but a deadly threat, and the Scots monarchy's task a
much more difficult one. Thus the conflict between Crown and
barons remained unresolved, and the Scottish feudal system with
all its centrifugal trends outlasted the English by some 200 years.
The maligned Stewart kings had atrocious luck, nearly every one
dying before his prime and with his tasks half done. Almost every
heir came to the throne in childhood, and each regency was a
period of virtual civil war among competitors for possession of
the Sovereign's person. A history of the many regents during the
minority of James VI reads like gang warfare in Chicago in the
1920s. Each king on reaching manhood had to begin by clearing
up the mess. The Stewarts' disastrous impetuosity and inflexibility
was probably due to a sense that time was against them. They
were never given a chance to build slowly or to play a waiting
game, 'again and again their work was unravelled in the chaotic

minorities of their children'.[12] The King's Peace was so feeble and intermittent that it was considered noteworthy of the reign of James I (1406-37) that 'the key kept the castle and the bracken bush the cow'. Don Pedro de Ayala, the Spanish ambassador at the court of James IV, wrote in 1498 that 'the Scots are not industrious, and the people are poor. They spend all their time in wars, and when there is no war they fight with one another.'[13]

The ever-present threat of English invasion meant a state of war-like readiness and so feudalism was bound to endure. To mount a large-scale expedition into the Highlands, over non-existent roads, and at the same time risk an English influx from over the Border was a gamble Scottish kings dared not take. So the barons retained their private jurisdictions, civil and criminal, with power of life and death not only over their own vassals but over any stranger in their territory.

For over six centuries the barons dominated Scottish life and in over a hundred heritable jurisdictions their wish was law. More especially in the inaccessible Highlands, but in the Lowlands also, the power of the chief or baron was absolute, and whatever verdict he desired was given by his tacksmen or tenants, who formed the jury. Sometimes a hereditary sheriff would act as both judge and jury and sentence as he pleased, and some even hanged the accused and afterwards called in the jury to convict. The courts were presided over by the baron or his baillie or both. All cases were supposed to be judged by the whole body of the court or the representative section called the jury. But too often an unscrupulous baron could bring undue influence to bear and act as the sole judge himself.

In the barony and regality courts summary justice was swift, and the fearsome pits and dungeons of the heritable jurisdictions were seldom occupied by any individual for long. The barons were realists and did not indulge in the unnecessary expense of keeping and feeding prisoners. The object of captors in this period (and all through the centuries up to the abolition of transportation in 1867) was to get rid of the offender with the least trouble and delay, to have him 'clenzit or conviktt' – freed or hanged; out of sight into the grave, the pit, or the next parish.

This was the general picture but there are indications that exceptions to such speedy justice were sometimes made, from sheer indifference or from private hate and vengeance. Thus the 'wicked Earl of Caithness' put his own son into the pit of his castle of Girnigoe near Wick, where he lay abandoned, filthy, half-starved, until he died a raving lunatic six years later.[14] In the baronial pits prisoners could be kept indefinitely with no questions asked – the length of time depended entirely on the whim of the baron.

In many surviving medieval castles one can still see the pit prison. At Threave Castle, the fourteenth-century stronghold of the Black Douglases on an island in the River Dee in Galloway, there is the pit in which the victims of Archibald the Grim languished without hope. (The Douglases boasted that the castle's gallows knob, a stone which projects from the outer wall at a giddy height, was never without a tassel.) Crichton Castle, near Edinburgh, has a classic example of this technique of confinement – pitch dark, sheer sides lost in the gloom below and an atmosphere calculated to strike fear into the hardiest beholder. Dunvegan Castle in Skye has a pit entered by a trap-door in the floor. It is sixteen feet deep, without light or air save what filters through the trap. Here in the late fourteenth century the wife of Iain, fourth chief of the McLeods, 'starved to death her own two daughters because they had sought to escape from the Castle with their lovers, MacQueens of Roag. The unfortunate young men were flogged to death, and their bodies thrown into Loch Dunvegan.'[15]

The 'pit' in the term 'pit and gallows' has sometimes been misunderstood as referring to the place used for drowning malefactors. In the records of Baron Courts, those found guilty of theft were sometimes drowned.[16] Drowning was in fact the most usual method of executing women, being considered 'more respectful' than hanging.[17] Thus in 1530 Katharine Heriot, accused of theft and bringing contagious sickness from Leith into the city, was ordered to be drowned in the Quarry Holes at the Greyfriars' Port. In cases of very heinous crimes, burning at the stake would be their fate.[18] Men too were sometimes drowned instead of hanged; in July 1568 the Regent Moray 'rode to St. Andrews, and causit drown a man callit Alexander Macker and six more, for piracy'.[19] It is possible that in the very early period wrong-doers were drowned in some form of pit which, like the gallows, may have been outside the castle, but later the fossa or pit within the castle walls was nothing more than the baron's dungeon. It obviously afforded the lord satisfaction to sit at ease in his castle with his enemy secured in the pit below.[20]

In the course of time the power of the despots was curtailed by withdrawing the Crown Pleas from their jurisdiction, and later still by limiting their power over homicides to cases where the slayer was taken red-handed, and over theft to those where the thief was taken with the fang (with the stolen goods in his possession). The minor proprietors who held of the barons may never have possessed the power of life and death over their vassals, and for the most part their authority in matters criminal was restricted to punishing petty thefts and exacting 'bludwites' (penalties for the shedding of blood, short of killing). Their relative impotence left them often at the mercy of their own tenants, for 'It would appear to have been esteemed no felony to pilfer from the laird ... in spite of all that he could threaten or devise, his greenwood fell before their thieving hatchets. They stole his peats, they trespassed in his hainings.'[21] Thanks to the strong construction of medieval castles, we know more about the pits in which the owners of heritable jurisdictions put their prisoners than we do about any other Scottish prisons of the period. In a village there might be a place of custody, simply 'the theivis hoill'. Like the average domestic building of the time it would consist of a small thatched hut with a damp earth floor and a small opening through which meagre rations would be pushed (if the prisoner was lucky). But it was virtually impossible to keep prisoners secure, there being no regular jailer, and breakouts were easy and frequent. As prisons were of limited usefulness, poverty-ridden communities would not construct elaborate and permanent structures even in the smaller towns, where any empty hovel would be deemed adequate for the temporary housing of malefactors.

Some of the larger towns however could boast of two prisons. There were the castle dungeons, appalling places hewn out of the living rock, where throughout the centuries state and political prisoners were kept, Edinburgh, Blackness, Falkland and Doune. There were also the Tolbooths, where less important prisoners were sent. A 'tolbooth' was originally a booth at a fair, where dues or tolls were collected and offenders against the fair regulations were detained. Gradually it became the building in which the

courts of justice met and criminals were imprisoned. In any early
Scottish burgh 'after the Church, the Tolbooth or Town House
was the principal edifice. It comprised council chamber, court
room and prison and was at first a tower structure, as at Tain, and
later a hall and attached tower, approached generally by a fore-
stair.'[22] The late-sixteenth-century three-storeyed Tain Tolbooth
is one of the few surviving buildings of this class. Canongate
Tolbooth in Edinburgh is of the same period. Criminals were
punished at the town cross from which also proclamations were
made. The thieves' hole in the Old Tolbooth of Edinburgh was
presumably the 'sext buith' (sixth booth), which was 'maid a
presoun' in 1480-1, and which was occasionally referred to as 'the
nether (lower) hole'.[23]

Fifteenth-century statutes certainly assume the availability of
prisons. An Act of James I states that if a man is guilty of 'forthocht
felony or throw suddande chaudemellay' (a fit of rage) then 'the
life and the gudes of the trespassour to be in the Kingis will, to
quhais preson he salbe sende incontinent'.[24] By an Act of James III
in 1487 entitled 'Of the keiping of arreisted trespasseures' (the
earliest authentic notice of prisons in the records of the Scottish
Parliament), the Crown undertook responsibility for safe custody
of prisoners before trial, either by imprisoning them in the King's
castles, or by handing them over to the Sheriff to be maintained at
the cost of the state, failing resources of their own.[25] It has been
said that 'There is little doubt but that the King's prison was the
King's castle, while the Sheriff's prison meant that the transgressor
was warded in the house of an officer of the Crown or of the
burgh.'[26]

The general term for confinement came to be 'warding', and
the term 'in ward' was applied for several centuries to all those
sent to prison.[27] A prisoner might be warded in the Castle, Tolbooth, his own house or private lodgings, and the confinement
might be 'close', or within an area of two to four miles; and
generally those in ward had to 'remayne upon thair awin expenses'. In ordinary cases full liberty could be procured by getting
some responsible person to become security for the reappearance
of the individual in ward when required.[28] Often those committed
to ward in a prison were kept there only until they had paid or
found security for payment of a fine, frequently in kind. Warding

in the Tolbooths was often 'open and free ward', which meant that the door was not locked, the prisoner being free to come and go as he pleased.

Edinburgh's was the best known of all the Tolbooths. By 1555 the Old Tolbooth of 1480 now consisted of an iron room where prisoners sentenced to death were immured, secured by irons and shackles, a thieves' hole, a jailer's house, and possibly one or two other rooms as well. By 1561–62 it had become so ruinous that the magistrates were ordered to demolish it. The new Tolbooth was erected on a site covered by part of the Signet Library, and provided accommodation for the Lords of Session and the Town Council. A section of St. Giles' Cathedral was partitioned off and converted into a prison, municipal offices etc., and was also called tolbooth. Parliament and the Court of Session met there and communications between the two buildings was by a covered passage. Thus there were three tolbooths at this time in Edinburgh; the Old Tolbooth was never wholly taken down, 'The eastern and first prison-part, originally known as the Belhous, remained down to 1817 much as it had existed prior to 1560, in which year it became wholly a prison, while the western portion was restored in 1610–11 and, undergoing repairs from time to time, also survived till 1817.'[29]

In Dundee in 1325 Robert I granted permission to build a Tolbooth with cells for prisoners in the Sea-Gait. In 1359 David II granted ground for an extension because by that time the Castle of Dundee, used for confining prisoners, had gradually crumbled away, the stones being used for other purposes.[30] This extended Tolbooth was abandoned in 1440, when a new one was built facing the Nethergait; it was used for meetings of the Town Council and the Burgh Courts. By 1550 this too was crumbling and yet another Tolbooth rose on the site of the later Town House, incorporating stones from the Franciscan monastery destroyed at the Reformation. This Tolbooth was used as a Council House and jail until 1730.

In Perth the 'old jail' stood at the foot of the High Street near the old bridge. It incorporated part of the ancient St. Mary's Chapel, destroyed by the great flood of 1210 and rebuilt on the same site. It is not known when it was converted into a prison, 'but it was sufficiently gloomy for this purpose',[31] In addition to the Tolbooth, use was made of the 'Spey Tower', which was 'a fortress, upon the city wall, near to Earl Gowrie's Palace, and had in it a strong prison.'[32]

Since the tolbooths were often in disrepair, church steeples were frequently used to imprison delinquents[33] until they had paid to be redeemed from ward. In some prisons there were cages of strong wood and iron to hold prisoners of special importance.[34]

In medieval Scotland planned imprisonment did not come within the scheme of things. Our ancestors would have thought us crazed to imprison men – and clothe and feed them – for ten, twenty or thirty years. Rehabilitation is a costly luxury which relatively under-developed societies cannot afford. And originally the transgressor was simply a menace to be disposed of, incorrigible, an outcast. Those in authority had neither time nor wish to try to transform him into a 'useful member of society'.

If prison did not loom large in the early period, savage and brutal punishments did. A wretched thief, caught infang (red-handed), received short shrift. If a notour or common thief he had his ears cropped and cheek branded, and it only remained – and he had not long to wait – 'that he be "whipped at a cart-tail and hangit till he be deid" upon the neighbouring gallows'.[35] In addition to the death penalties by beheading, hanging, drowning, and burning, tortures included wrenching of the head with cords, tearing off the nails with pincers, scourging with branding, cutting out tongues or boring them through, cutting off ears and hands. Common forms of milder punishments were branding and mutilation, banishment (often preceded by public whipping), nailing of ears to the tron (a public weighing machine), penance in the kirk, chaining to the jougs (iron rings at the end of a chain attached to a wall of the kirk), or the branks (an iron helmet with a spike to enter the mouth and prevent speech – a favourite punishment for scolds and slanderers), the pillory and the stocks. The object of the last two was to expose the culprit to public ignominy and humiliation. Banishment was vaguely 'furth of Scotland', or simply and very popularly 'to the next parish' where the neighbouring township could cope with the delinquent. A man could be denounced 'at the horn' and pronounced an outlaw if he did not appear to stand trial.

The most barbarous tortures of all were inflicted on the hapless witches (this with the strong approval of the populace) and on political prisoners (usually by members of the royal family). In 1437 the murderers of James I were put to death with the most inhuman and revolting cruelty, 'perhaps the most appalling that is recorded in our country's history',[36] being devised by the dead King's widow, the English Lady Joan Beaufort, his gentle 'milk-white dove'. Sir Robert Graham, the leader of the conspiracy, had his right hand nailed to a gallows set up in a cart in which he was then dragged through Edinburgh; the executioners ran hot iron spikes into his thighs and arms, and finally, after seeing his son slain before his eyes, he was quartered. The Earl of Athole, another of the plotters, suffered horrible agonies for three days. He was set in a pillory, on his head a red-hot iron crown inscribed 'The King of Traitors'; next day he was bound on a hurdle and dragged at a horse's tail through the streets; on his last day he was laid on a plank and disembowelled alive; his heart was cut out and cast into a fire. His head was cut off, exposed to the view of all, and set on a pole in the highest place of the city. His body was divided into four quarters, which were sent to be hung up in the chief Scottish cities.[37] The earl's grandson was 'only' hanged and quartered. 'After this manner was the death of James revenged, barbarous indeed, and which exceeds the bounds of humanity.'[38]

In cases of very heinous crimes like witchcraft, unnatural offences and (in the fifteenth century) heresy, those convicted were usually condemned to be bound to 'ane staik and wirreit' (strangled) and the body to be burnt to ashes. In even more atrocious cases sentence was 'to be brunt in assis, quick (alive) to the death.' In cases of treason a man would be executed with barbarous rites, a female by burning. In 1537 the Lady Glamis was condemned to be burnt on the Castle Hill of Edinburgh on a trumped-up charge of witchcraft and plotting to kill James V, who hated her Douglas brothers. 'Barrels tarred and faggots oiled' were piled around her and she was burnt to 'assis' in sight of her husband and son.[39]

In the fifteenth century there was still nothing that could be called a regular system of public prosecution. In crimes of public concern, such as heresy, witchcraft, unnatural offences and treason, the charges would be instigated by one or other authority, but in offences against an individual the right to prosecute belonged to that person or his relatives. In such cases, but not only in these, criminals might be allowed to compound their felonies. Pitcairn's *Trials* illustrate (in 1493, in the reign of James IV) the great number of crimes for which an accused person was permitted to compound by heavy fines. These included slaughter, theft, 'intercommuning with the English' (always heavily frowned on, but surprisingly frequent), horse- and cattle-stealing and adultery. Fines were paid to the King; compensation to individuals was a matter for private negotiation. 'Assythments and "letters of slains", which were a device to prevent violent reprisals for wrongs already committed, were a "familiar part of Scots Law" '[40] in the sixteenth century. The next-of-kin of the victim would subscribe letters of slains and in return receive assythment or compensation, the price which the culprit had to pay. An entry in the Records of the Privy Council for 1605 gives an example of assythment, 'William Linlithgow against Hamilton of Stenhaus for payment to him of 1,000 lib, as the assythment appointed to him for losse of his luggs.'

If sureties were not found, then the accused was 'hangit or drownit'. For the poor with no sureties there was no possibility of compounding, only one end after forty days, even if guilty only of 'pikry' or petty theft. But 'Probably banishment was more popular ... because it was simpler, and also cheaper, than the penalty of death. Hanging an undesirable was a costly business with little or nothing to be gained in return by way of escheats or otherwise'.[41] Nevertheless the death penalty was often meted out.

Imprisonment as a form of punishment is mentioned only occasionally; in 1510, for deforcing a King's messenger at Selkirk, some 200 persons 'shall be put in sure prisons for the space of a year and a day ... and their lives to be at the King's will; and all their moveable goods to be escheated to the King'.[42] In the same year, when John Dalglese was tried for burning Branxham and Ancrum, intercommuning with the English, theft and common treason, he could not find sureties to satisfy the parties and judgement was given that he should be warded by the Sheriff forty days – and 'if he could not find sureties ... should be hanged'.[43]

Sentencing anomalies are inevitable under any judicial system, but in Scotland it would seem that if the accused was very poor and unable to find surety, he paid dearly for his crime. If on the other hand he had money or influence he might hope to escape the harsher consequences. This is illustrated by Pitcairn's stern comments that 'The conduct of the Sheriff of Wigtoun ... affords a melancholy picture of the state of society ... the highest legal functionary in the district, appears to have vied with the most desperate of the Border thieves in the commission of all sorts of crimes; expecting doubtless that his high office and influence would sufficiently protect him from merited punishment for his odious oppressions'. And so it did, for in 1513 the Sheriff and two others were granted remission for the slaughter of two men, for the mutilation of another, and for stealing cows. Their surety was the Sheriff. Earlier, in 1509, he had been fined five merks for taking a bribe to acquit a murderer. But he stood no nonsense from other malefactors, and in 1510 a man who stole twenty oxen from him 'under silence of night' was beheaded.[44]

Scotland was a poor country. Froissart, describing the expedition thence (as Scotland's allies against the English) of Sir John de Vienne and his nobles in 1385, reported that 'Scotland is a very poor country and the people generally envious of the good fortunes of others and suspicious of losing anything themselves', and the French knights, accustomed to better things, 'were by no means pleased at the poverty they had to encounter'.[45] When Aeneas Sylvius (later Pope Pius II) visited Scotland in 1435 he was disturbed by the great numbers of beggars he saw everywhere. 'In this country I saw the poor, who almost in a state of nakedness begged at the church doors.'[46] But 'The poverty of medieval Scotland has been exaggerated, mainly because travellers' tales are easier to quote than the more reliable evidence of records'.[47] and it must be noted that there was an improvement in the general standard of living in the late fifteenth century which 'saw the foundation of many collegiate churches, a considerable development in domestic architecture, and the erection of many burghs of barony'.[48]

Yet the chaotic years of royal minorities between 1406 and 1528 and a sequence of bad harvests all swelled the numbers of hungry beggars who swarmed over the countryside, these numbers probably increased by the frequent sentences of banishment from various parishes and the consequent rootlessness and destitution of the offenders.

The constant stream of measures against beggars contain occasional references to imprisonment. By an Act of James I (1425) the sheriff was to 'inquire diligently' if any idle men with nothing to live on were at large. He had power to arrest them and keep them in 'festynance' (confinement) while enquiries were made. If they were unable to find employers within forty days the sheriff was to arrest them again 'ande sende thaim to the Kingis preson to byde ande be punyst (punished) at the Kingis will'.[49] In 1455 beggars were to be treated as common thieves, or reivers.[50] An Act of James II in 1457 forbade anyone between the ages of fourteen and seventy to beg unless provided with a 'tokyn' from the sheriff or baillies certifying that they could not work; beggars without tokens to be branded and banished – not imprisoned.[51] When licensed to beg they wore tokens or pewter badges and blue gowns, and were known as the 'gaberlunzies' or wandering beggars. Scott's Edie Ochiltree in *The Antiquary* is an example. However the numbers of vagrants, 'sorners and masterful beggars', continued to increase, and later fifteenth century Acts enjoined the cropping of ears and banishment; if they returned to the district they risked death by hanging. But the Scottish penal clauses were not as severe as contemporary English ones, and an Act of James IV in 1503 allowed begging by 'cruiked-folke, seik-folke, impotent folke and weak folke.'[52] An Act of 1535 revived the legislation of the previous century, with an 'additioune' confining licensed beggars to their parish of origin.[53] 'It can hardly be doubted that in sixteenth-century Scotland life was so precarious for the mass of the people that there were always many who were on or near the level of poverty or even starvation, and the numerous paupers are often alluded to in legislation and in contemporary writings.'[54]

2
Crimes or Sins?
1560-1747

A wild world, my masters, this Scotland
of ours must have been . . .
'For treason, d'ye see,
Was to them a dish of tea,
And murder bread and butter'.
                              Scott's Journal★

2

In sixteenth-century Scotland there was no shortage of crime. 'Men were accustomed to violence in all forms, as to their daily bread ...'[1] They were ignorant, superstitious, full of vehement intolerance. A contemporary historian in 1571 gave the grave opinion that 'All people were cassin sa lowse and war becum of sik dissolute myndis and actions, that nayne was in accompt bot he that could ather kill or reve his nychtbour'.[2] The country was said to be 'in sik deformitie that Justice appeirtet ruggit up be the rutes'.[3] The Highlands and the Borders were in a chronic state of lawlessness and disorder, but fighting was also common in the Lowlands. 'Churchmen fought hand-to-hand in Glasgow Cathedral',[4] and Edinburgh in the time of James VI was said to be 'the ordinary place of butchery, revenge and daily fights'[5] for nobles and their followers provoked many savage brawls in the 'Hie Gait'.

The Privy Council records a list of violent family feuds which took place within five miles of Holyrood. James VI tried vainly to put a stop to them, particularly in 1587 and 1595. In his *Basilikon Doron*, published in 1599, he commented that their honour required the nobility for any evil done to them 'to take up a plaine feide against him, and (without respect to God, King or Common-weill) to bang it out bravelie, hee and all his kinne against him and all his'.[6] 'Banging it out bravely' seems at this distance in time to lend a romantic gloss to what was a brutally destructive way of life. This chronic disorder accounts for the great number of Acts of Parliament against such common crimes as umbesetting of ways (waylaying), robbery, stouthrief (theft with violence), theft, rapt (rape or, more often, kidnapping), hamesucken (assaulting a man in his own house), and violence of all kinds.[7] Competing jurisdictions also accounted for much hindrance to law and order. If the accused was powerful he would present himself at the bar with as many armed friends and retainers as 'would do for him'. So did Bothwell appear at the mock trial for Darnley's murder. Maitland of Lethington contrasted the excellence of Scots laws with the violence with which their execution was too often oppposed:

> 'To make acts we have some skeil;
> God woteth if we keip them weil!
> We come to Bar with jack of steil.'

The whole nation would seem to have spent their time, as one malefactor expressed it, 'in drinking deep, and taking deadly revenge for slight offences'.[8]

The Bloody Roll of Perth lists the names of persons dwelling in Perth indicted for crimes punishable by death committed in the period 1556–1580. These include murder (on one occasion by drowning in the Tay), sedition and riots, witchcraft, importing false coin, mutilation.[9] Execution could be a costly process, and a letter to the Provost of Perth on behalf of the Duke of Athole in 1719 illustrates this: 'I have a letter from my Lord the Duke of Athole, desiring I might wryte to you hoping to allow the hangman of your toun to go to Logyrate and execute the two thieves, condemned and lying prisoners there, and that you will deliver him to Alexander Mitchell, his Grace's Chamberlain here, who will bait [feed] him and send some men with him to guard him up the country. I doubt not but you ... will comply with this.[10]

Edwin Muir described the prevailing mood well when he wrote of 'the stubborn anger that burns through Scottish history'[11] and it is against this sorry background of rage and violence that we must discuss the place occupied by crime, prison and punishments generally in Scottish society. Attitudes to crime are usually dictated by expediency, society's self-protection being the paramount consideration. In the absence of any effective central authority one would expect to find an ill-assorted record of arbitrary punishments for the usual run of crimes, varying from one part of the country to another and dependent on the idiosyncrasies of the local dispenser of justice, his vindictiveness, his degree of practical authority and his enlightenment or otherwise. Such was precisely the case in Scotland before the mid-sixteenth century.

The Reformation and the discipline exercised by the General Assembly and the Kirk Sessions transformed that pattern. The catalogue of crimes expands and the emphasis placed on the peculiar atrocity of certain offences rather than others shifts, as does the severity of their punishment. The new religious establishment was not primarily concerned with protection from violence or with crimes against property but with weeding out and punishing behaviour thought to fall short of the ways of God. The accent had shifted from expediency to a moral code. The sixteenth and seventeenth-century Scottish crime sheets illustrate the contemporary attitude which held the most pernicious crimes to be those against religion and morality. Throughout the period public opinion was coloured by religious influences. While the general picture of the country remained apparently unchanged in the universal lawlessness, ferocity and licence, and lack of any powerful central authority (which was the cause), a new influence had in fact exploded upon the scene.

It is impossible to understand the period and its attitude to crime without reference to the power of the General Assembly and the Kirk Sessions. Dictatorial, formidable, inquisitorial as the Kirk Sessions were, their efforts had an important effect on public order. 'The most important curb on outbreaks of violence may have been provided not by any of the older courts, still less by the new justices, but by the Kirk Sessions, which had existed here and there since 1560 but which first became generally effective in the early seventeenth century ... It may well be that one important factor in the reducing of Scotland to order was the persistent work of the Kirk Sessions in the parishes up and down the country. The Kirk Session was apt to be closely linked with the secular magistracy in the burghs ...'[12]

The 'crimes' of fornication, adultery, blasphemy, sabbath-breaking, slanderous language, drunkenness, 'horrid' swearing, witchcraft, and unnatural offences figure largely in the Kirk Session records and the Kirk was zealous in tracking down and punishing offenders. They manifested a peculiar delight in investigating cases of 'licentious intercourse' and in 'dealing with' offenders.

The Kirk Sessions used imprisonment in a way hardly known before and for this they had statutory authority. After the pro-

scription of Popery by Parliament in 1560 one of the first acts of
the legislature was to impose a punishment for the 'filthy vice of
fornication'. The penalty for a first offence was a fine of forty
pounds Scots and, on failure to pay, eight days in prison on bread
and water and two hours in the pillory. For a second offence the
fine was a hundred merks and a shaven head. For a third offence,
a hundred pounds Scots and to be ducked thrice in the deepest and
foulest pool in the parish and to be banished therefrom for ever.
In 1582 Perth Kirk Session ordained one John Ronaldson who had
in his custody 'fornicators, to put every one of them in ane sundry
house in time coming, to give them but bread and small drink; to
let none of them come to the nether window, and when they
come to the Cross Head that they be fast locked in the irons two
hours' – this under pain of loss of his office. And in the same year
a woman, after confessing her fornication, was put 'in the ward of
the fornicators, above the North Kirk door'.[13] Adultery was first
made a capital crime in Scotland by an Act of 1563: 'For-sa-meikle
as the abhominabil and filthie vice and crime of adulterie, hes bene
perniciously and wickedly used within this Realm in times by
gane ... It is statute and ordained ... that all notour and manifest
committers of adulterie in onie time to cum ... sall be punished
with all rigour unto the death, alsweil the woman as the man.'
However the supreme penalty was by no means invariably ex-
acted. In 1579 a man charged with the 'filthie cryme of adulterie
... hes bene keipit straitlie in ward within the tolbuith of Edinburgh' for more than sixteen weeks.[14] And in 1619 it was reported
that 'For as meikle as William Marshall, an auld doyted man, has
confessed his adultery with Janet Ramsay, and because that his
compearance publickly in sackcloth at the Kirk door and repentance stool would be an reproach to the toun [perhaps on the
theory that grey hairs should not be ridiculed] therefore it is
thought expedient that he be put in ward and detained therein, ay
and while he willingly consent to be banished this toun for ever'.[15]
These offenders could count themselves fortunate, for cases are
reported of others being hanged. Thus one John Gutherie, a
'notair' adulterer before the Kirk Session of Kirkliston in 1617, did
penance in sackcloth for his 'impurities' and was later hanged.[16]
In 1627 a man and woman guilty of 'adulterous commerce' were
hanged on the same day on a gibbet on the Castlehill.[17]

Hanging, banishment, and prison were not the only penalties imposed upon fornicators and adulterers. In 1585 a Perth man, for fornication with three women, was ordered to be 'warded, shaven and doukit.'[18] Also in 1585, for 'filthy fornication', a couple were ordered to be 'carted backward through the toun... having paper hats on their heads', and were then to be kept in prison till the next Sunday when, still wearing their paper hats, they were to sit on the stool of repentance in church.[19] It was important in the Church's eyes that sinners should be *seen* to be disgraced. Thus a pronouncement in 1605: 'Because that the sins of fornication and adultery do increase more and more among us, to the great offence and dishonour of God, and slander of this congregation; therefore ... the Session ordains a more public place of repentence to be biggit with all dilligence ... that therein fornicators and adulterers may be distinguished and better discerned, both by their place and habit.'[20] With this object the stool of repentence in every church was placed in a prominent position before the congregation and upon it the unfortunate penitent was perched, the scorned cynosure of the righteous, while the minister thundered of the hellfire to come. (In 1590 in Perth an order was given 'to buy timber to make a substantial ladder to the cockstool', thus indicating the height to which it was advisedly raised.) First offenders were 'delated' (or accused) of the offences, appeared before the Session, confessed and repented before the whole congregation. The number of appearances depended upon the heinousness of the offence. For example in 1648 the General Assembly laid down that fifty-two appearances be required for incest, and lesser numbers for other offences.

Members of the public could be pruriently eager to testify against sinners. Thus 'comperint George Kilgor student in the old colledge who being sworn deponit that in the last vacance in east Lotithian he and Mr. Thos. Wylie being walking ane day up through the fields at the back of Tranent they found a woman gathering peiss who desquit us to walk mair quicklie and we wold find twa sinners lying togither in the wayside qlk we did and found ane man and ane woman lying togither in the act whether of adulterie fornication or utherwqifs we know not...' The male culprit made an attempt to avoid the shame that awaited them. He said, 'What know ye but she may be my wyiff'. The woman,

Margaret Steward, was reported to the Kirk Session of Preston-pans.[21]

John Knox is often blamed for the austerity of the Scottish Sabbath. Professor Donaldson points out that it was not until 1579, seven years after Knox's death, that a statute imposed penalties for both working and playing on Sundays.[22] Sabbath-breaking, drunkenness, and swearing were usually placed in the same category and punished by fines and repentance on the stool before the congregation, or by a few hours in jail. In 1587, for profane swearing, David Innes was threatened with banishment from Perth if he should offend a second time. Stern efforts were made to repress boys who played football or 'the gowf' on the Inch of Perth in 'the time of preaching'. Zealous elders would sometimes find backsliders drinking on the Sabbath, as in 1612 when Isabell Murdoch, found 'drinking with an Highlandman in time of preaching', was committed to ward. In 1611 a deacon of the Kirk, called to answer for his wife's 'dicing and drinking' in his house on the Sabbath while he was in the Kirk, refused to present his wife to the Session and was therefore put in ward, 'there to remain while he should be better humbled.' In 1621 John Hynde, accused of 'uttering of disdainful speech' against the minister, tried to excuse himself by answering that 'in his rough humour after drink he spoke it', but was committed to ward. In 1622 Margaret Melling was apprehended 'for stiffening ruffs and over-lays on a Sunday. Being sickly ... she was admonished on her knees'. In 1675 merchants were delated for selling unnecessary goods on the Sabbath and had to promise not to sell 'except neidfull tobacco or bread'.[23]

The decision to imprison convicted persons seems sometimes to have depended on their ability to maintain themselves there. In 1602 a couple having admitted fornication, the Session 'understood that they are both poor bodies, having nothing either to pay in penalty or to entertain themselves in ward ... therefore ordering them to be put in ward, while [until] Saturday, on their expences'. The unfortunates were then to be 'carted about the toun together, and thereafter to be banished'.[24]

The Scottish Parliament of the reign of Charles II obediently passed statutes against Sabbath-breaking, swearing, drinking and other profanities and immoralities. One of these prescribed death for 'railing against God'. Scots Law thus followed both Jewish and Roman Law in making blasphemy a capital offence, and in 1697 an Edinburgh student, Thomas Aikenhead, was hanged for repeatedly declaring that 'theology was a rhapsody of ill-invented nonsense'.[25] Robert Louis Stevenson commented that 'Aitkenhead was hanged for a piece of boyish incredulity'.[26] A statute of 1661 ordained that a child over sixteen years who 'not being distracted, shall beat or curse either their father or mother, shall be put to death without mercy.' And the Chronicle of Perth relates that in 1618 the minister at Cargill 'for sum infamous writtingis and railling aganes the scottis natioun, werie onnaturallie, he being on of the sones of the hous of Craigie'[27] was beheaded in Edinburgh and his body quartered and transfixed upon the city gates.

The energies of Kirk Session and Assembly were not exhausted by the harrying of such offenders. They invaded every corner of their parishioners' lives to the extent that no independence of thought or action was permitted. In 1586 for example Perth Kirk Session decreed that unmarried sisters were not to live together but were to go out to service, 'under pain of warding their persons and banishment of the town', while in 1595, for travelling to the Roman Catholic country of Portugal, a man was censured and 'admonished not to travel to these parts again except that they were otherwise reformed in religion'.[28]

Although the sentences for fornication and adultery are shown to vary, in severity as well as form, these meted out for 'unnatural offences' and for witchcraft and heresy were usually merciless and of the utmost savagery. David Hume catalogues a series of these 'horrid crimes' or unnatural offences. Thus John Swan and John Litster, convicted in 1570 of 'the wild, filthie, execrabill, detestabill and unnatural sin of sodomy', were strangled at a stake and their bodies burned to ashes. Michael Weir, for incest, bestiality and sorcery in 1670, was 'wirreit' (strangled) at a stake and his body burned. Three 'abhorred offenders' in 1662, 1702, and 1719 all suffered the same fate for bestiality. But for the same offence in 1675 James Mitchell was drowned in the Nor' Loch 'between four and five in the morning, that the public eye might not be offended by the spectacle of the death of so vile a criminal'. George Sinclair was drowned for incest in 1628,[29] and in 1649 fate caught up with James Wilson who, being found guilty of incest committed thirty-five years earlier, as well as of adultery, was ordered to be beheaded next day on Castle Hill and his estate forfeit.[30] There are references to 'wild incests' – a strange description. One thinks of incest as essentially furtive, but the adjective somehow suggests the accompaniment of fiddle music or a fanfare of trumpets.

In 1675 at the court of Inveraray, Duncan McKawis in Knockantymere was convicted of having 'comitted the vyle and abominable crime of Bestialitie with ane whyte mear pertaining to Thomas Weir in Knockantymere ... the said Duncan wes sein in the verie act of that horreid cryme'. He was strangled at a stake and then burnt. The mare also was 'killed and burnt' – presumably on the assumption that she was a consenting party.[31]

Much energy was expended by the Kirk Sessions in hunting out young women suspected of infanticide and old women suspected of witchcraft. In January 1681 four women were hanged for murdering their illegitimate children. A few months later another woman was hanged in the Grassmarket for murdering her child, having declared that she had committed the deed in order to escape the ignominy of the church pillory. The frequency of such cases attracted the attention of the Duke of York, later James VII and II. He was disturbed by the practice of displaying these unfortunates on the stool of repentence and stressed that the custom was used in no other Christian country. He urged the substitution of fines or corporal punishment, but to no avail. In 1690 concealment of pregnancy resulting in the death of the child was made capital. Imprisonment was not a penalty usually imposed for this crime.

There are many sad examples of girls, some very young, shrinking from the horror of public shame and driven to desperate measures. Scott's *The Heart of Midlothian* and Galt's *Annals of the Parish* give harrowing descriptions of such cases. The Argyll Justiciary Records tell in vivid and poetic language of a case in 1679 at Inveraray. 'Mary McMillan, shaking off all fear of God last year, fell in the filthy crime of fornication with Donald McInlea of Ardlarich in Islay, being with child to him, for avoiding public slander and punishment, concealed the same so that none knew, and about the month of May last ... she under silence and cloud of night, past forth of her father's house to some place nearby it, and brought forth a man living chyld and there betook herself with the bairne to one of the burns ... remote and quiet, to prosecute her damnable and wicked intention, and there most barberously and unnaturally murdered the said infant, her own chyld, with her knife or strangled or smoored him some other way that he immediately died. She then hid him in straw under her bed until her brother buried him.' She confessed, but surprisingly was declared 'cleansed and acquitted of murder specified notwithstanding the Judicial confession but was found guilty of fornication'.

Another girl, Margaret Campbell, was less fortunate. In 1705 she too had an infant son 'which either stifled or left exposed in the condition he came to the world or other wayes put violent hands on him that he quickly perished and died. She immediately wrapped up the chyld in a little linnin cloath and hidd or buried him in the cleft of a rock and covered him with fagg and stone'. She was found out and confessed, and they 'searched and found the baby and sent it alongst with her to the tolbooth of Inveraray'.[32] She was hanged a month later. There are recorded convictions before the Court of Justiciary at Edinburgh of twenty-one women for child-murder from 1700 to 1706.

The hunting of witches was a popular pastime throughout this period, and the records of the Privy Council are full of commissions to take account of witches – fourteen separate commissions at one sederunt. 'Our ancestors were not alone in their belief in witchcraft; they were warranted in that opinion by the law and custom of all the nations of Europe.'[33] They harked back to Exodus 22, 18 – 'Thou shalt not suffer a witch to live' – and to Roman Law, which condemned sorcerers to die by fire. An Act of 1563 made the practice of witchcraft or consulting with witches a capital crime. There are many cases of witches suffering imprisonment while awaiting trial. Thus in Perth Kirk Session Records, 1582, 'Ordains James Sym to give the witch in the tolbooth 8 doits in the day'.

Those accused of witchcraft had small hope of acquittal. For them prison was very often a step to death. They were frequently kept there for lengthy periods and tortured with diabolic cruelty until they confessed their 'crimes' before the Session. The witches' mark was 'discovered amongst us by a Pricker, whose trade it is, and who learns it as other trades; but this is a horrid cheat' said Sir George Mackenzie in his *Law and Customs of Scotland in Matters*

Criminal (1699). Arnot gives the 'Expence of burning a witch woman, 1649:

> To William Currie and Andrew Gray for the watching of hir ye space of 30 days ... xlv lib.Scotts.
> To John Kinked for brodding [prodding] of her ... VI lib. Scotts.
> Mair for meat and drink and wyne to him and his man, IIIJ lib.Scotts'.

The accused were hung up by their thumbs, lighted candles were set to the soles of their feet, hair shirts dipped in vinegar were put on them to 'fetch off' the skin, needles were thrust up to the heads in their fingers. In 1596 a poor woman accused of witchcraft made her 'pretended confession' after being kept forty-eight hours in the cashielaws (an iron case for the leg to which fire was gradually applied till it became agonisingly painful). Her family were tortured in front of her, her husband in the 'lang irons', her son in the 'boots' and the daughter in the pilnie winks (which crushed the fingers).[34] The many more detailed descriptions of the tortures make sickening reading. It should be noted that it was the Church which inflicted these agonies and it was only after confessions had been extorted that the victims were handed over to the magistrates for final disposal.

This relentless hounding was to continue throughout the seventeenth century, which saw a dismal procession of women strangled and burnt. In 1590 a group of women were believed to be members of a North Berwick Kirk witches' convention with the Devil. Not only the aged, the poor, and the friendless were accused. Eupham McCalzeane, daughter of one of the Senators of the College of Justice was included in the group. She was accused of helping to raise a storm to prevent Anne of Denmark, Queen of James VI coming to Scotland. The King was fascinated by witchcraft and showed eager interest in all trials of witches and wizards. The unfortunate Eupham, for sorcery and treason by plotting the King's death 'by enchantments', was condemned to be burned quick (alive) in 1591. Some of her forfeited lands were bestowed on the King's favourite, Sandilands, and it is a striking illustration of the state of justice at that time that Sandilands in the same year murdered another Lord of Session in an Edinburgh street and suffered neither trial nor punishment.[35]

Perth Kirk Session Records mention 'ane great number of witches brint through all the partis of this realme' in 1597, and in the same year 'the Session ordains the magistrates to travel with his Majesty to obtain a commission to execute James Robertson, sorcerer, who lang had been detained in ward'; in 1598 three women were 'brint in the Southe inch'; and in 1623 a woman is 'committed to ward in the Tower till she be tried anent sorcery'.

The function of imprisonment in these cases was custodial only, however long the confinement might last; trial and conviction over, execution followed swiftly. Robert Chambers cites cases in 1662 of witches dying in jail of cold and starvation, and of others being kept there for forty weeks though nothing could be brought against them.[36] These last the Privy Council eventually freed. In 1667 the Privy Council noted that a woman had been in ward in different prisons for three years under the charge of witchcraft, 'haveing been most unjustlie apprehended and imprisoned in severall prissins, viz. off Dumblain, Edinburgh and Stirling, be the space of these 3 years last bypast for the alleadged cryme of witchcraft'. In 1678 ten were condemned on the same day, and in 1697, for 'bewitching' an eleven-year-old girl in Renfrewshire, seven men and women were burnt. The last witch to suffer death in Scotland was executed in Sutherland in 1722. An Act of 1735 repealed the former statutes against witchcraft, and a generation later witches and the 'muckle black de'il' were subjects of jest rather than dread to Burns and his farmer friends.

As in the earlier period, summary justice was swift, both in the heritable jurisdictions and where the King's writ ran. The object of captors continued to be to dispose of the wrongdoer as quickly and cheaply as possible. Thus in 1581 the Regent Morton, tried for his part in Darnley's murder, was executed the next day,[37] and in 1584 the Earl of Gowrie, tried at Stirling for treason by a jury of his peers, was found guilty and beheaded the same evening. And in 1689 the murderer of the President of the Court of Session was hanged three days after sentence. 'At this period, and long after, the sentences of the Court of Justiciary frequently express no time for these being carried into execution; it being customary to take the convict directly from the court to the scaffold.'[38]

Great lords continued to dispense their own peculiar brands of justice. The Register of the Privy Council has some alarming examples. In 1578 Lord Maxwell put an offender in prison at Caerlaverock for ten days and then tied him to a tree and "tuke ane small cord and band about his heid and threw the same about with ane pin quhill his ene [eye] lap out upoun his cheikis [cheeks]', and then returned him to prison. Maxwell was ordered to release the prisoner or be put to the horn (declared an outlaw). Ross of Balnagowin in 1580 seized prisoners and detained 'thame in ward in irnis tormenting thame maist cruellie'. And there were other cases where the victims of capricious holders of heritable jurisdictions successfully appealed to the Lords of Session. In 1613 for instance Alexander Marton complained that Kennedy of Crugilton seized him and 'committit him to strait prisone within the pit of the same' and kept him there 'in grite miserie'. Since the petitioner appeared personally and the defender did not, the Lords ordered the defender to be denounced rebel. In 1619 a complainer says that Sir George Elphinston of Blythswood, a JP, imprisoned him 'in his pit or thevis hoill of Gorbellis' and struck him in the face. The Lords found that the pursuer had been justly committed to ward, but that Sir George in striking his face perpetrated 'a grite oversicht and neglect of dewtie in the execution of his chairge and office" and ordered him to remain in ward at Edinburgh until relieved.

In the treatment of the crimes discussed prison does not loom large, save in the case of witches and fornicators. Possibly because of the chronic insecurity of prisons, imprisonment could seldom be considered a practicable punishment. There is no consistent pattern in the developing concept of prison as a penalty as distinct from its custodial function, partly because the central authority was more effective in some places than in others. It seems likely that in small remote communities where the royal writ did not run effectively the poverty-ridden inhabitants would regard the cost of building a secure prison and paying a jailer as a luxury quite beyond their means; there were cheaper and more satisfactory ways of disposing of malefactors. In the country districts it was probably only in the gloomy pits of the feudal barons that prisoners were kept for any length of time. However, in the larger towns like Edinburgh and Glasgow the royal authority or the burgh authority might be alive to the advantages of a strong prison building from the point of view of law and order, and its staffing and maintenance would not bear so heavily on a more prosperous community.

The custodial rather than penal function of prison did not necessarily mean that one's stay there would be short. Its length might vary enormously and depend on a variety of factors. Authority could commit a person to prison and having done so either deliberately delay or simply not bother to take further action, and if the prisoner was without money, influence or friends he might languish for months or even years. From 1660 onwards the Justiciary records are full of petitions for release by those awaiting trial, which, if it was followed by conviction, would mean not further imprisonment but some other punishment such as a fine, finding assythment or caution, or execution. Certain classes of offenders could find themselves left in prison for a very long time. Among these were political offenders, religious dissenters, debtors, and those accused of witchcraft.[39] In the case of political offenders especially, the authorities often tended to procrastinate, either from inertia or from a reluctance to embark on complicated investigations or proceedings which might have awkward political repercussions. It was often easier quietly to forget about such prisoners and to hope that they might rot away and the problem thus solve itself. In some cases the unfortunates really were forgotten. Without a Habeas Corpus procedure, as yet unknown in Scotland, a prisoner had no effective means of reminding the authorities of his existence, since petitions were frequently ignored. For example the notorious Sir James Macdonald was a prisoner in Edinburgh Castle from 1604 and under sentence of death there from 1609 for a career of crime and adventure dating back to 1587, but he eventually escaped in 1615. Patrick Stewart, Earl of Orkney, was imprisoned from 1609 to 1615, when he was executed. At a lower social level, one William Drew in 1666 petitioned for trial or liberation after five years in a Glasgow jail on a charge of murder. A group of Quakers was imprisoned under stringent conditions, one of them for more than four years (1666–70).

Debtors (or 'dyvours') could be imprisoned for long periods, and scourged or put in the stocks. By several Acts between 1606 and 1688 debtors were ordered to wear on release distinctive clothes; 'ane hat or bonnet of yellow colour', and in the case of bankrupts a coat half yellow, half brown. In prison they were allowed no fresh air or exercise.

Various alternatives were used to thin out the number of prisoners in jail. Firstly transportation, a mode of disposal first considered by James VI in 1617, was conceived with the double purpose of draining off the ever-present multitude of wandering beggars and relieving pressure on the jails. But transportation was not in fact begun until 1648, when the Scots were defeated by Cromwell in north-west England and Scottish prisoners were transported to the plantations of Virginia. And in 1650, after their defeat by Cromwell at Dunbar, 900 Scottish prisoners were shipped to Virginia and 150 to New England. In 1665 strong and idle beggars, gipsies, and criminals were transported to Jamaica and Barbados.[40]

Secondly, men could escape death or prison for theft by being bound in perpetual servitude in the mines or as servants to great lords. Thus at Perth in 1701 four prisoners in the Tolbooth under sentence of death had their sentences commuted by the Commissioners of Justiciary to perpetual servitude. One of the four was given to the Earl of Tullibardine, 'recommending to his Lordship to cause provide an collar of brass, iron or copper, which, by his sentence or doom ... is to be upon his neck, with this inscription, "Donald McDonald, found guilty of Death for Theft, at Perth, Dec. 5th 1701, and gifted as a Perpetual Servant to John, Earl of Tullibardine" '.[41]

Thirdly, from 1621 until the end of the seventeenth century all able-bodied males were at the risk of being forced into the army. Recruiting officers searched the prisons for likely lads. Prisoners in Edinburgh Tolbooth for the capital crime of maiming cattle found their sentences commuted to transportation to Flanders for service in the Scottish levies. According to the Register of the Privy Council they were to be 'transportit to the wearis [wars]' , never to return under pain of death without the King's licence. 'Idle rogues' had no right of appeal against such sentences, but those with a trade could appeal to the Court of Session.

Conditions in the prisons, though no worse than in England, were wretched enough. Life was miserable except in a few small

county jails where prisoners were allowed out if they promised to
return. If they had money they could buy food and drink and
carouse with the jailers. Often there was no proper supervision.
Again the Privy Council Records are a rich source. At Pittenweem
in 1601 a female was put in ward in the tolbooth, guarded by
officers. Two nights later her rebel husband and sons burst in and
freed her, leaving the officers in the stocks! In 1626 a burgess of
Crail with his own ideas of justice had to answer for having taken
the keys of the tolbooth from the officer and putting 'certain
persons as prisoners therein'. In 1628 complaints are made of lax
security and overindulgent kind treatment when two women
thieves in Canongate Tolbooth were fed and entertained with
wine and 'maist delicious fair' and allowed out as they pleased by
collusion of the jailer. The request was made that they be handed
over to Edinburgh Tolbooth where 'thair is sure and straitt waird
for sic persones'.

The problem of the maintenance of prisoners was especially
acute in the case of beggars, who by definition could not pay for
their upkeep. As we have seen in the previous chapter, the Act of
1579 for the punishment of 'strong and idle beggaris' ordered that
those between the ages of fourteen and seventy years should not
be allowed to beg unless carrying tokens permitting them to do
so. Perth Burgh Records show a list of beggars for 1741 with
sixty-seven names, their ages ranging from six to eighty-two
years. Those in breach of this law were to be committed to prison
until tried. The Act went on to make provision for poor prisoners,
in the expectation that the prisons might become filled with a
continually renewed supply of beggars. It was ordered that their
expenses be paid by the parish in which they were apprehended,
'allowand to ilk persone daylie ane pund of aitbreid [oatbread] and
watter to drink'. Before the passing of this Act the burden of
maintaining poor prisoners before trial was on the Crown, but it
was now shifted to the parishes. The subject appears in the Privy
Council Records in 1611, note being taken of the great numbers
of prisoners without means of maintenance and thus likely to
starve to death before they could be brought to trial, it being
decreed that they be supported by each parish at a weekly rate of
not less than one and not more than five shillings Scots.

These provisions for the maintenance of needy prisoners awaiting trial did not meet the case of those in prison after conviction, and no direct provision was made by law for the aliment of the convicted until well into the nineteenth century. Legacies were sometimes made for the relief of poor prisoners: 'Item the soume of ane hundredth merks ... to the distressit prisoners in the Tolbuith of Edinburgh June 23rd 1637'.[42] In 1614 a jailer in the Edinburgh Tolbooth complained that 'divers poore miserable personis ar committit to warde ... sua that the burdyne of thair interteynment lyis upoun him, to his grite hurte and wrak [misery].' The Lords of the Privy Council thereupon undertook that if such 'poore creaturis' were in the ward by their direction they should each be paid the sum of five shillings daily by the Treasurer-Depute.

In 1588 measures were taken for the more effective execution of the 1579 Act. All wandering beggars were to return to the parishes where they were born, and if found wandering were to be kept in prison or stocks, scourged, or 'brynt thraw the earis with hett irnis [hot irons]'. And all judges-ordinary and others commissioned were to prepare common prisons, stocks and irons within their jurisdictions for offenders against the Act.

Soon however responsibility for prisons was put specifically on the burghs. An Act of 1597, 'understanding that through want of sufficient and sure prisons, jails and ward houses sundry rebels and transgressors of the Laws, as well criminal as civil, escape unpunished ... ordained that within the space of three years in all burghs within this Realm there be sufficient and sure jails and ward houses built, upheld and maintained' by the burghs.

Some burghs had in fact already made efforts to build prisons. The Privy Council Records show that in 1572 the Bailies and Council of Musselburgh decided to build adjacent to their tolbooth 'a house to have for their council house, a warding place and a place of prison for keeping malefactors'. In 1579 there was a petition from the Dumfries magistrates regarding the rebuilding of the town prison for the safe-keeping of prisoners that would be committed to ward in the future, and they argued that the most secure part of the general prison would be in the middle or upper part of the building, to stop the possibility of prisoners working under the wall and undermining it in order to escape.

From 1597 until an Act of 1839 it was established law in Scotland that burghs were bound to receive prisoners under a warrant granted by the persons authorised to commit in the county in which the prison was situated. The obligation to provide prisons having been thrown entirely on the burghs by the earlier Act, responsibility for their maintenance became a necessary consequence, yet Acts of Parliament requiring magistrates to build tolbooths were often ignored. As late as 1620 there were none in Ross, Sutherland, or Caithness.

Such tolbooths as were built were often ramshackle affairs from which escape was ludicrously simple. In 1590, because 'the house of justice otherwise called the tolbooth of the Canongate is altogether become ruinous, decayed and fallen down ... malefactors have often freed themselves furth thereof and so escaped punishment'[43] a tax was levied on the inhabitants of the burgh of Canongate and the Regality of Broughton to build a new tolbooth.

Despite iron bars and shackles for desperate inmates, escapes continued. The law held the magistrates responsible and liable to imprisonment; for example, in 1612 when an untried prisoner escaped from Brechin Tolbooth the magistrates were summoned and imprisoned. In 1700 a Caithness man in debt for the then large sum of £1400 was lodged in Tain prison, from which he escaped in 1702, taking advantage of its insecure state. His escape made the Tain magistrates liable for his debt, so they pursued and caught the fugitive. He was cast into the vault of the steeple of Inverness, which was evidently more secure than Tain. He was still there in 1709, when he petitioned the Inverness magistrates that he was living 'with greatest severity ... and affliction ... not having the use or benefit of the least fire, or little candlelight allowed me ... tho' ever so sick or unwell. The said vault being so cold and obnoxious to the health ... that it is a wonder ... that a person of my age has continued alive so long in it'. Rain ran down in it 'and when there are dry snow and wind it will cover white the floor and the bed and bed clothes'. He goes on to plead that his privations have brought on several dangerous distempers and he 'may die here like a beast'. He begs to go to the Tolbooth, where he may have the 'use of a fire and administration of some doctor'. So in 1709 he was removed to the inner Tolbooth, but as the Town Council was at the time burning great quantities of peat in it to counteract the evil effects of the frightful insanitary conditions the prisoner was probably no better off.[44]

The county jail of Inverness had two small cells, one for criminals and one for debtors. A vault of the old stone bridge over the River Ness, erected in 1685, was also used as a prison, being thought more secure than the 'frail tolbooth'. The bridge vault was a fearsome place, twelve feet square. Entrance to it was by a hatch in the roadway of the bridge and the wretched prisoner derived all his air and light from an iron grating in the upper pier. In this dismal den, 'sometimes waist-deep in water, half-devoured by rats', the prisoner languished. So great was the impression made by the harrowing tales about this hole that the Inverness people christened it the Black Hole.

In many towns, including Edinburgh, Perth, Dundee, and Inverness, the steeples of the parish churches continued to serve as prisons, being regarded as more secure than the tolbooths. St Giles' in Edinburgh was so used until complaints were lodged that the prisoners dropped pebbles on the heads of the congregation. Pitcairn quotes a macabre description of suicide in a steeple-prison in February 1612, 'heiring that Jock Ellate was hingund in the stepill [steeple], came ... into the steepill, quhair he saw the defunct hingund in his awin belt'. Pitcairn comments, 'Steeples were often fitted up with fetters ... riveted into the wall, where these luckless victims were detained until Trial, without any Jail allowance. In cases of witchcraft, etc., iron collars were added; and it is highly probable that cases of suicide were by no means infrequent, owing to the desperate circumstances of these miserable creatures.'[45]

The general insecurity of Scottish prisons is illustrated by an incident in 1682. The magistrates of Dumfries were forced to have a man on a murder charge removed to Edinburgh because several Border friends daily threatened to force the prison and the magistrates were put to considerable expense to guard him. In 1690 the Privy Council were anxious about the security of the Edinburgh Tolbooth because escapes had taken place from the Canongate jail. They decreed that 'the shutters towards the North should be nightly locked, to prevent communications with houses in that direction' and a 'centinel' should stand all day at the head of the iron stair.

Gradually during the seventeenth century the primitive

tower-like tolbooths were replaced or, if still in use (like Crail's), remodelled and enlarged, most of them now having three storeys and a steeple. During the second half of the century more formally-designed buildings came into vogue, with three storeys and tall square towers; Linlithgow and Culross are examples. Stirling's new Town House (1702) designed by Sir William Bruce, had three storeys and a six-storeyed spire, the prison there being the 'holl beneath the steeple'. Dumfries Town House (the Mid-steeple) closely followed Bruce's design a little later.[46]

Political prisoners and religious dissenters, those whom the King regarded as serious threats to himself, were thrown into the State Prisons. These (often the King's castles) posed the biggest problem for prisoners trying to escape, but even they varied greatly in their strength. Edinburgh, Stirling, Doune, Dunnottar, Blackness were far more secure than the town tolbooths, while the Bass Rock, a natural island stronghold which could, with a garrison of two dozen men, hold off an army, was the most impregnable.

Robert Lauder built the castle on the Bass in the Firth of Forth in the fourteenth century. No prisoner ever escaped from it save by death and its strength passed into a local proverb:

'Ding doun the Bass,
Mak a brig to Tantallon'

signifying the impossible. The English tried in vain to seize it. By 1405 the bleak and rugged Bass had been fortified, and the first state prisoner there was Walter Stewart, son of the Duke of Albany. A Frenchman visiting the Rock in 1548 found a garrison of about a hundred men. The only means of egress from the fort to a boat was by a basket. 'Old prints of the Bass in a fortified state during the seventeenth century show the Rock ascending steeply from the sea to a level platform. Behind was the governor's house, and the towers connected by curtain walls. The prisons were situated in the centre of the enclosure. Only the roof and chimneys were visible from the exterior, thus shutting off the prisons from any possible signalling with the outer world'.[47] From 1676 the imprisonment of Covenanters became more rigorous, and the state prison on the Bass was deemed a fitting place of incarceration for the most persistent of the field preachers. These included

Robert Gillespie and Alexander Peden, imprisoned there in 1673–74, and the number of prisoners from the ranks of Coventiclers had increased in 1676 to seventy-seven. The Bass was a prison of hideous discomfort, and the prisoners' privations were increased by bad and insufficient food as it was often too difficult for boats to land in stormy weather. 'The prisoners were severely kept, not being always allowed to take exercise. John Blackadder, minister of Troqueer in Galloway, one of the most notable of the Martyrs of the Bass, endured a captivity of five years and died on the Rock.'[48]

After the landing of William of Orange the state fortress of the Bass was the last place in Scotland to hold out for the Stewarts. A few daring young Jacobite officers led the life of pirates, plundering passing ships for supplies, craning their boats up the face of the Rock, resisting all attempts to dislodge them. A London broadsheet of 1694 gives the 'Welcome Advice that the Rebels in the Island and Castle of Bass had actually surrendered that Impregnable Place after having been in Possession of it above Four years and from time to time supplied with Provision, Necessaries and Ammunition from France, the French King taking great Cognisance of this place, as designing to make it a Receptacle for Spies, Ingineers and Incendiaries' and to store great quantities of arms for future attempts to restore King James. The rebels sent to the Government Articles on which they would surrender the Bass, and all seven Articles were, rather surprisingly, accepted, including that a 'sum of 200 l. sterling might be paid them to enable them to subsist when out of the Place, and that all those who aided and abetted them to be pardoned, and all rebels to go free'.[49]

Blackness, the castle near Edinburgh built in the shape of a ship, and Dunnottar near Stonehaven were to play their part in the incarceration of the Covenanters. The discomfort and misery endured by the state prisoners was intense. Blackness had been a state prison for many years. Cardinal Beaton had been warded there before being sent to his own castle of St Andrews in 1543. In 1579 Lord Hay of Yester promised that 'he will enter himself in ward in Blaknes Castle . . . under pain of 10,000 merks', and again in 1584–85 the Earl of Morton was charged under pain of treason to enter in ward in the Castle of Blackness for failing to appear before the Council as committed, on various charges. Dissenting ministers were imprisoned there, for example James Fraser of Brae in 1681.

Conventiclers were frequently detained for long periods without trial, although they could obtain release if they gave bonds of caution not to attend conventicles in future. Finding surety against breaking this bond was difficult for the very poor, 'but refusal to take the bond rather than failure to find caution, appears to have lain behind most extended confinements'.[50] It should be remembered that 'the coercion used against those "solemn-leaguers" was no more severe than the coercion which they themselves would have applied had they been in power'.[51]

After the defeat of the Pentland Rising and the Battle of Rullion Green in 1666, eighty covenanting prisoners were taken, many being put in the 'Haddo's Hole' part of St Giles', while those of higher rank were thrown into the Edinburgh Tolbooth. At their trial ten were condemned to death by hanging, the sentences being carried out two days later; more executions followed in succeeding weeks. A bond of peace was offered to the others, transportation to Barbados or Virginia being the penalty for refusal. Those who agreed were freed from prison. From 1678 onwards transportation to the plantations of the East Indies and Virginia 'became a recognised means of dealing with Conventiclers, whereas previously this punishment had been used but sparingly'.[52]

Again after the defeat of the Covenanters at Bothwell Brig in 1679 over 1,400 prisoners were taken to Edinburgh, but these suffered far less than has sometimes been asserted. Their confinement in huts in a vacant part of Greyfriars Churchyard was less uncomfortable than in any of the insanitary and overcrowded prisons, particularly since the majority were imprisoned during the summer months only and lack of adequate security allowed quite a number to escape. The huge number of prisoners posed a problem and it was decided to transport some 300 or 400 of them, but with the exception of two field preachers all were offered their liberty if they promised never to rebel again. By August a start had been made in freeing them, but 400 refused, although a hundred of these gave in later. In November 258 sailed for Barbados, but they were shipwrecked off Orkney and all but thirty or so were drowned.[53]

The final solution of transportation for obdurate Presbyterians took time to effect, and in the meantime the prisons grew even more crowded. To ease the problem the Council decided to use Dunnottar Castle as a state prison, and in May 1685 over 150 prisoners taken up for acts of recusancy 'were gathered out of the prisons, driven off like a flock of sheep ... and huddled into a vault of Dunnottar Castle, where they lived for a few weeks in circumstances of privation, as to food, air, water, and general accommodation, truly piteous'.[54] Many of them were later transported. For refusing to take the oath of allegiance nearly a hundred men and women were 'gifted' to Scott of Pitlochie for settlement in his colony of East New Jersey. They sailed from Leith in September 1685, seventy of them dying on the voyage.

The Revolution brought another party to power, but it was as ready as its predecessors to punish dissidents. One of the first Acts of the Government of William III was for the securing of suspect persons. All through the summer of 1689 the Register of the Privy Council was crammed with petitions from political prisoners calling for relief from the miseries of Edinburgh Tolbooth, Stirling Castle or Blackness, where they were locked up, often with no cause given. Some, on giving their parole, were moved to private lodgings, but many were still in prison years later. Men alleged to be Popish priests languished in Blackness and in Edinburgh Tolbooth, until in 1693 they were freed on caution of their promise to accept banishment.

In the parishes the penalty of banishment was as popular as ever. It is recorded in the Court Book of the Barony of Balnakeilly at Moulin near Pitlochry, that in 1741 Isabelle Scott, accused of house-breaking and of stealing four shillings sterling, and meal and two cheeses, which were found in her possession 'save for one cheese which she had eaten', had to make restitution. She was fined twenty pounds Scots, put in the choggs [stocks] and was 'thereafter furthwith to betake herself furth of the grounds of Balnakeilly, not to be seen therein for the space of three years hereafter ...', and further 'ordains her Mother and others in the grounds of Balnakeilly, under pain of ten pounds Scots, toties quoties, not to lodge or harbour her by night or day in their houses or by giving her any manner of entertainment and victualls at any time'.[55] The realistic, down-to-earth pattern continues: let the offender go away and be a nuisance in some other parish, anywhere, so long as his own parish is no longer inconvenienced. The continual shifting of the population due to these numerous sentences of banishment swelled the hordes of beggars who so troubled the country, their numbers being increased by the 'dear years' [the famine] of King William. To deal effectively with them Fletcher of Saltoun unsuccessfully advocated compulsory servitude, an extension of the serfdom endured by those men, women and children who worked the coal and salt mines and were called 'black folk'.

All this concerns mainly the Lowlands of Scotland. It should be remembered that Scotland was a two-nation country, a fairly clear-cut division separating the Highlands from the Lowlands; two races, two languages, two entirely different ways of life, traditions and loyalties. There were no roads in the Highlands until General Wade built them, and the bad state of those in the Lowlands kept people from travelling unless from necessity. 'Thus the burghs and villages were largely isolated communities, self-interested and practically self-supporting, with wide differences in manners and customs.'[56]

During the first half of the eighteenth century, conditions remained similar, so much so that Edward Burt, a young surveyor who acccompanied Wade on his roadmaking, found in the Highlands in 1726 that the 'heritable power of pit and gallows, as they call it, which still is exercised by some within their proper district, is, I think, too much for any particular subject to be entrusted withal'. He found also, when in Inverness, that most of the murderers and other 'notorious villains' in the Tolbooth during his stay escaped, and in his opinion, 'this has manifestly proceeded from the furtherance or connivance of the keepers'. The excuse was 'the prison is a weak old building and the town is not in condition to keep it in repair; but, for my own part, I cannot help concluding, from many circumstances, that the greater part of these escapes have been the consequence, either of clan-interest or clannish terror. As for example, if one of the magistrates were a Cameron (for the purpose), the criminal (Cameron) must not suffer if the clan be desirous he should be saved.'[57]

The Highlands continued to be a law unto themselves until the defeat of the Jacobites in the rising of 1745. A typical incident is found in the Balnakeilly Court Book. It took place in 1745 when Adam Ferguson, the Whig minister at Moulin, preached against the Jacobites, thus giving offence to some clans, whereupon a party of Camerons from Blair plundered his house of food, goods, silver, linen, and silks. He wrote to the Governor of Atholl asking for restitution, protesting somewhat plaintively that if they had taken only 'beef, honney, ale and whiskey ... or even Body Linnen, shoes, stockens, it might have been thought tolerable, but to go to the length they did showed an ever rapacious disposition, and is, what I am well convinced, Lochiel [the chief of Clan Cameron] would as little allow or approve as any man alive ... my wife goes to make her moan to the Duke of Atholl and you'. It was probably a pointless exercise on her part.

The Jacobite risings of 1715 and 1745 each brought a spate of imprisonments but again, in the old tradition, they were nearly always custodial by intention. Jacobites taken prisoner in Scotland after the Fifteen seem to have fared better than those captured in England. Immediately after their defeat at Preston several prisoners were tried by drumhead court-martial, condemned and shot; the remaining leaders taken there were marched south and, after being paraded through London with their arms tied behind their backs, were imprisoned in various jails. Many death sentences were passed at their trials, but in the event only two executions were carried out, those of the Earl of Derwentwater and Viscount Kenmure. Several, including the Earls of Nithsdale and Winton, escaped from jail.

The Jacobites captured in Scotland were imprisoned in Edinburgh to await trial, but popular sympathy for them was so widespread that the Government feared that if they were tried in Scotland no jury would bring in a verdict of guilty. So in 1716 advantage was taken of the treason law for Scotland, which had been passed immediately after the Union of 1707, to transfer eighty-nine prisoners from Edinburgh to Carlisle to be tried by English juries. In September 1716 they were marched down the West Bow from the Castle, en route for Carlisle. This aroused fury among all classes in Scotland as being proof of their country's enslavement. But in strong contrast to the sufferings of the Jacobite prisoners after the Forty-Five, these prisoners were well treated and received fair trials, and while a number of death sentences were passed none was carried out. Some however were transported, 600 being sent as indentured servants to the American plantations, and 'in 1716 the governor of South Carolina bought thirty highland rebels at £30 apiece'.[58] The Balnakeilly Court Book has a reference to the number of Athollmen captured at Preston and transported for seven years' slavery in the American plantations, 'from which many a poor fellow was destined never to return, or if they did so, were mere wrecks of their former selves'. In 1717 an Act of Grace and Pardon was passed, by which those still in prison were allowed to settle at home or abroad.

Before and after Culloden the prisons were overcrowded with Jacobites. A combing-out of the Scottish prisons in the summer of 1746 resulted in the dispatch of 270 of the more important prisoners to Carlisle. 'It is practically impossible to arrive at the number of rebels in the Scottish prisons on any particular date because although monthly returns were required only some of them are available, but (with the exception of Inverness) the total cannot have been less than about a thousand.'[59] In some prisons there was considerable overcrowding and much resultant illness. Women Jacobite prisoners were sent to Edinburgh Castle, whence Lady Ogilvy escaped in the guise of a laundress; the clothes were brought in by a friend, who remained in her place and was afterwards allowed to go free. Less fortunate were the Duchess of Perth and Viscountess Strathallan and her two daughters, who in 1746 were for a year 'confined in a small, horrid and unhealthy chamber above the portcullis, used for many years as the "black hole" of the garrison'. Some unfortunate Jacobites suffered protracted periods of imprisonment in the Castle. The aged Macintosh of Borlum died there after a captivity of fifteen years for his share in the Fifteen and Macdonald of Barrisdale too died there in 1750.

Of fifty-eight Jacobites who escaped from prisons in England and Scotland only thirteen managed to do so from English jails, although the number confined there was about four times as great. The most obvious reason was the structural superiority of the English prisons, many of the Scottish being merely insecure burgh tolbooths. From Dumbarton Castle, whose insecure condition had been remarked on as far back as 1690, twelve out of thirty Jacobites escaped. Scots jailers too were more likely to look the other way during escape attempts than were English turnkeys, and the proximity of homes and friends would act as a natural spur to escapers.

Inverness prison was directly under the military authority and after Culloden held some 1,200 Jacobite prisoners, many of them wounded. 'Butcher' Cumberland 'never had any intention of treating his captives as prisoners of war, but rather as persons already proved guilty of high treason'.[60] Their treatment there, in the transports to London and in the various English prisons to which they were dispersed was often brutal and inhumane. In the transports and at Woolwich, starvation, overcrowding, ill-treatment, and an epidemic of typhus which took heavy toll of them added to the misery of defeat and captivity. An English doctor inspected the 'Pamela' at Woolwich in August 1746 and found horrific conditions. On looking down into the hold containing the prisoners he 'was saluted with such an intolerable smell that it was like to overcome me, though I was provided with proper herbs and my nostrils stuffed therewith'. Fifty-four prisoners emerged on deck, many 'very ill as appeared by their countenance and their snail-creep pace in ascending the ladder, being only just able to crawl up'. Another eighteen could only lie in wretchedness below decks.[61] Many died.

In the English prisons the Jacobites of 1745 soon found that possession of money was essential to secure the barest comforts of life, and some prisons were more expensive than others. At the Tower, where the titular Duke of Atholl died in 1746, it had cost him ten guineas a week to live. It was not until January 1746 that the Government started to make financial arrangements for rations for the prisoners in England. The authorities in Scotland had had standing orders on the subject which had been drawn up long before the outbreak of the Forty-Five and which had proposed four pence per day per man. On the other hand it was reported that the principal Keeper of the Edinburgh Tolbooth had compassion for the many cold and sick Jacobites there and out of his own pocket provided them with blankets.

The Jail Returns and the State Papers quoted in *The Prisoners of the '45* disclosed that eighty-eight deaths occurred in English and Scottish prisons and in the transports, but it seems clear that many more deaths in Inverness and in the English prisons went unrecorded. Only eighteen deaths in Scottish prisons were actually reported.

The policy of transportation of prisoners after the Fifteen was also adopted after the Forty-Five, when the numbers involved were considerably larger. About 800 Jacobite prisoners were transported between March 1747 and November 1748. They were sentenced to compulsory service for life, but in practice after serving for seven years they were freed, though they were still obliged to remain in banishment for the rest of their days. Also, in the Act for disarming the Highlands after the Forty-Five, it was provided that those convicted a second time for refusing to give up their arms should be liable for transportation for seven years, and that those guilty of wearing the Highland dress should also be liable for transportation in a second conviction.[62]

In the earlier part of the period covered by this chapter the harshest measures, as we have seen, were applied to offences against a code of religious morality rather than to crimes properly so called. By the end of it, Presbyterian fanaticism had lost its impetus and its hold on public opinion, and in consequence control passed to a secular, central authority which was concerned rather with offences more properly designated crimes, in the sense that they threatened the basis of society and the safety of persons and property. 'One of the most important and enduring achievements of the seventeenth century was the transformation of Scotland from a country in which the law had often been ill-enforced into one in which the law was generally obeyed.'[63]

Although prior to 1707 Scotland had her own sophisticated legal system, derived from quite different sources than those of the corresponding system in England, and differing from it in many respects, such as courts and jurisdictions, rules of procedure and evidence, and the specific crimes with which offenders could be charged, the system had never been fully effective. Even a perfect legal system cannot maintain law and order unless the judgments and sentiments of its courts can be enforced by a strong central government. It was only after 1707, and more particularly with the removal of the Jacobite threat and the end of heritable jurisdictions in 1747, that the firm control of all Britain by the Westminster Government endowed the Scottish legal system with the sanctions it required to operate effectively.

3
The Humanitarian Reformers
1747–1835

Punishment is not for revenge, but
to lessen crime and reform the criminal.
Elizabeth Fry ★

In prisons 'there must be a great deal
of solitude; coarse food, a dress of shame;
hard, incessant, irksome, eternal labour;
a planned and regulated and unrelenting
exclusion of happiness and comfort.'
Rev. Sidney Smith †

3

I   The English Background

Before looking at conditions in the Scottish prisons of this period, we should look at the situation in England and the conclusions and proposals of the English reformers or would-be reformers, since the two systems were to interact and eventually draw close together.

The middle of the eighteenth century found the prison conditions in England, as on the Continent, virtually unchanged since the preceding centuries, though some attempts at reform had been made. In 1702 the Society for the Promotion of Christian Knowledge carried out an enquiry into the state of London prisons[1] but this proved abortive. A Parliamentary Committee of 1729 was instructed to enquire into the state of the jails in the country, but despite its report that the more 'they proceeded in their enquiries the more dismal and shocking was the scene of cruelty, barbarity and extortion which they disclosed'[2] it had no effect. Prison reform aroused no concern in a complacent public.

The function of prisons was still merely to detain offenders in safe custody pending execution, transportation or the payment of debts. Towards the end of the century however three factors combined to bring the problem of prisons to a head. The most obvious, and most urgent in its effect, was the ending of transportation to America. After the War of Independence (1775-83) the British Government had to accept the unpalatable fact that America could no longer be used as a convenient dumping ground for undesirables. For some ten years after 1775 no satisfactory alternative method of disposal was found and the dilapidated hulks of the convict ships which had served as transports were moored in English estuaries and used as floating prisons. This measure was intended to be temporary but the hulks continued to be so used, *faute de mieux*, for almost a century.

Secondly, the resultant overcrowding of the prisons was made worse by the soaring crime rate, which may be attributed to the Industrial Revolution and the consequent rise of congested towns, to poverty, and to the large number of unemployed soldiers from the wars. The death penalty was less successful than might have been expected in restoring the balance. Although in 1760 no fewer than 164 separate crimes attracted the supreme penalty – a number which had grown to over 200 by the beginning of the next century – the theoretical severity of the law was greatly mitigated by the attitudes of both judges and juries, the former recommending mercy for more and more offenders, the latter committing what was known as 'pious perjury'.

The third factor – of least immediate but ultimately of most permanent effect – was the movement for reform. As part of the general humanitarian movement the whole question of punishment had been examined on a liberal philosophical basis by Continental writers such as Montesquieu (*L'Esprit des Lois* 1748), Beccaria (*Crimes and Punishments* 1764), Rousseau, and Voltaire. By the end of the century their criticisms had achieved some penal reform in Continental countries but the brutality of the English system remained untouched. For the Industrial Revolution had completely altered the English social scene long before the rest of Europe experienced anything similar and the resulting unrest as well as the fear of any innovation, induced by the alarming example of the French Revolution, made the Government wary of relaxing any deterrents.

In the face of public apathy and official resistance the English penal reformers found the going hard. Samuel Romilly (1757–1818), neither philosopher nor prison visitor, fought against the savagery of the English law. Despite years of effort, encouraged by his friend Dugald Stewart of Edinburgh, he succeeded only in pushing through Parliament Acts which abolished the death penalty for stealing more than a shilling from the pocket and five shillings' worth of goods from bleaching greens. He attacked the House of Lords (which included seven bishops) for the pronouncement that: 'Transportation for life is not sufficiently severe punishment for the offence of pilfering what is of 5s. value, and that nothing but the blood of the offender can afford an adequate atonement. . . .'[3]

Romilly had evidently no first-hand experience from visits to prisons, but John Howard, Sheriff of Bedford, had. In *The State of the Prisons* (1777) he published the results of his visits to all the English prisons and several Scottish and Irish ones. Appalled by the conditions he found, he urged improvements on a mainly deaf public. His recommendations illustrate by contrast the existing state of affairs.

Howard argued that prisoners should be classified according to sex and the degree of their criminality. There should be separate confinement by night, when (he believed) solitude might lead to repentance, but they should work together by day, grouped according to their classification. (Howard has been misquoted as advocating continuous solitary confinement.)[4] Health was high among his priorities and he urged the provision of adequate bedding, food and fresh air, along with baths and infirmaries. (Typhus, known as 'jail fever', was rampant, killing more prisoners than did the executioner.) Spiritual health was not overlooked and he recommended a chapel for every prison. Jailers should be forbidden to sell liquor, and should be paid regular salaries. (As we shall see later, this was a necessary reform, since many had to rely on the profits from liquor sales and such customs as 'garnish' and 'chummage' and payment for 'easement of irons', involving extortion from prisoners for necessities and ordinary comforts.)[5] To ensure proper administration, prisons should be regularly visited by magistrates. It was clear, however, that before the majority of these proposals could be put into effect new buildings were essential, and Howard himself designed a penitentiary house to embody his ideas. Here we have the three emergent factors mentioned above coming together; the first two (the abandonment of transportation and the rising crime rate) involving an urgent need for new buildings, and the third, the reform movement, presenting opportunities for the architects.

In 1779 the Penitentiary Houses Act was passed, providing for the establishment of a national penitentiary, and it constituted both prisons and bridewells penitentiaries pending the erection of such an institution. Houses of Correction had been established in 1576 on the model of Bridewell, a house given by Edward VI where vagrants and the unemployed were kept in harsh conditions and made to work (so called from its being near St. Bride's Well in London). By Howard's time the distinction between jails and bridewells had already become blurred, although it was not abolished until 1865.

But in the eighteenth century, with virtually no central control over prisons, the passing of an Act of Parliament was not sufficient to secure reform. 'It is not so much for want of good laws, as from their inexecution, that the state of the prisons is so bad.'[6] The 1779 Act had authorised the construction of Howard's proposed penitentiary and appointed a committee to choose a site with Howard himself one of the Commissioners, but they were unable to agree, and when Howard eventually resigned, the whole scheme lapsed. Apart from the quarrel among the Commissioners, and public apathy, another factor militated against the scheme's success. The policy of transportation, roundly condemned by Howard, was revived in 1786 when it was realised that Australia, the new continent discovered by Cook ten years earlier, could provide a large-scale outlet. It was easier, cheaper, and altogether more comfortable to get rid of criminals by banishment rather than by imprisonment. It was a long-established custom (banishment from the realm being a logical extension of banishment from the parish) and public opinion was strongly in its favour. Thus in 1787 the first draft of convicts reached Botany Bay, the start of a miserable procession which was to continue unchecked until the mid-nineteenth century.

Although Howard's proposed penitentiary was never built, its design, along with others of the period, was ultimately to have a profound effect on the structure and administration of today's prisons. Jeremy Bentham (1748–1842) also designed an ideal prison, a 'Panopticon' or inspection house, a circular building with a keeper positioned in the centre, unseen by the prisoners but able to watch constantly by an arrangement of windows. Howard, on a visit to Scotland, persuaded the Lord Provost of Edinburgh to institute a competition for plans for prison building, and the winning entry was that of Robert Adam, who had made a study of Bentham's Panopticon design and used some of his ideas. The Edinburgh Bridewell which was eventually built was a compromise - work cells formed the immediate semi-circle nearest the keeper's tower, with separate night cells behind these.[7]

Howard's ultimate aim was to create in the prisons an atmosphere conducive to reform (an ambition which was not to be realised in his lifetime nor for many years after his death). Since existing conditions, not to mention public opinion, made this unattainable he took as his immediate and more realistic objective the alleviation of the actual treatment of prisoners,[8] a concern which was shared by his successors in the reform movement, Elizabeth Fry, her brother J.J. Gurney, her brother-in-law Fowell Buxton, and James Neild.

Elizabeth Fry, a Quaker, and subsequently the mother of eleven children, started her work in 1813 among the wretched women and children in Newgate and between then and her death in 1845 achieved remarkable results. She campaigned for separate prisons for women, for classification, for the appointment of women warders, for religious instruction and above all for work, her theme being 'The enforced idleness, the dreadful *ennui* of prison, was worse to them than its other miseries. It was in itself a direct incentive to vicious behaviour, as a relief from intolerable mono-tony'.[9] Like Howard she was totally opposed to solitary confine-ment. She preached that 'Punishment is not for revenge, but to lessen crime and reform the criminal'.[10] She concerned herself not only with the prisons in England but also with the convict ships for females who were to be transported to New South Wales, and here she succeeded by determined and indefatigable efforts in alleviating the appalling conditions which women, often accom-panied by children, endured on board.[11] Her labours achieved order and cleanliness, classification and employment, and the abol-ition of the cruel 'ironing'. But she was admired rather than imitated. Her arduous tours of inspection at home and abroad, and her belief that it was society's duty to reform prisoners rather than to degrade them were generally regarded as evidence 'of a soft heart rather than of a practical mind'.[12]

James Neild in 1812 and Fowell Buxton in 1818 published books describing vile prison conditions. Buxton stressed that in many prisons there was still not available much of what Howard had advocated as necessary – 'instruction, classification, regular employment and inspection'.[13]

It is therefore against a general background of incipient intellec-tual and moral reform, and an indifferent if not directly hostile public, that the more or less static conditions of the English prisons of the time should be examined. The reformers were to see comparatively few results in their lifetimes. Their achievement was in sowing the seeds of a humanitarian spirit and in setting out practical proposals for establishing reforming conditions when the time should be ripe.

II The Scottish Background

Before the middle of the eighteenth century, few travellers were intrepid enough to penetrate the Scottish fastnesses. But after that came a perfect spate to inspect the prisons – Howard, Neild, Elizabeth Fry and Gurney, to name only the famous. The most objective and reliable accounts of conditions in Scottish prisons which exist are from such outside observers, who have no axe to grind. Their efforts were generally as ineffective as in England. Public attitudes were not yet favourable to the ideals of Howard and Mrs Fry.

Public indifference and intellectual hostility had combined to challenge the movement for reform. As late as 1831 Elizabeth Fry wrote, 'My interest in the cause of prisons remains strong, and my zeal unabated; though it is curious to observe how much less is felt about it by the public generally'.[1] In the *Edinburgh Review* of 1822, the Rev. Sidney Smith said that although he considered Mrs Fry an excellent woman 'hers is not the method to stop crimes'.[2] He would 'banish all the looms of Preston Jail and substitute nothing but the treadwheel ... or some species of labour where the labourer could not see the results of his toil ... where it was as monotonous, irksome and dull as possible ... no share of the profits – not a single shilling'.[3] He advocated prisons where 'there must be a great deal of solitude; coarse food; a dress of shame; hard, incessant, irksome, eternal labour; a planned and regulated and unrelenting exclusion of happiness and comfort'.

Many Scots would have agreed with him and Sir Walter Scott was equally reactionary. His entry in his *Journal* for 20 February 1828 is illuminating: 'A certain Mr MacKay from Ireland called on me – an active gentleman, it would seem, about the reform of prisons. He exclaims – justly, I doubt not, about the state of our lock-up houses. For myself I have some distrust of the fanaticism even of philanthropy ... The philanthropy of Howard, mingled with his ill-usage of his son, seems to have risen to a pitch of insanity. Yet without such extraordinary men, who call attention to the subject by their own peculiarities, prisons would have remained the same dungeons which they were forty or fifty years ago. I do not, however, see the propriety of making them dandy places of detention. They should be places of punishment, and that can hardly be if men are lodged better, and fed better than when they were at large ... As to reformation, I have no great belief in it, when the ordinary classes of culprits, who are vicious from ignorance or habit, are the subjects of the experiment ... The state of society now leads to such accumulations of humanity, that we cannot wonder if it ferment and reek like a compost dunghill ... A great deal, I think, might be done, by executing the punishment of *death*, without a chance of escape, in all cases to which it should be found properly applicable; of course these occasions being diminished to one out of twenty to which capital punishment is now assigned ... When once men are taught that a crime of a certain character is connected inseparably with death, the moral habits of a population become altered, and you may in the next age remit the punishment which in this it has been necessary to inflict with stern severity.'[4]

This then was articulate Scottish opinion, not necessarily that of the common man, but his views are not on record. What were Scottish prisons like? Did they fall short of the stern standards regarded by Sidney Smith as just? Were they the 'places of punishment' approved by Scott? From Howard we have a detailed account of Scottish prisons. He visited Scotland and Ireland in 1779 and again in 1782 and 1783 and inspected the prisons of Edinburgh, Glasgow, Perth, Inverness, Nairn, Stirling, Jedburgh and others; he found them generally to be 'old buildings, dirty and offensive, without courtyards and also generally without water'.[5] He cited the following defects in the Scottish prisons. First, they had no courtyards. The original cause of this seems to have been the customary harsh treatment meted out to debtors in Scotland by which they were strictly confined and denied even the benefit of fresh air. Thus debtors were treated with a severity curiously out of harmony with the comparatively lenient penal code, and were liable to stocks and scourging. Second, prisons were very dirty and there was a general lack of water and sewers. Water was carried in by keepers who often did not live on the premises.

Inverness he found 'the most dirty and offensive prison that I have seen in Scotland'.[6] Third, the prisons were not visited by the magistrates. Fourth, too little attention was paid to the separation of the sexes or to classification. Fifth, keepers were allowed licences for the sale of liquor and 'the county allowance being paid in money to the prisoners, they generally spend it on whisky instead of bread'.[7] Of Edinburgh Tolbooth Howard says severely, 'Such as have money have too much liberty. For in the same prison, I lately saw some, who were confined for a riot, drinking whisky in the taproom, in company with many profligate townsmen, who were readily admitted, as they promoted the sale of the gaoler's liquors.'[8] Sixth, as in all prisons, there was much sickness.

When Howard revisited Scotland he found that 'The new journies to Scotland, now extended as far as Inverness, afford little but censure for the neglect of the prisons in that country'.[9] Referring to the prisons in Edinburgh, Howard remarked to the Lord Provost that 'the splendid improvements carrying on in their places of entertainment, streets, squares, bridges, etc. seemed to occupy all the attention of the gentlemen in office, to the total neglect of this essential branch of the police'.[10]

Nevertheless Howard found much to praise in Scottish prisons compared with those in England and on the Continent. All criminals were tried out of irons, and women were not ironed at all, unlike English prisons and some Continental ones where jailers demanded payment for 'easement of irons'. Also, when acquitted the accused were at once discharged in open court and no jailer had a fee from any criminal.[11] With regard to debtors, if a debtor 'declares upon oath that he has not wherewithal to maintain himself, the creditor must aliment him within ten days after notice is given for that purpose, with at least 3d a day, but generally the magistrates order 6d. By the process of *cessio bonorum* a debtor after being a month in prison, may obtain his liberty . . . by making a surrender of all his effects to be divided among his creditors: though if he afterwards comes into better circumstances his effects may be attached for the payment of those debts. This compassionate law prevents a creditor putting his debtor in prison, unless he has good reason to believe he is acting fraudulently',[12] whereas in English prisons a debtor was not released until he had paid 20/- in the pound. The English debtor was thus often robbed of all hope, languishing in jail for twenty years or more. In 1729 more than 350 debtors died of starvation in the packed Marshalsea jail. In a previous year 300 had died in three months.[13] Men and women competed with rats in vile cellars for food occasionally thrown to them through trapdoors. Debtors in England were supposed, by an Act of George III, to get 4d a day maintenance, but Howard did not discover in all England and Wales twelve debtors who did, although felons had an allowance. 'Some debtors are the most pitiable objects in our gaols.'[14] Further, almost half the English local jails were in private hands with consequent abuses; this was not the case in Scotland, where the heritable jurisdictions had been abolished by the time of Howard's visits.

The clerk of justiciary told Howard that from January 1768 to May 1782 only 54 executions took place.[15] On 'an average for 30 years preceding the year 1797, the executions for all Scotland had not exceeded six in a year'.[16] These figures compare favourably with the English ones for the period; from 1749 to 1772 the annual average of executions in London alone was 29 or 30.[17]

Stern as the Scottish penal code was, it was infinitely milder than the English. To take only one example, ordinary thieving or 'pickery' was not a capital offence, unless the thief was one 'by habit and repute' or was committing his third offence. It is doubtful if our system was ever as sanguinary as that of England. Besides the milder code, the more lenient Scottish system allowed the judges discretionary power to give alternative and modified sentences according to the youth or circumstances of the accused, whereas in England every crime had its assigned penalty which was inflicted despite any extenuating circumstances. Thus Hume declared with some complacency, 'I repeat it therefore, without fear of contradiction, that generally speaking, and with a view to the ordinary course of vulgar practice ... our custom of punishment is eminently gentle'.[18]

Howard found relatively few prisoners in Scotland as compared with England and he attributed this to the beneficial effects of the parish schools and to the solid front presented by the ministers, parents and dominies in enforcing firm discipline. He probably overestimated Scottish piety but says, 'There are in Scotland but few prisoners; this is partly owing to the shame and disgrace annexed to imprisonment ... and partly to the general sobriety of manners produced by the care which parents and ministers take to instruct the rising generation'.[19] No parish was without a school and in some there were four or five. Howard added, 'It is scandalous for any person not to be possessed of a Bible'.[20]

James Neild, following in Howard's footsteps, published in 1812 his *State of the prisons in England, Scotland and Wales*, declaring 'Whoever visits the gaols in Scotland will, generally speaking, be forcibly struck with that "Destitution" which Hooker declares to be such an impediment to virtue, as, till it be removed, suffereth not the mind of man to admit of any other care'.[21] On two tours Neild conscientiously visited many Scottish prisons, and more than thirty years after Howard's journey north, he found them largely unchanged. The same filthy conditions persisted, with prisoners living in wretchedness. They wore their own clothes – sometimes for a year without changing them – and often subsisted on bread and water or a penny worth of small beer daily.

When Joseph Gurney toured prisons in North England and Scotland with his sister Elizabeth Fry in 1818 his findings were similar to Neild's and Howard's. As regards general conditions, 'There are certain peculiarities in the construction and management of many jails in Scotland . . . they may shortly be enumerated as follows: no airing-grounds; no change of rooms; tubs in the prisoners' cells for the reception of every kind of filth; black holes; no religious service; jailers living away from their prisons; consequently, an impossibility of any inspection, and an almost total absence of care'.[22]

Apart from aspects dealt with specifically later in this chapter, the overpowering impression which the prisons made on Neild and Gurney was of dirt and discomfort. Terse descriptions such as 'very dark – excessively dirty', 'no sewers are provided', 'tubs . . . extremely offensive', 'no bedding whatever or coals is here allowed', 'no fireplaces or bedsteads or bedding, except for a little loose straw on the floor', 'very damp and almost entirely dark', are commonplace in their reports.[23]

The Old Tolbooth of Edinburgh, the 'Heart of Midlothian', which may be regarded as epitomising most of the evils of the eighteenth-century Scottish prison, was described by Scott as 'a high and antique building, with turrets and iron grates',[24] and again, 'with narrow staircase, thick walls, and small apartments'.[25]

Lord Cockburn writes, 'A most atrocious jail it was, the very breath of which almost struck down any stranger who entered its dismal door; and as ill-placed as possible, without one inch of ground beyond its black and horrid walls. And these walls were very small; the entire hole being filled with little dark cells; heavy manacles the only security; airless, waterless, drainless; a living grave. One week of that dirty, fetid, cruel torture-house was a severer punishment than a year of our worst modern prison – more dreadful in its sufferings, more certain in its corruption, overwhelming the innocent with a more tremendous sense of despair, provoking the guilty to more audacious defiance.'[26]

On the wall of the upstairs Hall was a blackboard on which were painted the dismal verses originally designed for the King's Bench Prison:

> 'A prison is a house of care,
> A place where none can thrive,
> A touchstone true to try a friend,
> A grave for men alive.'[27]

The place of public execution was the flat roof of a low building attached to the western gable, and to reach it convicts were conducted across the Hall. William Chambers, the publisher, often visited debtors there in the last three years of the Tolbooth's existence. Criminals were confined in the East End and civil prisoners, including debtors, in the West End. The latter group could move about from the Hall to the apartments on the two upper stories. Chambers says, 'My experiences of Tolbooth life were in the days of the free-and-easy prison arrangements. As yet, neither county prison boards nor prison inspectors had been heard of ... So far as the debtors were concerned, the prison was little else than a union of lodging-house and tavern, under lock and key. Acquaintances might call as often and stay as long as they pleased. The inmates and their visitors, if they felt inclined, could treat themselves to refreshments in a cosy little apartment, half tavern, half kitchen, superintended by a portly female styled Lucky Laing, whence issued pretty frequently the pleasant sounds of broiling beefsteaks, and the drawing of corks from bottles of ale and porter'.[28] Chambers mentions the 'kind governor'; till his time condemned men and women were fed on bread and water for the six weeks between sentence and execution, but he broke this harsh rule and afterwards it was relaxed.

The Tolbooth was pulled down in 1817, the building of the new jail on the Calton Hill having begun in 1808. Cockburn deplored both the demolition of the Tolbooth because of its great historic interest and the siting of the Calton because 'It was a piece of undoubted bad taste to give so glorious an eminence to a prison'.[29]

Official surgeons were as rare as official chaplains, and even where there was an infirmary in the prison, as in Perth, it might not be used.[30] Edinburgh Calton shines by comparison. 'The infirmary is commodious and is regularly attended by the surgeon; there is also a small room fitted up for the reception of infectious cases.'[31]

Shackling, though less widespread than it had been, was still frequent, particularly in the case of condemned prisoners or refractory felons. Neild describes the Iron Room in Glasgow Tolbooth in 1809, to which 'the Prisoner, after sentence is immediately conducted. There, a blacksmith fixes an iron strap round his leg, again fastened by a ring, which encircles a strong iron bar, called the Goad; and this, running across, is rivetted down to the stone floor, so that he cannot raise that foot one inch from it. In this situation I beheld two wretched criminals, who had been condemned at the Justiciary Court in September 1809, and were to suffer on the 8th of November, on a platform in front of the Prison, which has a door conveniently adapted for the decent performance of that awful ceremony.'[32] 'The Magistrates, in addition to the 4d. a day paid in money, had humanely ordered them a hot dinner, to be sent from a tavern every day, and each had a wooden stool to sit upon. The Criminals appeared sensible of the kindness, and resigned to their tremendous doom.'[33] Neither was shackling confined to the condemned. In Ayr, Neild found one James Fisher who, imprisoned for stealing apples, had been in legbolts for sixty days. He had apparently shown signs of insanity, but as none of his relations was prepared to look after him he was kept indefinitely in prison.[34]

Added to the general squalor and inhumanity were the particular problems of lack of employment, lack of religious instruction, the peculiar misery of lunatics and debtors, and the power of

the jailer. It should be borne in mind however that the bridewells of Aberdeen, Edinburgh and Glasgow were exempt from
almost all the adverse criticism of Neild and Gurney. Employment
there was more or less constant and well paid, religious services
were regular, conditions were clean and baths frequent, bedding
plentiful and comfortable ('probably somewhat too comfortable').[35]

Like Howard, Neild and Gurney were favourably struck with
the relative paucity of criminals, particularly in the smaller county
jails. Neild visited more than thirty prisons in Scotland and in five
of them there were no prisoners at all. Of the rest, only the jails
and bridewells of Edinburgh, Glasgow and Aberdeen had more
than a dozen inmates (taking into account both felons and debtors).
In Greenlaw prison, for example, he found only one, a runaway
apprentice who 'had been for several months the only inhabitant
... decent-looking, well-behaved young man, of about 18; but
preferred remaining there in solitude, rather than return back to
his master'.[36] Gurney and Mrs Fry found no criminals in Dunbar,
Forfar, Brechin and Kinross. In Montrose was one unhappy de-
serter, in comfortless, total solitude; in Stonehaven there was only
one criminal, who had stolen ten shillings; in Kirkcaldy a woman
and her son, criminals confined together; and Cupar county jail
held only one occupant, a poor girl who had stolen a few potatoes
out of a field. Gurney asks: 'Where are we to find a parallel to this
paucity of criminals in any county jail of England or Ireland?'[37] In
Dundee prison, which was the jail 'not only for the town of
Dundee (which is said to contain 35,000 inhabitants) but also for
a considerable district of the County of Forfar, we found not a
single criminal in it; and the magistrate who was so obliging as to
accompany us, stated that there had not been a criminal in it for
seven months'.[38]

Gurney goes on to speculate that 'the small extent of crime ...
may be attributed mainly to the universal religious education of
the lower orders, and to the general dissemination amongst them
of the Holy Scriptures'.[39] And again 'In many parts of Scotland,
such are the effects of the education and independence prevailing
amongst the people, that crime is but seldom committed: the
consequence is, that the criminal's confinement is generally solitary; evil association is avoided; the petty offender escapes the

contaminating influence of adepts in crime; there is no herding together of large and lawless and dissolute companies'.[40]

Southey in his *Letters From England* endorses this opinion and elaborates on it. 'More offences are committed in England than in other countries because there is more wealth and more want; greater temptations to provoke the poor, greater poverty to render them liable to temptation, and less religious instruction to arm them against it. In Scotland, where the puritan clergy retain something of their primitive zeal, the people are more moral, poverty is almost general there and therefore the less felt, because there is little wealth to invite the contrast.'[41]

It may be that these comments by Southey and the reformers tend to oversimplify; the scarcity of prisoners in certain parts of Scotland does not necessarily imply that the Scots were more law-abiding. Many Scottish communities were very isolated and remote, much more so than the English, and they exercised their own discipline. It was a matter of practical expediency as well as local pride to deal with trouble-makers themselves. Poor roads alone would have made for a difficult journey to the nearest court of justice and a couple of men would have had to escort the offender and lose a day's work or more, which in a poverty-stricken community they could ill afford to do. Also, as there was a great deal of antagonism between neighbouring communities, each one would be loath to put itself to shame by parading its offenders. Thus even after the heritable jurisdictions were abolished in 1747 the attitude of mind was still geared to summary local justice. The idea of wrongdoers being dealt with by the central authority in towns was new and difficult to assimilate. The practice of banishing the offender from the district also continued, even in cases where he would have been more severely dealt with if the case had come to court. Also deeply ingrained was the habit of submission to the discipline of the minister and Kirk Session which persisted in the small isolated communities even though their power was waning in the larger ones. A kind of rough justice prevailed, having something in common with some of the early settlements in America.

In the larger towns the position is different, although in Neild's time the number of felons was still remarkably low. In Edinburgh Tolbooth in 1802 there were 26 felons, and in the Bridewell 51; in

Glasgow jail 27, and in the Bridewell 90; in Aberdeen in 1809 there were in the jail 8 felons and 7 petty offenders.[42] But in 1818 Gurney found the new Glasgow jail crowded to suffocation. 'There are seldom less than 200 prisoners in the jail ... The number of criminals committed during the last three years amounting to 3,068.'[43] In 1819 an American visitor found more than 200 prisoners in the Glasgow Bridewell. The Keeper showed him the books stating that 'the daily average of prisoners during the last year was 210'.[44] Similarly Gurney remarked that the Edinburgh Bridewell was meant for 144 prisoners, but the persons committed were far more numerous, resulting in improper overcrowding.[45]

Gurney explains the comparatively large number of prisoners in Aberdeen in this way: 'I believe the fact may be accounted for, chiefly by some large cotton factories, in which upwards of some 5,000 persons of both sexes work together in large companies. The manufacturing poor at Dundee work separately each in his own cottage, and at Dundee there are no criminals.'[46] Southey came to the same conclusion. 'In consequence of herding together such numbers of both sexes who are utterly uninstructed in the commonest principles of religion and morality' inevitably the men became drunken and the women dissolute.[47]

Again the diagnosis requires elaboration. As long as the family exists as a vital authoritarian element in the community, there is less crime. In remote areas of Scotland the authority of the family tended to survive to a much greater extent than it did in the larger towns. In towns like Dundee where cottage industry was still the norm, the family was still the unit and there was little or no crime, for there were fewer opportunities for young people to break away and achieve independence, and in many cases it is a revolt against authority which so often leads to crime. In the Aberdeen cotton factories the same family loyalties were not adhered to. When living and working in a family business to steal from it is against all traditional ties of loyalty. But in a factory with a large number of strangers no such loyalty exists, and if an easy way, criminal or not, presented itself of augmenting their meagre wages many seized the opportunity.

With the exception of the bridewells, Howard's principle of keeping prisoners usefully employed during the day was hardly observed in the Scottish prisons of the period and even in the bridewells the choice of labour was very limited. The reason for this was obviously the practical impossibility of finding interesting work for a mass of people from disparate backgrounds and with few or no skills. The result was that the prisoners 'remained in an unchecked condition of idleness, riot, and vice of every description'.[48]

In the prisons generally, no attempt at all was made to find work for the prisoners. In the Edinburgh Tolbooth, 'No employment is permitted'.[49] In Montrose, debtors were not allowed to work 'even if they can procure it of themselves'.[50] Gurney found the Edinburgh Calton Jail 'quite deficient in one great point of vital importance ... no provision for the employment of the prisoners'.[51] In Glasgow Tolbooth he saw 'total idleness'.[52] Perth prison was one of the few exceptions, indeed the only one specifically mentioned by Neild. The felons were allowed to work and to keep all they earned. At the time of Neild's visit three of the five female prisoners were spinning.[53] This old prison at the foot of the High Street was abandoned in 1819 when a new one was built, but was later reoccupied as a small bridewell on the principle of complete separation, the prisoners working in cells at teasing hair or picking oakum. But in the new 1819 common jail, 'They are allowed to associate daily in the airing-ground, and in a dirty day room in complete idleness, thus neutralising all attempts at reformation'.[54] This was in 1836 and Mr Hill, Inspector of Prisons in Scotland, reported: 'Very little good effect can be produced by imprisonment in the Perth jail. The number of recommittals is very considerable ... no small number of the lowest class at Perth are well content to be in the prison occasionally, as they fare better there than at home, and are not required to do any work. The conduct of the prisoners is generally bad, and sometimes very turbulent.'[55] Whereas in the small bridewell a well regulated discipline reigned, 'The expense incurred beyond the prisoner's earning, including aliment, washing and a sum of money given to each at his dismissal, was $1\frac{3}{4}$d. each per day'.[56] Prisoners in the common jail cost 5d.

A different picture emerges from the bridewells, not surprisingly since they were intended for the 'correction' of vagrants and petty offenders by a course of labour. In the Edinburgh Bridewell there were thirteen workrooms in each of the four storeys.[57]

Gurney found the prisoners employed in weaving linen, cotton, and woollen stuffs. All the bedding and clothing used in the prison were made there. 'The produce of a prisoner's labour is applied to his own maintenance' and any surplus (which was common) was for the support of his family or given to him in three parts, (a) when leaving prison, (b) and (c) on certification of good conduct being received after six and then twelve months.[58] According to Neild, 'The accounts of this Prison both with respect to diet and to work, are kept on a plan of singular correctness. The diet of each Prisoner is estimated at 1/6 per week'; (which is considerably less than the average allowance to felons in the proper prisons), 'to which is added the expence of clothes during confinement: What the Prisoner's earnings exceed the above disbursements, is entered in a book for the purpose'.[59] In the Aberdeen Bridewell, the occupants worked at spinning and picking oakum, and their earnings were similarly applied.

On the other hand, in the Glasgow Bridewell, where the women prisoners were employed in weaving, tambouring, picking of cotton, and the fabrication of sprig-muslin, the prisoners' earnings in excess of expenses were presented to them *in toto* on discharge, sometimes with unfortunate results. 'During my visit in 1802, an account was given me of one Margaret Raymond, who at her discharge received no less than fifteen pounds ten shillings and eleven pence; Another Prisoner had eleven pounds five shillings; and a third, five pounds nine shillings. Poor Margaret, however, became too rich to be prudent; she unluckily took the whole of her money at one payment; and being ineffectually lectured by past trials, the consequence was, that want of sobriety, and riotous behaviour, soon sent her back to her old habitation.'[60] In another place, Neild points the moral: 'To characters indiscreet from ignorance, the exertion of strict economy, at their Liberation from a Gaol, is in fact the truest charity'.[61]

Neild put the moral principle in this way: 'The Salary of a Gaoler should ever be proportioned to the trust and trouble incident to his important charge. He should draw no Emolument whatever from Misery'.[62] This remark was made in the context of the Glasgow Tolbooth, where the jailer (who had a salary of £60) was obliged to pay £100.2s per annum in wages to his staff. In addition to his salary, however, he had a licence to sell porter, ale and beer and to provide the prisoners with bread, and Neild deduced that a large proportion of his income must derive from the taproom.[63]

In the county jails it does not seem possible to relate the salaries of the jailers to their responsibilities, though of course the latter were variable. In Greenlaw, for example, where for several months there had been only one petty offender, the jailer's salary was £20.[64] In Jedburgh, where there were two debtors and three felons, the salary was only £5.[65]

In addition to their salaries, the jailers were generally entitled to fees in relation to debtors. There was usually a charge of 2/6d or 5/- (paid by the incarcerating creditor) for 'caption', which was the warrant for the apprehension of a debtor. In Edinburgh Tolbooth the caption fee was 6d per £1 of debt.[66] In Glasgow Tolbooth the Burgess debtor *paid* a caption fee of 2/9½d, the non-Burgess 5/6½d.[67] This distinction between Burgess and non-Burgess was more frequently used in calculating the fees due by the debtor himself to the jailer. Such fees were charged in the majority of prisons, usually at a rate of 4d a night. In Dumfries, Kirkcudbright, Edinburgh Tolbooth, this was reduced to 2d for Burgesses. 'Gaolers frequently detain what effects the Prisoner may have had in Gaol, until they are paid their fees; and, for want of payment, sometimes obtain warrant, and sell the effects by auction.'[68] In most prisons liberation fees were obsolete, but in Edinburgh Tolbooth and the Canongate they persisted. Edinburgh Tolbooth allowed a welcome privilege. 'Any person imprisoned for Civil Debt desiring to have a room by himself shall pay for the same such sum as shall be agreed on with the Gaoler, and that in full of all fees, but such sum shall, in no case, exceed 10s weekly.'[69] Garnish fees seem to have existed only in the Glasgow Tolbooth. The 2s each, charged on the lower flat, went, Neild assumed, into a fund to provide coals and candles for the taproom.[70]

The jailers in Dumfries, Edinburgh Tolbooth, the Canongate and Glasgow Tolbooth had licences to sell porter, ale and beer. Neild remarks: 'I cannot approve of a practice so justly unsatisfactory' and 'what is a licensed tap, but the certain means of introducing drunkenness and profligacy?'[71] The situation was exacerbated in the Glasgow Tolbooth by the practice of giving the felons their 4d. per day in money. As a result, the taproom was 'generally filled both with Prisoners and Towns-people; so that the Tap is constantly kept running'.[72]

One of the Rules to be observed by the 'Jaylor and his assistants' in Glasgow Tolbooth was: 'The Jaylor and his servants are expressly prohibited, on any account, to sell, or suffer to be brought into any of the Prisoners, spirits or strong liquor, whereby they may be in danger of being intoxicated; and to use their utmost endeavours to promote sobriety among those under their charge.'[73] This contradiction between giving a jailer a licence, from which a substantial part of his income is to be derived, and at the same time enjoining him to 'use his utmost endeavour to promote sobriety', is perhaps an indication of the extent to which the provisions of these rules were put into practice.

'The spirit of the law of Scotland is mild, in regard to the imprisonment of debtors: while it is sufficiently vigilant to prevent fraudulent absconding.'[74] At the time of Neild's second visit in 1809, there were in the thirty two prisons he saw only 112 debtors in all. The chief reason for this was the humane principle of *cessio bonorum*, praised by Howard as we have seen, and the law (Act of Grace 1696) by which an incarcerating creditor had to pay an insolvent debtor aliment at not less than 3d. a day within ten days or consent to his liberation. After 1825 the incarcerating creditor had to pay a deposit of 10/- as security for any aliment that might be awarded. If it was, the debtor would be liberated when the deposit was exhausted unless the creditor had already lodged a further sum. If no aliment was awarded, the deposit was returned. Aliment depended on the rank of life in which the debtor moved.

'The privilege of giving sanctuary was anciently enjoyed by many places, as the Mint or "cunzie house" [coining house]. The Castle of Edinburgh seems also to have been at one time considered as a sanctuary.'[75] By this time however only the Palace of Holyroodhouse and its precincts was recognised by law as a sanctuary, 'not as an ancient religious establishment, but as a royal residence'.[76] William Chambers says that the Sanctuary of Holyrood 'was seldom without distinguished characters from England – some of them gaunt, oldish gentlemen, seemingly broken down men of fashion, wearing big gold spectacles, who now drew out existence here in defiance of creditors'.[77]

The privilege extended only to the non-fraudulent civil debtor. When he had entered the precincts he was protected against personal diligence for twenty-four hours. Thereafter he had to register his name in the books kept by the bailie of the Abbey, and Neild tells us that the registration fee was fifteen shillings[78] – a considerable amount for a bankrupt. The debtor was not protected against diligence (i.e. a method of enforcing payment of a judgement debt) for debts contracted during his residence within the sanctuary; there was for this purpose a prison within the precincts ('one room above stairs, about 15 feet square, with a fire-place in it, and a window that looks into the court').[79]

We come now to the second, slightly sinister, limb of Bell's dictum: 'while it is sufficiently vigilant to prevent fraudulent absconding'. It was this aspect of the law relating to debtors which roused the indignation of all the prison visitors. An act of Session 1771 gives this definition of *squalor carceris*, 'There are no courtyards to the gaols in Scotland where debtors are confined. The original cause of this seems to have been the following very severe maxim in the Scotch law: "After a debtor is imprisoned, he ought not to be indulged with the benefit of the air, nor even under a guard; for Creditors have an interest, that their Debtors be kept under close confinement, that by the *squalor carceris* they may be brought to pay their debt".'[80] Despite this it is perhaps worth noting that Neild says of Selkirk jail, completed in 1806, 'except that of Dumfries, it is the only one in Scotland which has courtyards for the prisoners',[81] and it may be that by this time debtors were not so much deliberately victimised as simply obliged to share with the other prisoners the general squalor. But from the debtors' point of view the result was the same. For example in Nairn, Neild thought that 'Both the prisoners' (one debtor, one felon) 'looked very squalid; and but too exactly exhibited that genuine "Squalor Carceris", already noticed with Horror'. The felon was 'a Woman, with her infant Child!'[82]

On the other hand Gurney draws attention to the jailer's interest in keeping alive the old principle: By Scots law, if a debtor escapes from prison, the jailer, and through him the magistrate who issued the warrant, become responsible for the debt; therefore the jailer and magistrate protect their own interest. Thus 'the Scotch debtor is consigned to the closest and most severe confinement. He has no yard to walk in ... he is kept like the vilest criminal', often crowded together in a close and fetid room which he is never allowed to quit. Should 'enactments productive of so much un-merited cruelty ... be any longer tolerated by a civilised and Christian community?'[83] The magistrates remained liable for the debts of an escaped prisoner until 1839.

In Haddington county jail Gurney found three debtors in con-ditions which he felt violated 'the common principles of justice and humanity'. He described 'the most objectionable point of this terrible prison, namely, its accommodation for those debtors who are not burgesses ... These unhappy persons, innocent as they are of any punishable offence ... are confined day and night, without any change ... in a closet containing one small bed, and measuring not quite 9 feet square'.[84]

An English visitor has left a grim picture of the Tolbooth in 1820: 'He ... entered the abode of misery, the worst and most circumscribed jail in Europe, the Edinburgh Tolbooth, which has neither a felon's yard for air or exercise or even an area for debtors to breathe anything but dirt and infection'.[85]

In Perth, in the prison at the foot of the High Street, built on the site of the ancient chapel dedicated to the Virgin Mary, there was the inscription:

> 'Think with thyself whilst thou art on the Vay,
> And take some course thy Creditor to pay
> Lest thou by him before a Judge be calld
> And by ane officer by here inthralld
> Till utmost farthing shall by thee be paid
> Thou shalt be close within this Prison staid.'[86]

This cautionary verse remained valid until 1880 when imprison-ment for civil debt was generally abolished, though imprisonment for debts under £8 6s 8d was made incompetent in 1835.

Considering Scotland's reputation for her attitude to religion and for the universal authority of her ministers (which indeed were the chief reasons advanced by Neild and Gurney for the relative lack of crime), it may seem strange that in almost all the prisons Neild visited there was little or no provision for religious instruction. Gurney remarked on the inconsistency: 'How dis-graceful is such an omission in a Christian country! and how extraordinary in Scotland, where the communication of Christian knowledge is, for the most part, an object of so great attention!'[87] It is possible that the Calvinist inheritance may have been in some way responsible; wrongdoers tended to be written off as not worthy of help. Certainly in England, in a great many of the prisons visited by Neild, prayers twice a week and a Sunday sermon were normal. Many Scottish prisons had no chaplains and no 'religious attentions' and in some, even those under sentence of death had no spiritual comfort 'unless gratuitously and voluntarily attended'.[88] Gurney said of Glasgow jail that although there were seldom less than 200 in the jail there was no public worship and no instruction. Thus the Glasgow jail is 'a fruitful source of very extensive evil ... the jailer assured us that they uniformly leave the prison worse than when they entered it. He reckons, that of those who have been once committed, two thirds come back again.'[89] Gurney added that 'Crimes have of late been rapidly increasing in Glasgow. The fact may be accounted for, partly by the vast increase of manufacturing establishments, partly by the large accession of uneducated Irish, but, perhaps chiefly by the powerful machinery of corruption.'[90]

Edinburgh Tolbooth seems to have evolved its own peculiar principle. 'From what I saw here, I cannot but think that very little attention is paid to reforming the prisoners of the Tolbooth. In the first place, an attendance on Divine service is singularly made optional with the Debtors, and not permitted to Felons,'[91] though the latter were allowed a Bible each or a Testament.

Apart from the bridewells, Aberdeen Tolbooth was the only exception to this extraordinary state of affairs. There the regular chaplain attended on Tuesdays, Thursdays and Sundays.

In Edinburgh Bridewell an official chaplain attended every Sunday. 'To each room ... a Bible is assigned; and those who cannot read, are every Sunday detained with those who can read.'[92] In Glasgow Bridewell the regular chaplain officiated every Sunday. Elizabeth Fry, on her visit to the prisons of the north with Joseph Gurney her brother, met the Glasgow magistrates and a number of interested ladies and encouraged them to 'attempt the same kind of reform and moral superintendence and instruction which had proved so satisfactory in the Metropolis.' In 1819 an American visitor to the Glasgow Bridewell and Lunatic Asylum observed the inmates of several cells 'drawn together, and one of the committee reads a portion of Scripture to the degraded objects of their care. In passing the door of one of their cells I noticed the profound attention of the prisoners to their amiable instructress. One of them was bathed in tears.'[93]

Prevailing conditions are further illustrated by the following accounts of two more Scottish prisons. As we saw, Gurney found no criminals at Dundee in 1818, but about 1823 'an epidemic of lawlessness broke out which proved too much for the few constables. Assault and robbery were so common that the jail could not hold all the prisoners.'[94] People who had to be out late went armed with loaded pistols, for bands of robbers were organised. By 1831 the situation became so bad that the inhabitants urged the magistrates to build a new bridewell, but it was not until 1837 that a new building in Bell Street was completed at a cost of £12,000. While it was under construction one of the large rooms in the Old Steeple was used as a temporary jail, as well as cells in the Town House. The Old Steeple was thought to be a safer prison than the Town House, whence yet another prisoner had escaped. The insecurity of those two prisons was so great that speed was made to finish the new one and discontinue them, and in July 1837 '92 criminals from both places were removed to the new Bridewell in Bell Street between 2 and 3 a.m. by a party of soldiers from Dudhope Barracks and a posse of police'.[95]

At Greenock 'the earliest prison of which there is any information was set up by the magistrates in a thatched house at the foot of Broad Close. Jougs were affixed to the wall ... Sometime thereafter a change was made to the old court-house and jail on a site between Cross-shire Street and Broad Close, now occupied by the Post Office. On this being found insufficient as a prison, the keep or Massimore of Greenock Mansion House was utilised until 1765, when the Town Buildings were erected in Hamilton Street. Later there was a guard-house in Market Street. In 1808 Sir John Stewart agreed to give ground behind the Mid Kirk for the building of a Bridewell, and private subscriptions were made for this purpose. The architecture was in the old castle style, with two towers in front and battlements on the top.'[96]

The early nineteenth century also saw the building of many new prisons, for example 'the rudimentary classicism of the unobtrusive little jail at Inveraray (c. 1820) and the fortress-like aspect of the complex radial lay-out at Jedburgh (1823) are illustrative of a wide range of style and plan-types'. The Old Calton Jail, of which only the Governor's house remains, was a 'spirited essay in the castellated manner'.[97] There seems to be a certain illogicality in the external embellishments of these castellated buildings. All these towers may not have detracted from the security of the prisons, but they were superfluous. It was part of Howard's principles that money should not be wasted on unnecessary ornamentation. He considered that prison architecture should be strictly practical. But the nineteenth century concept of external appearance was the result of some confusion between the objectives of the confinement of inmates on the one hand and the repulsion of invaders on the other. Scott's romanticism brought about attempts to revive this traditional Gothic castellated style of building, and these embellishments were adopted by nineteenth-century prison builders who saw in them ideal security patterns. The architects seem to have forgotten or ignored the fact that their principal object was to keep prisoners in, not to keep attackers out.

4
Prisoners of War
1756–1815

*The first time I ever saw a procession of French
prisoners, it frightened me. I thought the world
was at an end when I beheld so many skeletons in
motion.*

Mrs Oliver Elton*

4

Little has been written about the many thousands of prisoners of war in Britain during the years 1756–1815. This is curious because the prisoners, especially the officers on parole, formed an important feature of national life, mostly in the country towns, where their presence made a great though not a lasting impression. Few stories of their sojourn have been handed down, and only some graves and a few exquisitely carved bone and wooden ships and boxes survive here and there to testify to their presence.

The main focus of interest is on the French prisoners, since the numbers from North America, Spain, Holland, Denmark and other countries were insignificant by comparison. During the Seven Years' War (1756–63) the annual average of prisoners of war in Britain was 18,800, and the total had risen in 1762 to 26,137. In the Revolutionary War of 1798 the number of French prisoners had soared to 35,000. Between 1803 and 1814 a total of 122,440 prisoners was brought to Britain. 10,341 of them died in captivity and 17,607 were exchanged or sent back home sick or on parole. The greatest number of prisoners at any one time in Britain was about 72,000, in 1814.[1]

The prisoners were housed either in land prisons, in the hulks at Portsmouth, Plymouth and Chatham, or in private lodgings mostly in small country houses where they lived on parole if they were officers above a certain rank. The treatment of these men in the land prisons and on parole was similar in many cases to the treatment of British prisoners in France, but life in the hulks was grim. Those for whom no room could be found in the packed hulks were herded together wherever space was available, in borough jails, which were often fearful places, in common prisons like the Savoy in London, in adapted country houses like Sissinghurst in Kent, in adapted farmhouses in Cornwall, or in barracks as in Winchester and Edinburgh.

In 1760 the Government began to search for permanent land accommodation. The royal palace at Linlithgow narrowly escaped conversion to a war prison. Scott alludes to this in *Waverley*: 'They halted at Linlithgow, distinguished by its ancient palace ... whose venerable ruins, not quite sixty years since, very narrowly escaped the unworthy fate of being converted into a barrack for French prisoners.'[2] In 1806 Dartmoor was built, to hold 6,000 prisoners, although it was not occupied until 1809. The annual expense of a hulk to hold 700 prisoners was £5,864, while a prison the size of Dartmoor cost only £2,862 a year. But the hulks were kept in service throughout the Napoleonic Wars, and refractory men from land prisons all over Britain continued to be sent there.

By 1814 there were nine large prisons in Britain, including two in Scotland, at Perth and at Valleyfield depot near Penicuik, holding in all about 45,000 prisoners.[3]

The story of how the Perth Depot came to be built is a tortuous one. The ancient jail at the foot of the High Street had long been deemed inadequate, and the Town Council decided that the only possible place for the new jail was the ground on which the historic Gowrie House stood. There was however one apparently insurmountable obstacle: the Town Council had itself bestowed Gowrie House on the Duke of Cumberland as a reward for winning the Battle of Culloden. He, having no wish to own an historic Scottish building, lost no time in selling it to the Government. The Board of Ordnance used it as a barracks and proposed to house a regiment of foot there. In 1809 the wily Perth Council saw a way round the obstacle. They succeeded in buying nine acres of land (later increased to seventeen) from Moncrieff of that Ilk, and exchanged them with the Government for Gowrie House. The Government at once proceeded to build a Depot for French prisoners, and the Town Council to destroy Gowrie House.

This transaction which Penny indignantly calls 'one of the most shameful ever done in Perth'[4] enabled the Depot to be started in 1811 and finished in record time; part of it was ready for occupation by August 1812. It was intended to hold 7,000 men closely packed, including a hospital for 1,000 or 1,200 petty officers and invalids (later to house criminal lunatics and provide jailers' houses) and accommodation for troops on guard. One of the hospital wards was allotted to prisoners who had broken their parole. *The Perth Courier* reported on 9 July 1812, 'The Depot forms altogether the greatest establishment of the kind in Britain ... the ingenious and unusual mode adopted for ventilating, and introducing fresh air into the different prison buildings, and other means for ensuring the health and cleanliness of the prisoners and the secure manner in which every part of it is constructed, it is certainly the most complete Depot or Place of Confinement which has yet been erected ... While it is to be deplored that the necessity of such establishments exists, it is at the same time satisfactory, and credit-able to the country, also that such accommodation is provided for our prisoners as admits of their enjoying every comfort and con-venience, consistent with their unfortunate situation.'

The first division to arrive consisted of 400 men from Plymouth, landed from a frigate in the Tay at Dundee in August 1812, and marched up through the Carse, lodging for the night in a church. In Perth large numbers turned out to see this novel sight. In the winter, after Salamanca, great numbers were landed at Kirkcaldy and marched through Fife in foul weather. The roads were bad and many of the men in wretched plight. Many, half-naked in the bitter cold, gave up on the way. These were flung into carts one above the other, and when the carts were full others were tied to the back with ropes and dragged along.[5] But in Perth they were to find one of the healthiest prisons in Britain. In February 1814, despite the excessive cold, the prisoners in the Depot continued to be surprisingly healthy. There had been no deaths among them for a long time, and the sick in hospital numbered only between 10 and 20 (out of 7,000).[6]

In 1804 the old mansionhouse of Greenlaw near Edinburgh was bought by the Government and converted into a Depot for 200 prisoners. After 1814 Greenlaw was empty until 1846 when exten-sive, mainly wooden buildings were added, and it was used as the military prison of Scotland until 1888. In 1899 much of it was demolished, and the only relic now is a stone guard-house.

In 1810 the Government bought Esk Mills at Valleyfield near Penicuik, nine miles south of Edinburgh, and in 1811 the first 350 prisoners arrived. Soon there was accommodation for 5,000. The three-storey wooden buildings were surrounded by a stout wooden stockade. No fireplaces were provided, as it was considered that 'the animal heat of the closely-packed inmates'[7] would make them unnecessary, but the French felt the cold cruelly. Prisoners for Valleyfield were landed at Port Glasgow and marched by Glasgow, Bathgate and Edinburgh.

From 1756 till 1814 the vaults of Edinburgh Castle were used for the custody of French prisoners, especially those from privateers. In 1759 the Castle held 362 prisoners, and a correspondent wrote to the Edinburgh *Evening Courant* on behalf of the ragged miserable creatures seen trudging along the High Street to the Castle. Many who saw them were moved to tears. 'The City Hospitals for Young Maidens' offered to make shirts for twopence each, and sundry tailors to make a certain number of jackets and breeches for nothing.'[8] At the end of the Seven Years' War in 1763, the 500 prisoners then in the Castle sailed home to France from Leith.

The parts of the Castle where prisoners were kept are now military storerooms, but are probably very much as they were then. Steep flights of stone steps lead down to the subterranean chill beneath. In these dungeons the Frenchmen pined, with as many as forty men to a vault. Heavily-built doors and strongly-barred small apertures intensified the gloom. The initials of some of the inmates can still be seen carved on the walls.

Officers on parole enjoyed very different conditions and they played a large part in the everyday social life of many parts of England, Scotland and Wales for at least sixty years, leaving behind pleasant memories of gaiety, charm and courtesy. At one time there were 5,000 in Britain. The parole system was in practice from the beginning of the Seven Years' War and the rules were very strict. An understanding existed between Britain and France that officers who broke their parole and escaped should be imprisoned in their own country or sent back to the enemy. According to the parole form of 1797, officers could walk on the great turnpike road within one mile from the end of the town but not into any field or crossroad, and they had to return to their lodgings at 5 p.m. in winter and 8 p.m. in summer. (Sometimes the prisoners got round this rule by moving the milestones some distance further on.) Rewards were offered for the recapture of prisoners who had escaped, which often encouraged the riff-raff of the neighbour-

hood to tempt prisoners to break parole. Louis Garneray, captured
from a French ship and imprisoned in Britain for ten years until
1814, much of that time spent in the hulks, says, 'Any citizen who
sees a Frenchman clearly disobeying the parole regulations is entitled to seize him or strike him down like a wild beast; and he
gets a reward of a pound for doing it'.[9] Garneray escaped, was
recaptured and imprisoned in the Black Hole, swarming with
vermin. The agents, whose duty it was to guard and look after the
needs of the prisoners and censor their correspondence, were not
chosen from 'the ranks of shopkeepers' because the French complained that these were not fitted by position and background to
deal with officers and gentlemen. So in the later part of the war
agents were always naval lieutenants of not less than ten years'
standing. In Scotland agents seem to have been on excellent terms
with the prisoners.

Officers on parole were sent to small country towns, generally
on the Borders. In these pleasant places they contrived to make
the best of things. They were treated with kindliness and tolerance.
Scott entertained them hospitably at Abbotsford, though he always thought of them as foreign soldiers. Thus in a letter of May
1812 to Lady Abercorn he mentions 'the multitude of French
prisoners who are scattered through the small towns of this country, as I think very improvidently. As the peace of this county is
intrusted to me I thought it necessary to state to the Justice Clerk
that the arms of the local militia were kept without any guard in
a warehouse at Kelso that there was nothing to prevent the prisoners there at Selkirk and at Jedburgh from joining any one night
and making themselves master of that depot.'[10]

While the enemy governments all tried to treat their prisoners
humanely, their goodwill had no power over their subordinates
who dealt with the prisoners at first hand and were accused, often
with truth, of brutality, avarice and dishonesty. In Britain, prisoners were looked after by the 'Commissioners for taking care of
sick and wounded seamen and for exchanging Prisoners of War'
(abbreviated to the 'Sick and Hurt Office'). In 1799 the care of
prisoners of war was transferred to the Transport Office till 1817.

Contemporary accounts and the testimony of French prisoners
themselves seem to agree that the treatment of the latter in Scotland was good, and the health of the prisoners, particularly in

Perth, excellent and well above the national average throughout Britain, especially that of Dartmoor. This was the most hated land prison of all – measles killed off one fifth of the prisoners in the winter of 1809-10.

In France, British prisoners at times were subject to ill-treatment, much depending on the character of the local commandent and on local feeling. In 1799, at Calais and Dunkirk, Howard 'found that gross overcrowding and inadequate food were the worst features of the gaols in which British sailors were held'. But to balance this, when he inspected the French prisoners at Plymouth, 'The reports he had heard in France of their treatment were only too well founded. In the hospital . . . there was evidence of utter neglect', and in Winchester prison he found over 1,000 French prisoners 'confined is so small a space that the air itself was offensive'.[11] Howard himself had been a prisoner in French hands in 1756, when the ship in which he was sailing to Portugal was captured. He spent two months in France on parole and had ample opportunity to observe his countrymen 'being treated with such barbarity' that many died.

The experiences of prisoners of war on both sides of the Channel were similar in many ways. A British sailor, George Casse, was a prisoner of war in France from 1809 until 1814. He wrote of his arrival at Calais town jail, 'although I was faint and hungry I could not find an appetite for such miserable allowance. An earthern pan of hot greasy water, crammed full of miserable, coarse bread, sour, and almost the colour of my hat', and at Arras, whose citadel held 5,000 prisoners, he 'was particularly struck . . . with the sickly and squalid appearance of so many of my poor countrymen'.

Casse and several others escaped, were recaptured and marched in chains for days to a depot, sometimes lodged in 'the tower of an old ruinous church where, covered with sweat and dust, we were all crammed, regardless of the chilling damp that saturated its walls'. In a village which had no regular jail they were 'put into a hole under the church, which had been used as a charnel house . . . many human bones lay scattered about it,' and rats ran over them in the night. At the fortress of Bitche, where Casse was to spend many months, 'not infrequently a storm would beat in the lattices and cover our beds with snow'.[12]

It was a corrupt, hard, and callous age, generally indifferent to suffering: and viewed in the context of the time and bearing in mind our brutal behaviour to our own soldiers and sailors, prisoners of war could hardly expect tender treatment from government subordinates.

The dreaded hulks were worst of all. There the unfortunates dragged out lives of unbroken suffering. The hulks stand alone – nothing comparable to them existed elsewhere. But it should be remembered that many of the combatants on both sides who fought in the long wars were born and bred in bitterly poor conditions. They were inured to hardship, hunger and severe punishments while serving in the navy and in merchant ships. Such men, acclimatised to foul air, vermin and revolting rations in crowded ships, could endure philosophically the conditions in French and British prisons. A letter from a Scots sailor to his wife in Leith in 1813 begins resolutely, 'This is to let you know that I am well, in a dungeon in Dunkirk, God be blessed for it, hoping to hear the same from you and all friends ... I bought an anker of brandy and gin to ourselves, but, Jenny, that is gane, and a's gane; for the French dogs unrigged me in an instant, and left me nought but a greasy jacket of their ain. But, Jenny, I have my pay from the King of England, God bless him; and have bread and water from the French Emperor, God curse him! Out of my pay, I have saved as meikle as bought me a knife, a fork, and a wee coggie. Jenny, keep a good heart; for I'll get out of this net, and win meikle good sillar, and get a bottom of my ain too; and then have at the French dogs.'[13] There is no lack of spirit here whatever his privations.

It is difficult to understand the mentality of many women who came out from the shore in boats to visit the hulks, and from the quarter deck watched with eager interest the miserable wretches on the deck below.

It was customary for the French government to pay French prisoners in Britain, the British supplying them with food. A similar arrangement existed with our prisoners in France. During the Seven Years' War, the French King sent money monthly – the 'Royal Bounty' – which was supposed to be distributed by appointed agents. Often the French accused the British of misappropriating the money. In 1759 the care of French prisoners 'practically devolved entirely upon us, as their Government unaccountably withdrew all support'.[14] All prisoners suffered more or less from lack of food and clothing, and they were often in the power of extortionate and corrupt contractors, or at the mercy of famine prices owing to the prolonged wars. Many men, long imprisoned, went almost naked and suffered greatly from the cold. 'The true down-and-out has neither breeches, coat or shirt; he is simply naked.'[15]

During the American War of Independence Howard found that the French Government made an allowance of 3d a day to captains, mates and surgeons, 2d to petty officers generally, and 1d to all ranks below (almost the same as the British Government gave to its own nationals imprisoned in France). Clothes and shoes were also supplied by the French authorities. Howard found that Americans were well clothed and were helped by the liberality of their own Government. In 1798, during the Revolutionary War, the French Directory announced that they would be responsible for the feeding, clothing and medical attention of prisoners, and at once reduced the daily rations by a quarter. The Commons decided that an enquiry must be made to establish if complaints about the treatment of French prisoners in Britain were true or not. The enquiry's report of 1798 declared that all such allegations were grossly exaggerated and complained that all British proposals for the exchange of prisoners were rejected.

French prisoners were supposed to eat the same rations as British sailors. Garneray describes the daily menu. The week was divided into 5 meat days and 2 fish days. Each man had a pound and a quarter of black bread and 7 ounces of cow meat per day, as well as barley and onion soup. On the two fish days they had 1 lb of potatoes and 1 lb of red herring on Wednesdays, and 1 lb of potatotes and 1 lb of salt cod on Fridays.[16] (Tea and coffee, unless bought by prisoners, were luxuries and not on the dietaries.) But often the P.O.W.s did not get their full allowance. For obvious reasons there was eager competition for the position of contractor. These men were often greedy and dishonest. Copies of letters at Edinburgh Castle show correspondence between the Transport Office and a James Miller, contractor in Leith, written between 1808 and 1813. In 1808 he tendered to supply provisions to prisoners of war at Greenlaw for six months 'till three months notice shall be given'. From Greenlaw in 1813 the same agent was asked to send out 'herrings for tomorrow, potatoes, barley, salt and cod'. As well as supplying food '14 days' provisions for 200 prisoners', Miller also lists 'coals 10/-, cooking 9/-, carriage 48/-, attendance 20/-'. Miller in a letter to the Transport Office in October 1813 understandably shows concern at the rumour that 'it is contemplated to remove Prisoners of War' from the Castle. He asks anxiously for assurance that the Transport Office will 'be pleased to allow them to remain'. A brief reply told him 'it is not intended to remove the Prisoners from Edinburgh Castle'.[17] We have no means of knowing whether Miller was an honest man or not.

French prisoners however seem to have had far fewer complaints about food in Scottish prisons than for example at Norman Cross near Peterborough; Borrow declared after a visit there, 'much had the poor inmates to endure, and much to complain of, to the disgrace of England ... Rations of carrion meat, and bread from which I have seen the very hounds occasionally turn away, were unworthy entertainment even for the most ruffian enemy, when helpless and a captive'.[18]

In 1799 the French Consulate repudiated the Directory's arrangement for the support of their prisoners of war and again forced the responsibility on the British Government and the Transport Office, which now replaced the old 'Sick and Hurt Office'. The French defended their Act of Repudiation by declaring, rather pompously, that 'The generally received custom of leaving to the humanity of belligerent nations the care of protecting and supporting prisoners marks the progress of civilisation'.[19] As a result many Frenchmen presented the spectacle of walking skeletons, dying of debility. Many survived only through the generous gifts of the British. The Government blamed much of the prisoners' misery on their incorrigible gambling habits. 'The first time I ever saw a procession of French prisoners, it frightened me. I thought the world was at an end when I beheld so many skeletons in motion.'[20]

The behaviour of the prisoners was good on the whole, but the very length of time some spent in prison – languishing for ten or more dreary endless years – proved too much, even allowing for French natural gaiety and determination to make the best of things. Fierce quarrels would break out, frequently duels were fought with halves of scissors secured to the ends of sticks by resined twine. Often the quarrels and duels ended in death. Prisoners carried out their own courts-martial. The accused was tried by the whole body of prisoners. There was no appeal to mercy and sentences were executed with implacable severity. The penalty for violent behaviour was confinement by the authorities in the cachot or Black Hole, a deep dungeon opened only once every twenty-four hours. In France punishments were similar. If he wounded a turnkey, a prisoner had his hands handcuffed behind his back for twelve to twenty-four hours. If guilty of murder or forgery he came under the civil law.

Prisoners of war were not required to work but 'There was a great coming and going in this evil-smelling dungeon [hulk]; apart from a few men lying flat on the deck, at the point of death, ... not a single one was idle. Some were planing wood, some carving chessmen or ships from scraps of bone, some were plaiting straw hats and slippers, or knitting nightcaps.'[21] Many of the Frenchmen were gifted craftsmen and lost no time in producing works that were small miracles of dexterity; some can still be seen in museums up and down the country. They drew and painted, worked models in wood and bone, fashioned exquisite tiny chessmen, dominoes and draughts, backgammon, dice, papercutters and toys. Nothing was wasted, not even the bones from their meat. Model ships, as well as snuff spoons and straw-plaited boxes are in Edinburgh and Perth museums. *The Times* of 6 November 1976 reported that at a sale at Sotheby's many models by French prisoners of the Napoleonic Wars were included, the finest being a miniature boxwood model of a French 80-gun two-decker on a straw-work stand. It fetched £3,400, while a model of a 48-gun frigate was sold for £4,600. At Perth 'Vast multitudes went daily to view the market, and buy from the prisoners their toys, of which they had a great variety ... they had stands set out all around the railing of the yards, on which their wares were placed'.[22]

In the excellent museum of the Scottish Prison Service college at Polmont there are several articles made by French P.O.W.s at Perth. These include a figure of a girl curiously carved out of coal, a handsome pewter box and a long-stemmed pewter pipe with a minute bowl.

At Glamis Castle, Angus, there is a beautiful patchwork quilt, said to be the work of French prisoners 'somewhere on the Bor-

ders', and now adorning the Queen Mother's bed. It is intriguing
to speculate on the impression it would have made on the quilt's
creators if they could have known its future. After all, many
French P.O.W.s were romantically inclined, and despite the treatment by compatriots of their own royal family, they would
probably have been filled with incredulous pride at the thought of
their quilt being treasured for years and at length coming to rest
on the bed of their enemy's Queen.

In Perth Museum there are two volumes of great interest concerning French prisoners of war. One was written by a French
Bombardier and disposed of by raffle for the support of his family.
Titled *The Selector*, it contains 'a variety of interesting facts, pleasing anecdotes and biographical sketches'. The other is an account
book of the Depot at Perth. Its columns list from 1812–14 the
amounts of cash paid to the prisoners of war and the places (e.g.
Dumfries, Valleyfield) from whence they came. A bizarre entry
states that one unfortunate Frenchman on his death-bed made over
his pay to a friend. He had 'fallen into the boiler and died the same
day'.

At Perth they dug clay out of the yards and modelled little
figures. Some played the flute or the fiddle for half-pence, and
gave puppet shows or 'Punch's opera'. Those who had no talent
for teaching languages, or music, or dancing, or painting, or
making handicrafts, could earn 3d to 6d a day as sweepers or
barbers or washermen for their more affluent fellows. Those
officers recaptured after breaking parole (they were numerous), or
sent to prison for other serious offences, were glad to pay humble
prisoners 3d a day to be their servants. Garneray painted portraits
and became a commercial success. 'For every portrait I got 6d to
1/- and as I did 3 or 4 every day I began to lay by enough capital
to get proper brushes, oil colours and canvas. Now life was really
enjoyable. Every day I thought less of freedom.'[23]

Contemporary observers have remarked on the versatility, in-
genuity, and above all the industry of the French, and compared
these characteristics unfavourably with the indolence of their
opposite numbers in French prisons. These writers declared that
they favoured the French practice by which men of all social
grades, professions and trades were compelled to the colours,
whereas only the scum of the British population joined the forces.

The Americans were in a class by themselves. In 1778 there were 924 of them in Britain. There was not enough room in the jails for them all to be treated as prisoners of war. Thus there is the occasional mention of their arriving at Newgate, ironed, with murderers and highwaymen, and no allowance for food or clothing. In London large sums of money were raised by private charity for them. Many Americans were taken during the war of 1812. In April 1813 all Americans were ordered to Dartmoor, no doubt because of their persistent attempts to escape from the hulks. At Dartmoor there were already 5,800 French and by September 1814 there were 3,500 Americans there.[24]

An American taken prisoner from a privateer has left a vivid account of life in Dartmoor. During the war of 1812 the prison contained as many as 9,000 prisoners of war at one time. The writer spent seven months there in 1814 and describes his confinement in bad conditions after arriving in England on a frigate from Barbados, where he had been captured. During their march from Plymouth to Dartmoor, 'The spectacle seemed to be one of great interest ... The docks, the grog shops and ale houses sent forth their tenants to see us ... The people were civil enough; they did not insult us, either by language or gesture', the same reaction from the populace as the prisoners of war met with in Scotland.

This self-styled 'Yankee privateer' complains that the prison was adapted 'to keep their tenants secure and to make them as uncomfortable as possible'. Prisoners were housed in two storeys with capacious cock-lofts. There was no glass in the windows and so no light, unless the shutters were opened, which often meant intense cold for the prisoners. No fires were allowed and the weather seemed always dreary and drizzling. The inside of Dartmoor was very dirty, damp, dark and cramped. The men's hammocks were hung in three tiers to save space. The writer does not mince his words – 'this terrible climate'; never had he imagined a 'gloomier abode of incarcerated wretchedness'. Dartmoor was very unhealthy and the prisoners suffered from smallpox, measles, pneumonia and excruciating toothache. 252 prisoners died there, says the writer, who has however a good word for the doctor in charge, 'a very kindly one-eyed Irish gentleman'. By contrast with these conditions, Perth Depot shines. Dartmoor held some very rough types and the 'Yankee privateer', evidently 'a little man', disapproved of them and their ceaseless gambling.[25]

At first the British government furnished the prisoners with clothing, which the American writer described as grotesque. 'A coarse woollen jacket dyed a bright yellow colour, marked on the back with what is called the King's broad arrow which resembles the two sides of a triangle, the point turned upwards, and another straight line running from the point equi-distant through the middle. The letters T.O., being the initials of the transport office, were in staring black letters, one letter on each side of the arrow. Also a pair of pantaloons of the same color and material, with the same marks upon them; a conical cap made of coarse woollen stuff, and a pair of woven list shoes with wooden soles about one inch thick.'[26] Very few prisoners accepted this clothing willingly. Robert Louis Stevenson in *St Ives* describes the dress of the French prisoners in Edinburgh Castle, 'jacket, waistcoat and trousers of a sulphur or mustard yellow, and a shirt of blue-and-white striped cotton'.[27]

The Americans proved vastly annoying to their captors. They were so independent of rules and regulations; so constant with their complaints; so untiring in their efforts to escape; so averse to anything like settling down and making the best of things, as did the French, that Shortland, the Governor of Dartmoor in 1814, declared with heat, 'I never saw ... such a set of Devil-daring, God-provoking fellows, as these same Yankees. I had rather have the charge of 5,000 Frenchmen, than 500 of these sons of liberty; and yet I love the dogs better than I do the d—d frog-eaters.'[28] Commander Wilson of the hulk 'Bahama' said, 'These Americans are the sauciest dogs I ever saw; but d—n me if I can help liking them, nor can I ever hate men who are so much like ourselves'.[29]

There seems to be no record of any American prisoners in Scotland, perhaps fortunately for the authorities, who had to cope only with the more controllable Europeans; but the Yankee privateer's description of his life in Dartmoor can, with the exception of the unhealthy conditions, be applied to the Scottish prisons which housed prisoners of war.

As already observed, prisoners were allowed to dispose of their work at daily markets within prison walls. At Edinburgh Castle small sheds were erected behind the palisades separating prisoners from visitors, and the work was handed through apertures.[30] Often illicit trade went on in straw-plaiting; from smuggled-in straw, prisoners plaited charming bonnets and smuggled them out to be eagerly snapped up by the female population. But after a couple of years or so, the country people began to protest that unpaid labour by untaxed prisoners was injuring them (in much the same way as the Trade Unions protest today), so the Government prohibited straw-plaiting and the prisoners suffered accordingly. Soon however the smuggling of straw began again and it was sold later as manufactured articles. This trade was very profitable to the outside dealer, who often made a small fortune. One Matthew Wingrave found it very worthwhile to move from Bedford to Valleyfield, where he bought wheat and barley fields in order to engage in the straw-plaiting trade with the prisoners, bribing the guards to make his plan easier. In 1813 he found himself on trial. Soldiers who helped to smuggle the finished goods out were liable to be flogged severely.

Chief amusements of the French were games of cards, dice, and the occasional use of an old billiard table. The French prisoner generally was an inveterate gambler; he craved tobacco and to get it would stake his clothing, bedding and rations for days ahead, and sadly, even his cherished place on the exchange ladder. Prison surgeons who examined the emaciated corpses in the prison hospitals often testified to starvation as the cause of death. To visitors they presented a miserable picture of distress, often being naked except for a few rags. 'There was another class who gambled away everything, even the clothes from their bodies; and some of them were to be seen wandering about with a bit of blanket round them, without any other covering.'[31] Similar habits prevailed among British P.O.W.s in France, where Casse described 'Furious battles and drunken riots' almost daily, and much gambling. To get money the prisoners would 'dispose of every article of clothing from their backs and supply this deficiency by wrapping round them a prison blanket'.[32] *In extremis*, they would often draw the worsted out of the rags covering them in their hammocks, wind it into balls, and sell it to industrious knitters of mittens. The privateers were gamblers to a man. Many Edinburgh prisoners were busily occupied with forging banknotes, and in Perth too this went on with the manufacture of base coins.

In the parole towns, the amusements and recreations, as one would expect, were altogether more sophisticated than in the prisons. Before 1813, pay of officers on parole above and including the rank of captain was 10/6d weekly, and below captain 8/9d. In 1813 the sums were increased to 14/- and 11/8d. The French surgeons in 1806 were allowed 6d for a bleeding, and 1/- for drawing a tooth. Serious cases went to the prison hospital, where assistance for more than five days cost 6/8d.[33] There were many doctors on parole.

How did the prisoners contrive to feed and clothe themselves and pay for lodgings? The allowance from the government was about 1/- a day. Sometimes two officers shared a room, but this cost at least 2/6d weekly. They would have suffered severely if many had not got money sent from families in France; and the richer helped the poorer. They 'messed together', and William Chambers recollects how he and his brother reared rabbits in their backyard to sell to the Frenchmen's mess at 8d a pair – the money being spent on books.[34] Living was cheaper in Scotland than in England, and the talented could supplement their income by teaching French, dancing and music. The theatre and concerts were the favourite recreations of the parole officers and they lost no time in constructing a theatre wherever they found themselves. 'In letters from prisons in England and Scotland the money asked for from home is very often used to pay for lessons, as well as for tobacco and a taste of spirits. But the bitterest privation is the lack of letters. No home news, in too many cases for years, was to all prisoners of war a cause of dreadful anxiety and depression, filling their hearts with the fear of death or misfortune.'[35]

'The Scotch and the French were old allies in history, and however unlike superficially, they seemed never to have failed in experiencing a subtle attraction for each other. Certainly the foreign officers were made curiously welcome in the country town [Cupar] which their presence seemed to enliven rather than to offend. The strangers' courageous endurance, their perennial cheerfulness, their ingenious devices to occupy their time and improve the situation aroused much friendly interest and amusement.' They were treated by the residents of Cupar 'with genuine liberality and kindness, receiving them into their houses on cordial terms. Soon there was not a festivity in the town at which the

French prisoners were not permitted – nay, heartily pressed to attend.'[36]

At Selkirk, in 1811, ninety-three Frenchmen arrived, marching from Leith. They included many army surgeons. During their two and a half years there, they poured money into the town (£150 being the weekly average). Their weekly pay of 10/6d was ample for their lodging of 2/6d, board was proportionately moderate, and the rivers teemed with fish. The officers at once formed an orchestra and gave Saturday concerts, made a theatre and gave weekly shows – Molière and Racine. They used the old Selkirk subscription library and were voracious readers, especially of history and biography. Many attended masonic meetings. On each of the four main roads at a mile's distance from the town a notice read 'Limite des Prisonniers de Guerre'. The Selkirk townspeople were not friendly, but the country and gentlefolk round about made up for their chilliness by a warm hospitality.

This merry pattern was repeated in the other Border towns. In Kelso we hear of many balls and theatre shows. They did their own cooking and scared the landladies by chopping up frogs for 'outlandish' fricassées. Their most singular peculiarity to the natives of Kelso was 'their habit of gathering ... different kinds of wild weeds by the roadside and hedgeroots, making tea out of dried whin, and killing small birds to eat – the latter a practice considered not much removed from cannabalism'. They were frivolous, 'as many of them wore earrings and one, a Pole, had a ring to his nose; while all were boyishly fond of amusement and were merry, good-natured creatures'. The young misses of Kelso were intensely aware of the charm, glamour, and gaiety of the gallant prisoners. 'The French showed great mannerliness and buoyance of spirits.'[37] But they did not win universal approval. Fullarton says sternly that from 1810 to 1814 Kelso's average number of 230 prisoners of war 'inoculated the place with their fashionable follies, and even in some instances tainted it with their laxity of morals'.[38] The majority of the Kelso prisoners, although fighting under the French flag, were from Spain, Portugal, and the West Indies, with some twenty Sicilians.

In 1811 parole prisoners came to Dumfries. 'The town is pretty enough, and the inhabitants, though curious, seem very gentle', wrote one of them. An old man declared, 'The first siller I ever earned was for gathering paddocks [frogs] for the Frenchmen'.[39] In Jedburgh there were a large number of naval officers, many of whom were to rejoin Napoleon after his escape from Elba and to fall fighting for him at Waterloo. Peebles was not a parole town until 1803, but many French prisoners, mostly from frigates of the expedition to Ireland, were lodged in the town jail in 1798 and 1799. The first parole prisoners were Dutch, Belgian and Danish, and they were taught cotton handloom weaving to eke out their allowance. They fished in their leisure time. They were free to live and ramble where they liked, within reasonable bounds. In 1810 there arrived over a hundred French, Poles and Italians, captured in the Peninsular War. William Chambers describes how, as a boy, he went out to meet the new prisoners of war on the road from Edinburgh: 'They came walking in twos and threes – a few of them lame. Their appearance was startling, for they were in military garb, in which they had been captured in Spain. Some were in light blue hussar dresses, braided, with marks of sabre wounds. Others were in dark-blue uniform. Several wore large cocked-hats, but the greater number had undress caps. All had a gentlemanly air, notwithstanding their generally dishevelled attire, their soiled boots, and their visible marks of fatigue.' They were all naval or military officers and several were doctors. They managed to procure a billiard table and spent much time at it. They built a theatre – to the French an essential amenity. Chambers recalled, 'The remembrance of these dramatic efforts of the French prisoners of war has been through life a continual treat'.[40]

Escapes were frequent from all places of captivity, including the parole towns. Often there were desperate and futile attempts, from Edinburgh Castle particularly in 1761 and 1811. When caught, which they frequently were, the punishment was the Black Hole. A favourite method of escape was by tunnelling; men carried out earth in their pockets and dropped and trod on it in the airing grounds. In 1799 two prisoners sawed through the bars of their dungeon with a smuggled sword-blade, and the Episcopal minister of the Cowgate, an Englishman, helped them to escape in a Newhaven fishing boat to Inchkeith and thence to France. He was sentenced to three months in the Tolbooth.[41] In 1761 one prisoner was dashed to pieces on the Castle rock, and in 1811 fifty men

ьune Castle, Perthshire, a fine example of fourteenth-century domestic Scottish architecture and
raditional Stewart stronghold, was sometimes used as a state prison. Here the Jacobites imprison
eir captives after the Battle of Falkirk, 1746. *By courtesy of Edinburgh Central Libraries*

The branks, a skeleton iron helmet with a bit to
secure the tongue, was a medieval instrument used
mainly for ecclesiastical punishment. *National
Museum of Antiquities of Scotland*

ne jougs, a medieval neck-ring for
aining offenders to the wall of the
·k. *National Museum of Antiquities
Scotland*

Caerlaverock Castle, Dumfriesshire, dates from the late-thirteenth century. From here the Maxwells exercised feudal power over their tenants. *Crown copyright*

The pit entrance at Dunvegan Castle, Skye, showing prisoners' shackles. Measuring 16ft deep and 6ft × 4ft wide, this pit, dating from the fourteenth century, is typical of those in which the baron immured their captives. *Aberdeen University Press*

ackness Castle on the Forth near Edinburgh was used as a state prison. Cardinal Beaton was
.rded here in 1543 as was the Earl of Morton in 1584–85. Dissenting clergymen were
.prisoned here in the late-seventeenth century. *Crown copyright*

.reave Castle, fourteenth-century stronghold of the Black Douglases, on an island in the River
.e in Kirkcudbrightshire. *Crown copyright*

Old Tolbooth, Edinburgh, 'the Heart of Midlothian'. Demolished in 1817, it was replaced by Calton Jail, The railed platform was often the scene of public executions. *By courtesy of Edinburgh Central Libraries*

Brass collar of servitude dredged from the River Forth at Logie, Stirlingshire. Inscribed 'Alexander Steuart, found guilty of death for theft at Perth the 5th of December 1701 and gifted by the justiciars as a perpetual servant to Sir Jo Areskin of Alva'. *National Museum of Antiquities of Scotland*

Branding iron. *National Museum of Antiquities of Scotland*

e stool of repentance on which the
…itent, dressed in a sackcloth gown,
before the kirk congregation.
*…ional Museum of Antiquities of
…tland*

Canongate Tolbooth (Town House)
was built in 1591 and closed in 1840.
This view is circa 1800. *Royal
Commission on the Ancient and
Historical Monuments of Scotland*

Beggars' tokens issued in the fifteenth century by the sheriff or baillies
were a licence to beg. *National Museum of Antiquities of Scotland*

Elizabeth Fry (1780–1845) the Quaker prison reformer who first became concerned at the conditions of women prisoners at Newgate in 1813. *National Portrait Gallery*

John Howard (1726?–1790), himself prisoner of the French in 1756, advocated prison reform on his appointment as high sheriff of Bedford in 1773. *National Portrait Gallery*

Edinburgh Bridewell, designed by Robert Adam, was built 1791–96. Its fortress-like appearance led to a public fear that it might become a sort of bastille used for secret and excessive purposes. treadmill was installed. *National Library of Scotland*

Samuel Romilly (1757–1818), a barrister
• became interested in radical politics on
:ing Diderot and Franklin in Paris in 1781.
onal Portrait Gallery

James Neild (1744–1814) retired as a wealthy
London jeweller in 1792. His *State of the
Prisons* (1812) followed tours of prisons
throughout Britain. *National Portrait Gallery*

City Guardhouse, High Street, Edinburgh. Headquarters of the armed guard formed in 1679
:ep order in the city. After 1750 the guard numbered only some seventy men, mostly
landers and all old soldiers, armed with Lochaber-axes. It was disbanded in 1817. *Royal
mission on the Ancient and Historical Monuments of Scotland*

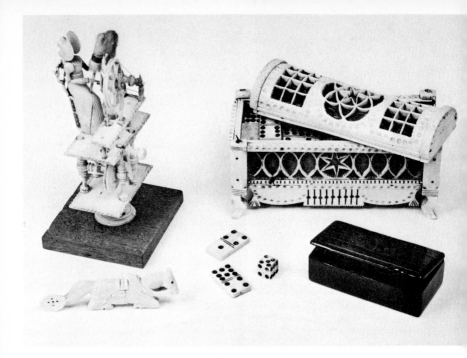

Examples of work by French prisoners of war: (*above*) working model in bone of a woman spinning, a carved bone box of dominoes, a bone snuff ladle, and a papier maché snuff box; (*below, right*) work box decorated with coloured straw. *Perth Museum*. The warship (*below, left*) modelled in bone, is 24 inches long and 18 inches high. *Royal Scottish Museum*

escaped from the Castle by cutting a hole through the bottom of the parapet wall, at the south west corner below the Devil's Elbow, and sliding down a rope smuggled in piece by piece for weeks before. One fell to his death and all the rest were captured in time.[42] Stevenson describes the 1811 escape in *St Ives*, but puts it in 1813, 'On anybody not a seaman or a steeple-jack, the mere sight of the *Devil's Elbow* wrought like an emetic'.[43] Sievwright says there were 14 escapes or attempted escapes from Perth Depot between 14 September 1812 and 24 September 1813. Sixty-one prisoners made a clean escape for a time, '32 of them, however, were re-captured and brought back to prison, leaving 29 ... who were never found'.[44]

The country people had been antagonistic to the prisoners of war during the early years of the parole system, and the prisoners were considered fair game for oppression and robbery; hundreds of complaints were made by the prisoners concerning very expensive and bad lodgings, and there were many instances of mobbing and stoning in England, where extortion and resentment seems to have been much worse. According to Garneray, in his village 'more than 1,200 Frenchmen were living in a block of broken down houses for which they paid an exorbitant rent to the English ... I managed to get for ten shillings a week, not a room, but the privilege of setting up my bed in a dirty garret with five other officers'.[45] But in the Napoleonic Wars this attitude moderated a great deal. The authorities found the sympathy of the people more difficult to combat than the daring of the prisoners. While the upper classes were often friendly, they did not aid escapes since that would have meant encouraging a breach of honour. The lower classes helped, usually for gain alone; and so profitable did escape-aiding prove that soon it had become as regular a pursuit as smuggling, with which it was closely connected. In 1812 an Act was passed to the effect that helping P.O.W.s to escape should cease to be a misdemeanour and become a felony, punishable with transportation for seven or fourteen years or life. Previously the punishment had been the pillory and two years' imprisonment. In France a decree condemned to the galleys all who were retaken, and the penalty for helping escapees was a fine of £12.10s per head, legal expenses and two months' imprisonment. In the three years before 1812, 464 officers on parole had escaped, but not one

British officer had broken parole abroad. Many high-ranking French officers, colonels and generals, saw nothing wrong in breaking parole.

Escapes from parole towns only became common when the alternative way of returning to France had to be stopped. This was when an officer on parole signed a declaration promising that unless he was exchanged for a British officer of similar rank by a certain date he would return to England on that date. He was then allowed to go to France, pledging himself not to fight. But it became so common for French officers to break parole and on gaining French territory to serve against the British that the Government stopped the practice. In 1804 the Transport Office complained that the French Government had not released one British officer in return for 500 French sent to France on parole. On this question of exchange of prisoners it is difficult not to come to the conclusion that the British were fairer to the French, Dutch and Danish than vice versa. Often the British would send over the cartel or exchange ships full and they would return empty.

Marriages between prisoners of war and local girls took place in the parole towns. Sometimes these marriages were happy but a large number of Frenchmen, knowing that in France such marriages were invalid, deserted their wives and children when they returned to France. The British Government paid for the support of wives and children of prisoners. In 1814 complaints were made to the Transport Office about the public burden which the illegitimate children of the French prisoners were causing. Prisoners of war were not amenable to the civil law and thus debts incurred were wholly debts of honour. Chambers' father had befriended many Frenchmen in Peebles and had given them extensive credit. They departed at the peace of 1814, promising to send the money owed. None did, which led to a severe financial crisis in the Chambers family.[46]

The departure of the prisoners for France began in June 1814. From Perth some sailed down the Tay, cheered heartily by the people. Others marched to Newburgh and on the thronged quay held their last market. It was during this march to Newburgh that the prisoners to a man sold the French New Testaments which had been distributed amongst them by the zealous missionaries of the British and Foreign Bible Society. Prisoners in Edinburgh were freed after the peace of 1814, and they marched down by torch-light to the transports at Leith. Cheering thousands lined the pavements as the pale and haggard prisoners tramped down the High Street singing the Revolutionary songs, the *Marseillaise* and the *Ça Ira*.

In many a Scottish country town there was regret when the prisoners had gone. No wonder, for the presence of two or three hundred young men, many of good family and private means, living there for months or years, was both a social and a commercial advantage to a small community.

In conclusion it can be argued that the long sojourn of the French and other prisoners of war in this country had a permanent effect on Scottish and English prisons. It seems reasonable to draw the conclusion that enormous prisons like Perth and Dartmoor (still two of the most important) probably would never have been built on such a scale but for the pressing need to confine huge numbers of prisoners of war. The Scots themselves had comparatively few convicts to house, transportation siphoning off the majority. Before the French wars any squalid hovel sufficed for malefactors, but national prestige required something better for the housing of foreigners, and the standards of our prisons were raised accordingly. The readiness with which the Government granted money and the speed with which the buildings were erected could only have been achieved in time of war.

After the French went home the vast prisons remained empty for years. Perth Depot was 'fully occupied for almost two years only, all the inmates being sent home after Bonaparte's first discomfiture when he was exiled to Elba, there being no occasion for it during the brief final struggle which terminated with Waterloo in 1815'.[47] Penny wrote in 1836, 'The prison has since been either empty, or let for granaries ... but it might be far better occupied as a national bridewell ... where convicted felons, instead of being sent out of the country at so great an expence, could be employed in labour to maintain themselves'.[48]

When transportation was ended in the mid-nineteenth century, the 'French prisons' reverted to their original use, but this time to incarcerate the natives.

5
Repression and the Separate System 1835–1877

Better to have hanged him in the beginning than brought him to this pass, and send him forth to mingle with his kind, who are his kind no more.
                                                          Dickens*

I do not believe that a despairing or stupefied state is suitable for salvation.
                                                          Elizabeth Fry†

Solitary confinement deprives a criminal of his force, of his energy . . . and at last exhibits a dried up mummy as a model of repentance and amendment.
                                                          Dostoevsky‡

5

Introduction

Attempts to reform British prison conditions in the late-eighteenth and early-nineteenth centuries were not successful. The whole oppressive punitive system was largely approved in both England and Scotland. The efforts of Romilly, one of the greatest and most selfless of the reformers, had been continually blocked. Very slowly however feelings began to change and in 1819 a committee was set up to enquire into the criminal laws, with the object of bringing about a revision of the criminal code. The resulting publicity kept the reform of criminal law in the public mind, and prepared the way for the work of Peel as Home Secretary; there was no inspection of prisons until Peel's Act of 1835. The period under review saw the important Prison Acts of 1839, 1860 and 1865, proponents of different systems of prison discipline, the great influence of American prisons, the end of transportation and the establishment of its substitute, penal servitude. The period ends with the landmark of the 1877 Act which brought all prisons in the United Kingdom under the control of the central government.

'The eighteenth and nineteenth centuries formed an era in which deterrence was firmly established in the centre of the penal system.'[1] Expiation and retribution were part of the religious climate of the mid-nineteenth century. Apart from members of certain professions who visited prisons regularly – sheriffs, advocates, magistrates – the general public were completely uninterested in prison life, and when a writer did give an opinion it was generally in favour of the severe treatment of criminals. The reactions of Thomas Carlyle and Hugh Miller are illuminating. Carlyle in his *Latter-Day Pamphlets* declares that nothing should be done for prison inmates, 'diabolic canaille',[2] 'thriftless sweepings of creation',[3] until much had been done for those honest poor yet struggling in 'dingy, poor and dirty dwellings'.[4] In 1850 a visit to a London model prison, housing some 1,200 prisoners, put him into a perfect fever of rage and resentment. The imprisoned Chartists angered Carlyle even more than the 'notable murderesses'; thieves roused him to heights of furious rhetoric. He envied the peace of the prisoners, 'the world and its cares quite excluded'.[5] He eyed the prisoners with angry revulsion and contempt: 'Miserable distorted blockheads, the generality; ape-faces, imp-faces, angry dog-faces, heavy sullen ox-faces'.[6] He advocated 'A collar round the neck and a cartwhip flourished over the back'.[7] He asked why reformers should work only on the 'rotten material',[8] and vituperated against the 'dull, solid Howard'[9] and his philanthropy. He refused to be associated with 'a universal Sluggard-and-Scoundrel Protection Society ... the scoundrel that *will* hasten to the gallows, why not rather clear the way for him?'.[10]

We can take from Carlyle's verbose and cantankerous rantings that he would greatly prefer efforts to be concentrated on the honest, deserving poor rather than on the criminal classes. Scott, as we have seen, put forward much the same view, only more moderately.

Hugh Miller, writing in 1856, was alarmed at the increase of crimes with violence, and explains it by the loss of our penal colonies, and the vast number of ticket-of-leave men let loose on society. He urged new penal colonies and suggested the Falkland Islands 'to rid us of a ... formidable class of wild beasts, – the incorrigible criminals. It is surely not at all necessary that a penal colony should be a paradise.'[11] He adds, 'We cannot put them in at the one end of a penitentiary in the soiled state and take them out white and pure at the other'.[12]

No voice seems to have been raised in Scotland in the cause of reform. Tight-lipped, unyielding in disapproval of wrongdoing, Calvin's followers held to the grim adage 'If he's made his bed, let him lie on it'. But it must not be inferred that there existed a deeper hostility to reform in Scotland than was perhaps the case. Only articulate opinion is available for reference; that of the common man is unknown.

I

The year 1835 saw a turning point in prison administration with the Prison Act for 'effecting greater Uniformity of Practice in the Government of the several Prisons in England and Wales; and for appointing Inspectors of Prisons in Great Britain'.[1] Section 7 of the Act was crucial: 'It shall be lawful for one of His Majesty's Principal Secretaries of State to nominate and appoint a sufficient number of fit and proper persons, not exceeding five, to visit and inspect, either singly or together, every gaol, bridewell, house of correction, penitentiary or other prison or place kept or used for the confinement of prisoners, in any part of the Kingdom of Great Britain'. By the same section, the Inspectors had to submit to one of the Principal Secretaries of State a yearly report on the state of every jail visited by them. Thus uncontrolled local government over prisons gave way to supervision by Government inspectors, which continued until 1877.

Different systems of prison discipline were at this time given prominence by their supporters. The congregate system which had prevailed for generations, i.e. prisoners in association by day and night (as in Newgate), was now universally condemned. 'The Victorian penal system was still chaotic – the majority of London prisons were ancient, insanitary and hideously overcrowded.'[2] Newgate was a populous school of criminals, segregation being quite impossible.

Some reformers went to the opposite extreme and advocated the 'Solitary Sytem', which meant no association at all during the whole term of imprisonment, and almost total deprivation of labour, books, and exercise. It was held that through solitary contemplation the prisoner would be led to a better life. Others campaigned for the 'Separate System' which was not so severe since it allowed work in cells, some books and exercise, and communication with prison officers. William Brebner, Governor of Glasgow Bridewell, established the separate system there in 1825, several years before its introduction into the Pennsylvania Penitentiary which has been generally regarded as the pioneer in this respect.

Later came the 'Silent System', which allowed work in association but in silence. 'Conscious that jails were usually nurseries of crime, Victorian reformers introduced the ghastly Silent System;

... the prisoner ... was reduced to the condition of a numbered and uniformed automaton, condemned to perform so many hours of entirely useless work upon the crank or treadmill. At exercise the prisoner was sometimes masked to preserve his anonymity, and was never known by name, only by number. But neither the sociable squalor of Newgate nor the segregated gloom of the prisons that had been reformed and remodelled could check the rapid expansion of the criminal and vagrant classes.'[3]

The treadmill or treadwheel, started at Brixton in 1817, was a big iron frame of steps around a revolving cylinder, which could be fitted to a mill or used for pumping water. The crank was a wheel like the paddle wheel of a steamer; it fitted into a box of gravel which the prisoner had to turn by means of a handle, and could, like the treadwheel, be used for productive purposes. But it was rarely that either of them was. 'Prisoners, male and female, trudging up the steps in their own separate compartments on the wheel might work ... for six hours a day and achieve nothing except the climbing of 8,640 feet, and others turning the crank worked for the same length of time to do nothing but break the resistance of the gravel in the box and turn the handle through ten thousand revolutions.'[4] Prisoners were required to do 14,400 cranks a day except on Saturdays, when the number was reduced by a quarter, and frequently they were refused food until the requisite number of revolutions had been completed.

The reformers who believed that prisoners should be separated all the time found that this could not be done in the old prisons because of their structure, but it was possible in the newer ones. The new system of prison discipline, that of solitary confinement, did not originate in Great Britain. For some time it had been operative in parts of America, where penal reform was taken seriously. New prisons were built with individual cells for solitary confinement, though in some the system had to be abandoned through time because of overcrowding. Owing to the influence of the Quakers (always strong on the power of solitude over the soul) two new State prisons were built in Pennsylvania and in both, solitary confinement was universal. They were the Western Penitentiary at Pittsburgh (1818), built on Bentham's pattern, and the Eastern Penitentiary at Cherry Hill (1829). At the famous

Auburn prison in the State of New York, built about the same time, convicts passed their days in solitary confinement and were given no work, while in other blocks they were separated at night but during the day worked in association in silence – Howard's plan. This had the advantage of making possible a greater variety of occcupations and it was hoped that it would enable prisoners to pay for their own keep. The main disadvantage was that prisoners could never be prevented from communicating with each other, unless there was a very big staff to supervise. The cruel and unnatural Silent System at Auburn was maintained by flogging. Here was first seen the inside cell, a sort of cage, which was to have a great influence on subsequent American, and later on British, prison architecture. Unfortunately it was the Auburn Silent System and Pennsylvania's Solitary System which had most influence on English observers.[5]

One of the newly-appointed Inspectors visited America in 1836 and on his return made an enthusiastic report to the Home Secretary. In consequence, at Pentonville, built in 1842, complete silence reigned as at Auburn, 'as the men tramped from their lonely cells wearing masks of brown cloth so that none should recognize them'.[6] Even in chapel each man was hidden from the others. Pentonville was 'a place of punishment and repression'.[7] The many attempts at communication were punished by immurement in the completely dark refractory cells for as long as three weeks on end. The most dreaded punishment was to be denied work. Many became mentally ill and there was a great number of suicides.[8] Pentonville had 520 cells, each with a table, stove, gas-burner, hammock, mattress and blanket, water-closet and unlimited hot and cold water. The water-closets were later removed because the pipes had been used as a means of communication. In America, W. Ellery Channing, writing in 1832 of a visit to the Philadelphia Penitentiary, says that all the prisoners were 'confined in solitary cells, and seldom see any countenance but that of the keeper. The system is thought by some to be too severe as human nature shrinks from nothing so much as from this utter loneliness ... I think that terrible effects might follow, if the poor secluded beings were not allowed to work'.[9] But he 'was much disposed to regard it as the greatest advance yet made in prison discipline'.[10] For after talking with some prisoners to find the effect on them of such seclusion, 'my fears as to its stupefying effect seemed to be wholly groundless'.[11]

Dickens was to reach a different conclusion. In 1842 he visited the same penitentiary and described it in burning words in his *American Notes*. 'In the outskirts of Philadelphia stands a great prison called the Eastern Penitentiary, conducted on a plan peculiar to the State of Pennsylvania. The system here is rigid, strict, and hopeless solitary confinement. I believe it, in its effects, to be cruel and wrong ... I believe that very few men are capable of estimating the immense amount of torture and agony which this dreadful punishment, prolonged for years, inflicts upon the sufferers ... I am ... convinced that there is a depth of terrible endurance in it which none but the sufferers themselves can fathom, and which no man has a right to inflict upon his fellow-creature. I hold this slow and daily tampering with the mysteries of the brain to be immeasurably worse than any torture of the body.'[12] Dickens saw all over the prison where absolute silence reigned. 'Over the head and face of every prisoner who comes into this melancholy house a black hood is drawn; ... he is led to the cell from which he never again comes forth, until his whole term of imprisonment has expired. He never hears of wife or children, home or friends, the life or death of any single creature.'[13] With the exception of the prison officers he would never see or hear a human being. The prisoner had an hour's exercise daily in a solitary yard attached to each cell. 'He is a man buried alive, to be dug out in the slow round of years ... His name, and crime, and term of suffering are unknown, even to the officer who delivers him his daily food.'[14] The convict had a Bible, some books, fresh water laid on, and in his cell he worked at loom or bench. Dickens found that the prisoners grew deaf in time, and those who had been in for years he found 'quite broken and crushed', and afraid to go out when the time came for their release. The prisoner had 'a burning sense of the years that must be wasted in that stone coffin'.[15] 'Better to have hanged him in the beginning than bring him to this pass, and send him forth to mingle with his kind, who are his kind no more.'[16] 'It is my fixed opinion that those who have undergone this punishment *must* pass into society again morally unhealthy and diseased ...[17] That it is a singularly unequal punishment, and affects the worst man least, there is no doubt.'[18] Elizabeth Fry concurred. In a journey to Scotland in 1834 she had become anxious about 'the solitary and silent systems; imported from America, where in many respects, and under the closest and most careful inspection they appeared well to answer, but which were to her feelings both liable to grievous abuses'.[19] In 1838 she came North again and 'was at this time extremely anxious as to the extent to which Prison Discipline was carried in Scotland. She greatly feared the enforcement of solitary confinement, and felt it her duty to make a sort of appeal against its possible abuses.'[20] In 1843, nearing the end of her life, she protested against the new prison of Pentonville with its grim, solitary confinement cells. 'Let them see the sky!' she begged, 'I do not believe that a despairing or stupefied state is suitable for salvation'.[21]

Dickens and Mrs Fry were not alone in their condemnation of solitary confinement – in America, humanitarian motives, combined with growing doubt about the efficacy of solitude and meditation as a means of reform, led to a search for alternatives to isolation. The annual report of a New Jersey keeper in 1839 contained an admirable analysis of the fundamental defects in the system of solitary confinement on the physical health of the prisoners through the impossibility of taking normal methods of exercise. But even worse was its effect on the mental health of the prisoners, leading to solitary vices and mental degeneration. The choice between the congregate and solitary type of confinement, he held, was fundamentally the problem as to whether vicious association is more to be deplored than mental and physical deterioration.[22]

In many respects the old, filthy, promiscuous prisons were less inhuman than the repressive, silent, cold-storage ones of the nineteenth century. Prisoners in the eighteenth century died from gaol fever, those in the nineteenth century went mad or committed suicide in terrifying numbers.[23] Today it is accepted that 'In a very fundamental sense, a man perpetually locked by himself in a cage is no longer a man at all; rather, he is a semi-human object, an organism with a number ... It was the recognition of this fact that played a large part in the abandonment of solitary confinement for the general inmate population of the American prison'.[24]

But this was still in the future, and the 1839 Prison Act showed strong American influence. Official circles favoured the separate system, largely based on isolation in cells. It laid down that 'to prevent contamination arising from association of prisoners in any prison in which rules for separation of prisoners shall be in force, any prisoner may be separately confined during the whole or part of his or her imprisonment'. Separate confinement was not to be deemed solitary confinement, and each cell had to conform in size, ventilation, light, and warmth, to a recognisable standard for health. Prisoners were now to be classified as:

1. Debtors.
2. Prisoners committed for trial.
3. Convicted men sentenced to hard labour.
4. Those not sentenced to hard labour.
5. Any other prisoners.[25]

In Scotland liability for management and custody remained with the burghs from the Act of 1597 until the 1839 Act to 'Improve Prisons and Prison Discipline in Scotland' provided that the general supervision and direction of all Scottish prisons should be committed to a General Board of Directors of Prisons in Scotland. County Boards were established which took over the local supervision and management of all prisons save the General Prison which was to be established at Perth. It was to be administered by the General Board of Directors as a government institution for the detention of criminals with long sentences. The cost of local prisons fell on the counties who were empowered to levy an assessment on the burghs in their areas. Prisoners with sentences of nine months and upwards were brought from every county to the new central prison at Perth. This was partly because the local prisons were inferior and inadequate, but the main reason for this centralisation at Perth was no doubt financial, for the government had at hand sufficient land for the new building as well as the old French prison,[26] the latter being closed in 1887. The General Prison, begun in 1840 and completed in 1859, is the oldest in Scotland. The first two wings were opened in 1843, and 'among the first arrivals were three children under twelve years of age serving 18 months to 2 years, and six children between the ages of twelve and sixteen with 2 years or more'.[27]

II

The Scottish Prisons Minute Book of October 1840 gives a table of prisons in Scotland; a detailed and comprehensive list, with the number, situation, and description of all prisons – jails, bridewells, houses of correction, lock-up houses, and other places used for the legal confinement of civil or criminal prisoners.[1] From the summing up by the Prison Board it is clear that although real concern was shown for cleanliness, ventilation, airing-yards, and visiting, the over-riding consideration was to ensure the smooth working of the separate system. For example Aberdeen Burgh Prison, the old jail in Castle Street, has 'little room for classification',[2] 'is capable of but not very well adapted to the separate system';[3] Dundee prison was used as a county burgh and police prison and as a bridewell; no classification was possible as the gaol was 'crowded and loathsome; new gaol indispensable'.[4] This was finished, built on the radiating plan with the Governor's house in the centre and five radiating wings, 120 cells and rooms, the principle of separation being acted on though 'not completely'.[5] At Inverness burgh jail, 'Bad condition ... dark, no airing-grounds, but secure'.[6] At Perth city and county jail, built in 1819, although it boasted twenty-nine apartments and a jailer's house, yet there was 'Imperfect classification'[7] and it was 'ill-arranged, overcrowded'.[8] Later, despite considerable alterations, the prison was 'not yet very secure or sufficient for the separate system'.[9] At Edinburgh Calton, though it had seven day-rooms and fifty-four sleeping-cells, yet there were three or four to a cell, classification was defective,[10] and there was no effective means of separation.[11] Edinburgh Lock-up House for criminals, behind Parliament House, was 'little better than a moral pest-house; young and old being crowded together in idleness and corruption'.[12] The County Board ordered it to be discontinued. Glasgow Burgh prison, built 1812–13, although it had '97 apartments; 62 for criminals and 37 for debtors, does not admit of proper classification'.[13] Some bridewells satisfied the required standards, e.g. Aberdeen Burgh and County Bridewell, criminal, 'contains 70 apartments, complete means of classification'.[14] 'Better than most prisons – affords means of complete separation'.[15] Also Glasgow, City and County Bridewell for criminals, erected 1823–24, had excellent management, separation and labour.[16] Working arrangements could be threatened or completely upset by a large increase of prisoners – 'system of separation broken in upon by an unusual influx of prisoners – 274 separate cells, while the average number of prisoners during the year was 330'.[17]

Discipline and management naturally loomed large in the reports. Glasgow Burgh prison was found to have 'an utter want of order and discipline',[18] while again Glasgow Bridewell is praised for being 'One of the best regulated of the kind in the empire'[19]; 'This excellent prison goes on most satisfactorily'.[20]

The situation of prisons was carefully noted, Perth being 'exposed to communications from without',[21] and Inverness 'inconveniently situated'.[22]

The conditions – cleanliness, ventilation and security – are commented on. Dundee new prison is 'clean and tolerably healthy';[23] Inverness is 'in bad condition – only 4 cells and 6 rooms all small – dark'.[24] Edinburgh Calton Bridewell, County and Burgh prison, built 1790, 'with 52 working cells and 129 sleeping cells; secure though very imperfect in construction, on a better plan than any prison in Scotland built so long ago'.[25] Edinburgh Canongate burgh prison, 'Ancient structure used only for debtors',[26] had a hall and eight rooms 'which might with advantage be given up altogether',[27] and was in fact suppressed later by the County Board. Generally bad conditions were the norm, but again Glasgow Bridewell is praised for its 'perfect security, dry and clean, and tolerably well ventilated'.[28] It is noted that many prisons still had no airing-grounds and no means of employment. For example, Edinburgh Calton showed 'want of means of work'[29] while Glasgow Bridewell had 'constant employment'.[30]

The running of the Glasgow Bridewell and its excellent management afforded 'satisfactory proof of the advantage in point of economy and discipline of the abolition of small prisons, and having prisons on such a scale as to ensure respectable management'.[31] Thus the County Board suggested that the Calton Prison and Calton Bridewell should be joined as one prison under the name of the Prison of Edinburgh, and the 'County Board being desirous to act on the principle of affording to all prisons the benefit of the separate system, which they are of the opinion can best be obtained in a large jail, such as the Prison of Edinburgh, therefore providing the Prison of Edinburgh be enlarged enough to take all those previously in minor prisons such as Musselburgh, Pennycook, Lasswade, Dalkeith, and these should be considered as mere lock-up houses'.[32]

As regards Scotland's small prisons, it is little wonder that the Boards were eager to close them, for many were no more than lock-up houses, cold, damp, and often only moderately secure. They held petty culprits under examination and vagrants for short periods. Many were seldom used.

Barony prisons were unpleasant places, Peterhead being a 'vault under the Town-House; never used; no gaolers':[33] while Melrose, the private property of the Duke of 'Buccleugh', consisted of 'a single stone vaulted cell on the ground floor of the Court Houses seldom used'.[34] Hawick was a 'wretched place, consisting of a single room ill-ventilated and dirty; males and females sometimes kept together'.[35] The small burgh and county prisons were frequently as mean and miserable as the Barony ones. There were only four prisons in the whole of Ross and Cromarty and of these Tain's consisted of 'a square tower, 200 years old, in the middle of the town; four rooms with a dungeon below ground, never used, insecure';[36] while Fortrose had 'a wretched place, quite unfit for use – consists of a single room, formed in the ruins of the cathedral; damp, cold dirty, and insecure'.[37] At Gifford prison, property of the Marquis of Tweeddale, there was one cell 'seldom used, except at fairs';[38] Lockerbie's was formed 'recently out of an old ruin';[39] Cockburnspath was 'a wretched damp hovel in churchyard';[40] Crail's '2 rooms forming part of a steeple, not very secure';[41] Falkirk's 'part of a tower on which stands the town's spire';[42] Wigtown's, part of the townhouse, 'very insecure so much so that magistrates call upon the inhabitants to keep watch upon it through the night'.[43]

In the islands, Portree had the prison for all Skye – 'very small, very bad';[44] for Stornoway there was no Inspectors' or Burgh Commissioners' report but 'one apartment not sufficient – the population of Lewis is 12–13000';[45] Kirkwall's prison was the townhouse, 'insecure, cold, damp, ill ventilated, communicates with the outside'.[46] Here there was 'grievous want of a proper prison'.[47] Selkirk was one of the few smaller prisons to find favour. Built in 1804, it was well situated with an airing-ground; its eleven apartments were 'sufficient in size, accommodation, security and repair'.[48] It was judged better than most small prisons and a 'credit to those concerned'.[49]

Many of those hovels, vaults, and damp, dark rooms up and down the country clearly did not justify the name of prison. The scandalous lack of care could have tragic results, as when the prison in Tain burned down and some prisoners were burnt alive; the keeper lived at a distance.[50]

III

The Governors' Journals of the General Prison at Perth 1845-55 make dismal reading. They describe the wretched frugality of the diet leading inevitably to sickness, often exacerbated by hardship, poverty and neglect before admittance. The dreary work, frequent grim punishments, the harshness of solitary confinement and the extreme youth of the majority of prisoners resulted in many cases of suicide and insanity. The picture that emerges is a miserable one. Prisoners fell ill, died, and were buried within the prison precincts, for although any known relatives were invariably offered the body, only one case reveals that they accepted. Babies were either born dead, died within a week or two, or, perhaps even more pitifully, survived the year during which they were allowed to stay with their mothers and then were sent 'outside'.

In 1851 the Government prisons and convict establishments in Great Britain were the Hulks, Parkhurst, Portland, Millbank, Pentonville, Dartmoor, and Perth. All convicts sentenced to transportation could be sent to Perth General Prison for their twelve and sometimes eighteen months probationary period in solitary confinement. Juveniles served a month in solitary before being transferred to the Juvenile Wing. Unlike the days of the old insecure prisons, escapes were now infrequent and solitary confinement had to be endured, but at great cost. A number of prisoners – a horrifying proportion of them very young – 'became incoherent in their minds' or 'their minds gave way'. There is a constant stream of prisoners crossing to the Imbecile and Lunatic Wing. Suicide attempts were frequent and often successful. If the imprisoned children were of very tender years (eight or nine) the initial month in solitary could be waived. Thus in September 1850 two 8-year-olds were admitted into the Juvenile Class and 'owing to their extreme youth',[1] the surgeon recommended that the prescribed first month in prison should be dispensed with. On 30 November 1847 sixty-nine juvenile males (under eighteen) 'were exercised in gangs of ten at a time in the Airing Galleries with a view to the relaxing of the separate system of confinement in accordance with the General Board's Order of date November 1847'.[2] Despite this isolated attempt to alleviate the prisoners' loneliness, the system was firmly adhered to and the Journals are full of entries of suicides or attempted suicides, sometimes two or three in one day by male prisoners between twelve and thirty. For example in 1846 a sixteen-year-old attempted suicide, while a prisoner 'who had scarcely been three hours altogether in the prison' hanged himself with his neckcloth and pocket handker-chief. In 1851 a twenty-five-year-old 'committed suicide by throwing himself over the Upper Gallery'. At times those threatening suicide were put in restraining gloves or handcuffs for several days. In 1854 an unsuccessful suicide had to be removed from solitary confinement to the Imbecile Prison a few weeks after the attempt.

Solitary confinement was obviously a large factor in cases of insanity in prison. All prisoners who were weak-minded on ad-mission became much worse in prison and eventually were bundled off to the Lunatic Wing. Frequently a prisoner would become 'incoherent in his language'; he would then be 'doubled up' (that is put in with another prisoner, a strong-minded one if possible), very often 'became violent', and from there it was a short step to restraint and the Lunatic Wing. The Journals are full of references to such cases. In June 1846 the surgeon reported four men and two women insane, and nine men very weak-minded or imbecile. The treatment of such unfortunates always followed the same pattern and was wholly arbitrary and oppressive. They were placed in coercion; doubled up; sent to the Lunatic Wing; pun-ished. Only rarely was a vague attempt made to alleviate or improve their condition.

Food is of paramount importance in any prison at any time. The diet has already been described but a fuller picture can be built up from the Journals. In 1846, on 10, 12 and 14 November, 'all infirm prisoners and all prisoners who had suffered five months of continuous imprisonment, whether in the General Prison alone, or partly there and partly in other prisons, received 4 oz of butcher

meat in terms of the Board's order'.[3] When there was a milk
scarcity a beverage called 'treacle water' was handed out instead.
Efforts were made to keep green vegetables in the diet. When the
number of prisoners increased as in July 1847, 'the work in the
cookhouse has become too much for the cook and his assistant,
and this day an additional prisoner was employed; the two cooks
are however kept separate from the prisoner in the bakehouse'.
When epidemics such as cholera broke out efforts were made to
strengthen the resistance of the ill-fed prisoners. Thus in November 1848, 'this day all the prisoners had an allowance of 4 oz. of
butcher meat in addition to the ordinary diet, which addition is to
be continued twice weekly, also the partial use of treacle water
instead of milk to prisoners who have endured less than five
months of continuous imprisonment was abolished'. The surgeon
added, 'this had no reference to those prisoners already having
butcher meat as part of their diet. This diet is to be continued as
long as cholera is epidemic in this country'.[4]

The scanty diet, the strain of the separate system, and the fact
that many prisoners were in a poor state of health on admittance,
led frequently to illness and death. 'Thysis' (pthisis) was a common
complaint (sometimes contracted before imprisonment), as were
bronchitis, pneumonia, and scrofula. In September 1853 a communication from Under-Secretary Waddington states: 'The attention of Lord Palmerston has been drawn to the number of cases in
which prisoners are affected by pulmonary complaints, and he
requests to be furnished with reports of medical Officers of the
various prisons of Scotland, stating whether they are able to assign
any particular cause connected with the Prison Regulations which
can be supposed to produce the tendency to this mode of disease'.

Frequently prisoners died of debility,[5] and diseases such as
smallpox, marasmus (a wasting illness), epistaxis (bleeding from
the nose), insanity, and palsy figure in the gloomy pages. Epileptic
fits were common and sometimes epileptic prisoners got so 'excited when handcuffed that they would have several epileptic fits
right off', and occasionally would have some of their punishment
remitted.

A curious malady afflicted male prisoners from time to time,
referred to as 'stiffness in the limbs'. (There is no record of females
being so affected.) Sometimes the prisoners would arrive at the

General Prison already stricken, sometimes the disability would develop while they were there. On 2 December 1845 the entry in the Journal refers to prisoners 'who have become stiff in the limbs since their admission to this prison or who were stiff previous to their admission'. There follows a list of nineteen teenage boys, all with previous jail records. An 18-year-old from Glasgow prison had been so stiff during his ten months there that 'he could not go to the cell door for his food'. The entry for 10 December says: 'Two boys were withdrawn from the sixteen stiff boys at present exercised daily in the large room adjoining the storehouse this day, both having recovered'. The entry for 27 January 1846 reads: 'The boys who have been exercised for some time past in the large room adjoining the store, for stiffness of limbs, having much improved, they were this day withdrawn and will in future be exercised daily in the ordinary yards and galleries'. In August of the same year 'Ten prisoners affected with stiffness of limbs were taken out and employed in wheel barrows and digging up weeds with spades in the airing-yard at the west of the hospital; they were masked and under constant superintendance of two warders'. On 10 September, 'The stiff prisoners continue to be exercised digging and wheeling barrows and also on gymnastic exercises – Horizontal vaulting poles have been erected in two of the airing yards for exercising the juvenile prisoners with a view to preventing their being affected with stiffness of limbs – The surgeon has this week reported "Prison tolerably healthy" '.

Occasionally prisoners would be temporarily liberated because their health was in a dangerously low state. Thus in 1846 a male prisoner was 'temporarily liberated – being so weak and worn out as to be in immediate danger of his life by further imprisonment', and another prisoner was in such bad health at the expiry of his sentence that he could not be removed from prison, and stayed in hospital until the surgeon allowed him to move. In 1852 a convict sentenced to seven years transportation was temporarily liberated for the same reason during his probationary confinement. In 1854 a prisoner was granted a temporary discharge on account of ill health, 'as long as he grants an obligation to return to the General Prison for his probationary confinement and seven years transportation for theft when better'. He had not much incentive to get well.

Punishments were frequent and of an unvarying monotony. A prisoner was either handcuffed in his own cell or in a dark punishment cell for periods not exceeding seventy-two hours. Occasionally diet was reduced. By far the greatest number of punishments were given either for trying to communicate with other prisoners[6] or for being noisy in the cell and disturbing the peace of the prison.[7] Both misdemeanours clearly stem from the unbearable strain of solitary confinement pressing on the very young. Prisoners often destroyed their cell contents,[8] used obscene language[9] and were disobedient, struck the warders,[10] and attempted suicide.[11] The youth of the delinquents makes disturbing reading. The year 1847 is typical. Whatever the offence, the Governor invariably justifies the irons and dark punishment cells. 'The Governor considered there was no other mode of punishment here adequate to the offence'; and again and again, 'the prisoner being an imbecile the Governor could not adopt any other mode of punishment'.

A truly desperate desire to communicate is apparent from these pages, coupled at times with an uncontrollable urge to smash and break up cells. A sort of frenzy would seize the prisoners, especially those under 25. In fact very few cases are recorded of misconduct and punishment meted out to the over 35s. Apathy and hopelessness by then had crushed the spirit.

Throughout the years 1851–53, ten-, twelve- and sixteen-year-olds spent hours in dark punishment cells. In 1853 one eighteen-year-old was repeatedly in trouble. In April he was given five days (three in handcuffs) in the dark punishment cell 'for destroying the dial and plate of a crank machine'. A few days later he got seven days for 'wilfully destroying the newly painted wall of his cell while at crank machine labour'. In May he had fifty-four hours in handcuffs and on third class diet 'for making a violent noise in his cell during the night and breaking window'; in July three days for destruction of his cell; in October three days 'for wilfully injuring and taking sand out of a crank machine while at hard labour'; and later in the same month he was twice given three days and third class diet 'for throwing a jugful of broth in a warder's face'. This youth's continued misbehaviour illustrates the futility of the punishment meted out to the prisoners and the completely negative approach of those in authority.

Occasionally an unusual misdemeanour is noted; for example in August 1850 a juvenile prisoner 'having repeatedly refused to allow of his hair to be cut, was handcuffed and otherwise coerced by order of the Superintendent until his hair was cut'. But the Governor evidently held this coercion to be an unwarranted interference with the rights of the individual for he 'highly disapproved of such proceedings' and ordered that in future such cases of disobedience be reported to him first.

The Governors seem to have had some difficulty in keeping warders in their employment. They arrived and left with astonishing rapidity. Certainly the authorities were averse to giving second chances to warders who displayed weaknesses such as unpunctuality, falling asleep at their posts[12] (frequent), turning up in a state of intoxication[13] (even more frequent), sheer carelessness,[14] or simply proving unsuitable for the job.[15] Sometimes warders resigned, for a motley variety of reasons. Thus in 1853 the warder of the Epileptic Rooms resigned on the ground of inadequate remuneration (12/- weekly with uniform). And in 1848 'the Head warder resigned his situation as he found the duties too irksome for him'. Finding the work too hard,[16] the authority too overbearing,[17] and moving to other occupations[18] are typical. Sometimes no cause was given.[19]

The Governors themselves were not infallible. In November 1849 the visit to the prison during the night as ordered by No. 4 of the General Board's Rules of 3rd October 1848 was not made during the week, 'it having escaped the Governor's memory'. And again in July 1851 'owing to inadvertence the Governor did not visit the prison at night during this week'. But, being the Governor, he apparently suffered no unpleasant consequences.

The Journals for 1851–55 break off in January 1855, and from that date until 1862, cannot be traced either by Perth Prison or the Scottish Record Office. During the period covered by the Governors' Journals at Perth 1845–55, the prison Visitors' Book lists the type of people who came there. They include governors of English jails and those of the Scottish ones, ministers, chaplains, Edinburgh advocates, provosts, knights and dukes, foreign dignitaries. Surprisingly, at a time when young girls were sheltered from the harsh and seamy side of life, 'a party of young females' would frequently be in the family party shown round the prison.

1843 was a busy year with 306 visitors. Sometimes their comments are included. Thus in 1842 a Greenock magistrate 'was quite delighted with the health and condition of the prisoners', and in 1844 a Glasgow manufacturer expresses himself 'very much pleased with the whole economy of the establishment', and a Berkshire J.P. considered the gaol 'very clean and orderly'. In 1846 a visitor from Berlin came to inspect the prison 'by order of the King of Prussia' and made no comment. In 1849, the prison was honoured by a visit from H.R.H. Prince Albert accompanied by Secretary of State Sir George Grey, and Sir James Clark, H.M.'s Physician. In 1852 came the Governors of Heriot's Hospital and officials connected therewith – seventeen in the party, and 'a family from Madras Civil Service with daughters'.[20]

The table of the whole establishment of male officers at the General Prison, Perth, with salaries, at 31 December 1868 is of interest:[21]

	Min.	Max.	Annual Increment
Governor	£450	£550	£10
Chaplain	£200	£300	£10
Visiting Roman Catholic Priest	£70	£70	
Visiting Episcopalian Clergyman	£50	£50	
Resident Surgeon	£250	£350	£10
Visiting Physician	£100	£100	
Scripture Reader	£100	£130	£3
Five Teachers	£70	£90	£2
Head Warder	£75	£100	£2/10/-
Two Trades Warders	£55	£75	£2
Thirty Warders	£52	£62	£1

Of these thirty warders only one was under 30 (28), one was 63, and the majority were in their 40s. The Head Warder was 55 and the Trades Warders 56 and 64. The Governor, chaplain and resident surgeon had 'house, gas and garden', and the warders 'house, after period of service, gas and uniform'.

The table of the whole establishment of female officers at Perth was:

	Min.	Max.	Annual Increment
Matron	£175	£225	£5
Sub-Matron	£80	£120	£4
Two Scripture Readers	£75	£95	£2
Seven Teachers	£55	£65	£1
Superintendent of Convicts	£52	£62	£1
Twenty-three Wardresses	£35	£45	£1

Of the twenty-three wardresses only four were under thirty but their average age was younger than that of their male counterparts, only one having reached fifty. The Matron and sub-Matron had furnished house and gas and the Matron had a garden. The wardresses had furnished lodgings, gas and uniform. The age limits of male teachers on permanent appointment was 20–40, and of females 25–40.

The staff of the Lunatic Department was:[22]

	Min.	Max.	Annual Increment
Male:			
Superintendent	£120	£150	£5
Senior Warder	£62	£72	£1
Six Warders	£52	£62	£1
Teachers of Music	£8	£8	
Female:[23]			
Senior Warder	£43	£53	£1
Two Warders	£35	£45	£1
One Sick Nurse	£45	£55	£1
One Housekeeper to Wardresses	£40	£50	£1
One Outer Gatekeeper	£15	£15	

The wages of warders, chaplains, teachers, and other prison officers are important as evidence (in money terms) of the value which contemporary society set on them. Certainly Governors, chaplains, and matrons seem comfortably off.

An inspector's report of July 1853 states, 'We this day visited the General Prison, dividing the duty of seeing the prisoners, every one of whom separately had an opportunity of stating any complaints'. The report continues firmly, 'A very few, and those troublesome persons who had often been in prison before, made statements as to the diet and the like, all of which on investigation proved frivolous or groundless'. The report gave the total number of prisoners in custody as:

	Males	Females
	419	9
Insane prisoners	26	9
Leaving male prisoners	393	
Of these male prisoners there are:		
Separate	323	
Boys in class	39	
Epileptics and prisoner nurse	4	
Imbeciles	7	
Doubled up in prison by surgeon's instructions	14	
In cookhouse (under warder)	2	
In outdoor work (under warder)	2	
Assisting weaving warder	2	
Total	393	
Total number employed is:	389	
Unemployed	30	9
Total	419	9

Thus, with the exception of the insane, only four were unemployed in the prison; only three were on the sick list.

The report gives the pleasing information that the person who for twenty-three years has been surgeon at Woolwich Prison, and lately visited Perth, expressed some surprise at the remarkable general state of health, which he attributed in a great degree to the excellence of the bread and to the proportion of milk allowed. He was struck with the circumstances that there were few cases of scrofula, a form of tuberculosis.

'No punishment has occurred in the prison for a week. The manner in which the prisoners expressed themselves generally indicated satisfaction with their treatment – one prisoner had a handcuff on which he seemed to admit that he deserved.' The visitors saw the 'weak-minded and epileptic, who all appeared contented', and reported that the Lunatic Department 'appeared to be in all respects in excellent order'.[24] Complacent reading after studying the Governors' Journals for the General Prison!

In October 1853 a meeting of the Board refers to 'difficulty experienced in various districts in finding persons willing to inflict the punishment of whipping on Juvenile Offenders'. The Board decided that the difficulty is 'very much, if not altogether attributable to the inadequacy of the remuneration allowed for performing the duty: and that the Government should take the proper steps for raising that remuneration'.[25] No time was wasted on idle speculation as to any principles that might be involved! In the Prison Service College Museum at Polmont examples are displayed of the severe treatment meted out to offenders in the not so distant past. The Dumfries register lists juvenile males sentenced to be whipped between 1852 and 1883. Not more than twelve stripes of the birch rod could be ordered for those under fourteen. A nine-year-old endured ten. Up to thirty-six lashes could be inflicted on those over fourteen and there is quite a long list of such sufferers in the book.

In October 1853 Sir John Kincaid, Inspector of Prisons, recommends a modification of the Rule as to Beds and Bedding of convicted prisoners in Scotland. He concludes from inspection that as regards 'results of the Guard bed system lately introduced for the sleeping of certain classes of prisoner I have found it to be the opinion of all the Prison officers that it has a strong deterring influence without damaging in any respect the health of those subjected to it, and I may add that I received no complaints from any of the prisoners'.

'As however there is reason to fear that a fatal epidemic is approaching with winter, I think it would be a prudent precaution to modify that portion of the Rule which relates to the Bed Clothes, as well as to discontinue the discretionary power vested in the Keepers of Prisons in the event of prisoners misconducting themselves, for such cases can be punished under the ordinary rules.'[26]

Kincaid reported 'the failures to complete Hard Labour Oakum tasks as being much more numerous than those of the Crank Machine',[27] and on the grounds stated by Kincaid the Board agreed to modify Hard Labour Rules 'for the present' to the extent of 'reducing by one half pound the minimum quantities of oakum which the Rule requires to be picked by the several classes of Prisoner to whom it is applicable'. It goes on to say that 'for the present the Governors of the other prisons, if a convict for some good reason cannot complete a task at either kind of Hard Labour, may mitigate in such cases the penalty of stoppage of food, so far as shall appear necessary'.[28]

There is reference to a relaxing of the separate system for certain convicts under sentence of transportation who were to be in the General Prison for longer than the usual twelve months of pro-bationary confinement. They were to have additional exercise daily, and to be associated together at some useful occupation for limited periods. The Governor at Perth reported that 'this system works well'.[29]

The Governors' Journals of the General Prison at Perth for the years 1862-65 show the same pattern as the earlier ones.[30] Both sexes endured the same punishments for the same offences of swearing, refusal to work, and breakup of cell furniture. Several times young female prisoners 'violently assault a teacher and ward-er, tearing their bonnets', and young males got hours in handcuffs for 'fighting on chapel stairs after Divine Service' and for 'forcing open his crank and removing the sand'. There are the same illnesses and suicide attempts, babies 'sent out', and the steady stream to imbecile wards. Trouble with the staff goes on. In September 1862 a male teacher 'was suspended by the Governor for his being addicted to the use of intoxicating drink to excess'.

In December 1862 'a serious riot took place attended with great personal violence' in the Chapel of the Female Convicts. The immediate cause was that a cell search ordered by the Governor, acting on information from the Matron, revealed eleven bottles of Porter and 'unauthorised quantities of articles.' To complicate matters a male prisoner with a false key was found at large in one of the galleries and the Governor recorded rather naively, 'I feared that an attempt might be made to reach the female Prison'. An informer next declared that 'about three dozen men ... were to break out at night and through the night choke the Night Watch and get into the Female Prison'. The whole prison was now near hysteria, and as a precaution the Governor took 'a small double-barrelled pistol but did not load it'. As the riot got out of hand, he loaded it with blank cartridges, entered the chapel and 'fired two shots towards the ceiling'. During a momentary lull a wardress was 'carried out bruised and insensible'. The Sheriff was sent for and arrived accompanied by 'a small detachment of soldiers without firelocks, and several constables . . .' a large body of armed soldiers arrived subsequently. The Sheriff's arrival aroused much excitement and noise but he addressed the prisoners and the chapel emptied. Tolerable quietness reigned by evening but a small guard of soldiers and constables remained all night.

Greenock Prison may be taken to be reasonably representative of the Scottish prisons other than the General Prison. From the reports of the Inspector of Prisons between 1834 and 1864 it appears to have been a very dreary place. There was no lighting, no bath, no exercise and in 1838 'a few dresses were procured for the use of such prisoners who had no proper clothes of their own'.[31] These were not lent to prisoners who were not likely to remain for more than a few days. Little money was spent on food, for although there were 846 prisoners during 1838, the net expense of the prison in that year was a mere £325. 11. 11½. The average daily cost of each criminal prisoner, including cooking, was 'nearly 3d.'.[32]

John Love was Governor of Greenock for thirty years from 1842-72, so most of the Greenock Journal is his. He was very much against the congregate system; thus in February 1848: 'The whole of the prison is exceedingly damp today which must be very injurious to the health of the prisoners on being turned into their cells at night out of the halls where they are kept so warm during the day'. And in April, 'The prisoners are now confined to their cells, the congregation of them in the large room is a most pernicious system'.

Later the same month he says 'congregating has a very bad effect', and he 'fondly hopes' that before winter a new heating apparatus will be set up which will let them 'keep them in their cells day and night'. Also improvements were to be made in cell windows to prevent the prisoners from communicating either with each other or with their associates on the outside. In November he noted with satisfaction that the heating apparatus was finished and the cell windows altered. But by August 1856 'Sir John Kincaid, Inspector of Prisons, visited this prison and suggested that the prisoners sentenced to hard labour should not be employed on the crank machine on account of the cells being so small and badly ventilated. I have acted on the suggestion'.

There were a few suicide attempts and Love also had his disciplinary troubles, with both male and female prisoners. In March 1848 a 16-year-old female 'was handcuffed for twelve hours for swearing by her maker that she would take Miss Gibson's life before she left the prison and for being otherwise noisy'. The usual punishments are listed for the usual misconduct, chiefly calling out or destroying walls, but not nearly so often as at Perth, and there is no record of dark punishment cells or of seventy-two hours in handcuffs. In October 1848, a 38-year-old was handcuffed for twenty-three hours 'for threatening to throw his water pot at the warder and calling him unbecoming names. This is one of the wickedest men that I ever met with in prison'. In 1849 a ten-year-old boy was handcuffed for seven hours for climbing up to his windowsill and calling out, and a fourteen-year-old handcuffed for seventeen hours for a similar fault. In 1850 a fifteen-year-old 'had on the respirator and irons for two hours for calling out at his cell window and being otherwise noisy and pretending to be in a fit while nothing ailed him'. In January 1851 an eighteen-year-old was 'put in irons for climbing up to the window-sill and sending up articles to the female in the cell over him'. The Governor on his inspection found 'all quiet save for this prisoner in irons (an 18-year-old) who was disturbing the whole prison until I tied him down to the floor'. In December 1854 a 13-year-old was 'handcuffed for fifteen hours for outrageous conduct'.

Rarely was there reduction of diet although in August 1850 a prisoner had 'dinner bread stopped for a day for using obscene language to a warder'. In August 1848 the Governor allows those prisoners 'awaiting trial and likely to remain in prison for a length of time, 6 oz. of meal for supper instead of 4, as they complained of hunger before breakfast'. In August 1856 a male prisoner stopped 'taking his food at dinner-time, alleging that it was watery; it only required to be stirred up with a spoon as it was early dished and the Barley and Milk had gone to the bottom'. Two days later the Governor wrote ominously that 'the prisoner commenced to take his food at dinner-time, having seen the Board'.

Epidemics raged at Greenock too. In September 1849 Love notes that 'there were a great many of those who were constant inmates of the prison carried off by the cholera', and he records, 'As cholera is very fatal in the town at present I have stopped the visits of the friends and relatives of prisoners during the prevalency'; but by October, 'cholera having subsided', visits were resumed. In 1854 a case of smallpox was mentioned. The Governor recorded occasional births in the prison and, as at Perth, stated when children could be safely removed from their mothers. Several are so listed in March 1854.

At Greenock Prison the Governor had quite a lot of trouble with his staff, and the reasons for dismissals make amusing reading. The difficulty of getting on with the redoubtable matron seemed to be the biggest problem with the female staff, and the perils of intoxication with the males. Thus in 1848 a female warder 'gives up her situation on account of some differences between her and the matron'. In March 1850 the housekeeper is dismissed 'for irregular conduct'; and in October the new housekeeper is dismissed in her turn 'for keeping up money belonging to a female prisoner'. In July 1851 another housekeeper gives up because of her health and in April 1852 the housekeeper resigns on account of 'some dispute with matron', as the Governor records a little wearily. In November 1853 a female warder 'gives up her situation being unable to live with the matron'. The male warders proved as unreliable. In November 1853 a watchman 'having come on duty in a state of intoxication gave occasion to put him out by force; I dismissed him from his office'. In May 1854 a 'warder gave up his situation; he considered it too confined for a married person'. In June a watchman who had been there only a few months 'gave up his situation as he would not get an advance of wages'. In September, 'two warders gave up to go to Australia', and in November a watchman 'gave up his situation as he did not like the place'. In November 1856 a warder 'gave up as he had taken a shop which he was going to open'.

Love had other difficulties to contend with. In 1865 he complained about the bad living conditions and insecurity of the prison. In March of that year the front boundary wall collapsed owing to undermining by excavations made by the tenement owner opposite. The main wall then fell into the excavation 'leaving the prison quite exposed'.[33] A night watchman had to be posted on the breach day and night until a barricade could be erected. In May, the north boundary wall collapsed, was rebuilt and fell down yet again. In 1869 a new prison was built in Nelson Street, adjoining the Court house, was occupied in 1870 and continued in use until 1910.

Very occasionally in the depressing entries of the Governors' Journals a small ray of light breaks through. It is pleasant to read in the Perth Journal for 26 October 1846 that one of the 'stiff boys' of an earlier entry, aged fifteen and having had five prison sentences, was liberated and 'went to Woolwich having received a situation on board a vessel lying there', and that he received '11/- in addition to ordinary travelling expenses which would have been allowed him on his liberation, by order of the Sheriff in consideration of good conduct while in General Prison – expected to do well'.

IV Transportation

An interesting correspondence[1] illustrates how sick Scottish convicts under sentence of transportation could be shuttled back and forth between Scotland and Millbank Prison in London. It was possible for one of the Secretaries of State to direct the removal to Millbank of any convict under sentence of transportation, but the convict had to be pronounced fit by the prison doctor before leaving it, and if when examined at Millbank he was found to be unfit, he was sent back to his original prison.

There are frequent protests by the Governor at Millbank to the Sheriff of Edinburgh stating that the medical certificates accompanying male convicts received from various jails in Scotland were not in accordance with terms of the Secretary of State's warrant. Reports of 1847–48 cite cases of ill-treatment and death among Scottish prisoners sent south. A letter from the Millbank doctor in

1847 asserts that two female convicts brought from Banff were not fit to be received into Millbank as they were too old and sick for labour in a penal colony, while an angry letter from the Clerk to the Prison Board in Banff insisted they were perfectly able-bodied, though one was 'adept at feigning illness', and that they were now back at Banff where there was no room for them. An accompanying letter from the Sheriff of Banff adds his complaints.

There is a letter of January 1848 from the man who brought twenty-nine convicts from Glasgow, Ayr, Paisley, Lanark, Hamilton, Kirkcudbright, and Jedburgh to Millbank. From Glasgow they proceeded to Granton in the usual manner 'per Railways, Omnibuses and Van', and were shipped on board the *Royal Adelaide* steamer. The voyage took two and a half days and all 'enjoyed good health (Sea Sickness Excepted) with the exception of one who took three convulsion fits', but recovered by the time they reached Millbank. One of the party was rejected as ill and sent back to Glasgow.

Sometimes the convicts were too ill to undergo the voyage north again and were sent to Millbank hospital. Thus in January 1848 the doctor at Millbank reported on the state of 'Patrick McGinty being in the last degree of Emaciation and debility', and 'very great danger would attend his removal from London to Glasgow'. His letter was accompanied by one from the Millbank Governor to the Sheriff of Edinburgh, couched in strong terms, 'I cannot avoid expressing my regret that convicts should be sent to this establishment under circumstances which oblige me from motives of humanity to act in violation of the regulations framed for my guidance'. Next the Crown Office at Edinburgh sent notice of the inevitable inquest on McGinty, the proceedings to be taken against the Glasgow doctor who authorised his removal south.

In March 1848 a letter came to the Lord Advocate, at the direction of Sir George Grey, Home Secretary, from the Inspectors of Millbank prison, reporting on the improper removal of a convict from Dornoch Gaol to Millbank, and calling the attention of the Home Secretary to 'the objectionable mode in which Convicts are generally removed from Gaols in Scotland to that Prison'. They felt it their duty to report it 'as another instance of the want of proper care on the part of the officers entrusted with the removal of Transports from the Scotch Prisons'. (They added that Scottish female convicts are never accompanied by a female warder on the journey South but are under the supervision of a male assistant which is 'highly improper'.) In March it was reported by the Millbank medical superintendent that the Dornoch prisoner was dying. He was brought from Dornoch to Aberdeen via Inverness, three nights on the way, 'without going to bed, had no place to lie down on, but passed these nights in Irons with scarcely any fire, being all the time chained to a female convict . . . During the first day he made the journey in an open Gig and the second on the outside of a coach . . . The weather at the time was very severe'. In April the Lord Advocate took the matter up with the General Prison Board who wrote to the Sutherland Prison Board. They sought to justify the treatment of the prisoner, saying he was convicted of horse-stealing and the female convict of house-break-ing, declaring they were only chained together at Aberdeen in case of attempts to escape when going on board in the dark. They add as a further justification that the female convict 'was a person very different from the general run of her sex . . . an uncommonly stout muscular woman', and quoting a statement from the keeper of the Prison to the effect that she was unmanageable and 'on one occasion she threatened to knock out the brains of the Matron'.

It is difficult to escape the conclusion that there was a conspic-uous lack of humane care at the Scottish end of the transportation journeys. Still the dominant feeling in Scotland was, 'Get rid of the offender at all costs, in whatever state he may be, to the next parish, the next county, or beyond the seas'.

Meanwhile the transportation chapter in our history was draw-ing to a close. The Australian penal colony had had a turbulent existence and transportation became unpopular both at home and in Australia. In Britain there was a growing tendency to condemn transportation as wastage of manpower and to ask why convict labour should not be utilised on public works in the UK. There was some doubt too as to whether transportation was in fact a punishment. The ubiquitous Sidney Smith argued that it was not and that neither was it a deterrent. Many were inclined to agree with him, further stating that transportation had proved to be in no sense reformative.

Objections were considered by a Select Committee in 1837 which proposed the ending of transportation to Australia as soon as possible and the substitution of confinement with hard labour at home or abroad. This was impossible to implement at once for there were too few prisons and the hulks were already unhealthily overcrowded. It was decided to stop transporting convicts to New South Wales but to continue to Van Diemen's Land (Tasmania). There, savage punishments and inhuman tortures were commonplace.[2] If transportees escaped and returned home before serving their term, they were liable to be executed.[3]

Sir George Grey, the Home Secretary, suspended transportation in 1846 for two years and instead sent all transportees to undergo a period of separate confinement at home in an institution like the new Pentonville. Transportees between eighteen and thirty-five years spent 18 months in solitary confinement there and were taught a trade in their cells. In 1857 the 18 months was reduced to 9 months for all sentences of penal servitude. There are many instances of convicts coming from prisons all over the UK to do their 12 or 18 months probationary confinement in solitary at Perth and then being sent south to the hulks to await transportation.[4] When their solitary confinement was over, convicts were sent to labour in association on public works in Britain, Gibraltar, or Bermuda, then on ticket-of-leave (licence to be free before ending of sentence) to any colony which would take them. This plan was the origin of the sentence of penal servitude which was to dominate British penal treatment at the end of the nineteenth century. In 1852 Tasmania, swamped with the British criminal classes, firmly refused to accept any additions, and Bermuda and Gibraltar with more than 8,000 convicts already, clearly could not absorb many more. Western Australia continued to be used but the last convict ship sailed there in 1867.

In 1853 the Penal Servitude Act had been passed, substituting sentences of four years penal servitude for the existing ones of seven years transportation. A frantic hunt revealed no new dumping ground for criminals – the Falkland Islands, Labrador, and New Guinea were all tried unsuccessfully. The discharge of many ticket-of-leave holders in Britain led to public unease and agitation, and the second Penal Servitude Act, 1857, was the result. It recommended that the terms of Penal Servitude should correspond exactly to the previous sentences of transportation and that there should be remission if behaviour warranted it; one-sixth remission in a sentence of three years and one-third in a sentence of fifteen years or longer. This Act continued in force until the Criminal Justice Act of 1948.

V Towards Centralisation

In the nineteenth century the general public, if they thought about it at all, largely held the opinion that prison must be oppressive and punitive. As this was in line with the views of officialdom, it was only when some particularly scandalous incident of prison life found its way into the press that any public interest in the treatment of prisoners was aroused. Such an incident was the suicide by hanging in Birmingham Jail in 1854 of a 15-year-old boy to escape further tortures by the inhuman governor. Maconochie, the former Superintendent of Norfolk Island, had been Governor of Birmingham Prison from 1849 to 1851 and had introduced the marks system he had started in Australia. His methods were not popular with the justices, who forced him to resign and replaced him by the Assistant-Governor, a man of savage propensities. Now began a period of incalculable suffering for the Birmingham prisoners under the new Governor Austin. Ignoring all the prison rules, Austin carried out a reign of terror over his unfortunate charges. Failure to complete the stipulated 10,000 revolutions of the crank was punished by starvation.[1] Thus enfeebled, over-tasked bodies found it impossible to labour at the crank, which led to more savage punishments such as removal of bed and light, flogging, the black hole, solitary confinement, and, most feared of all, the frequent use of the strait-jacket, an instrument of medieval torture. Many became insane, some dying under the bestial treatment they endured.

After the Royal Commission's report on the Birmingham atrocities, and the publication in 1856 of Charles Reade's *It's Never Too Late To Mend*, in which the daily tortures inflicted on hapless prisoners from the age of nine upwards were vividly described, the public became uneasy. Reade's almost unbearably realistic exposure of jail abuses forced people to accept the unpalatable fact that such barbaric cruelties could be practised in prisons under the care of local and unpaid visiting magistrates. This realisation led to a growing demand that all prisons should be placed under national control.

By the 1839 Prison (Scotland) Act a General Board of Directors was empowered to erect a central prison at Perth, a General Prison for long-term prisoners, and, although administration was still in local hands, the central government was strengthened by the appointment of a Board of Managers. In 1839 there were in Scotland 178 locally-administered establishments, many of which were in a deplorable condition and did not possess even the rudimentary standard of accommodation or classification. Gradually the number of these had shrunk until by 1860 many were closed. 'The decision to make certain local prisons good and sufficient was really the death of the idea of centralisation at Perth.'[2] And the Prisons (Scotland) Administration Act 1860 abolished the General Board of Directors of Prisons in Scotland and brought Perth General Prison under a body of managers, i.e. the Sheriff Principal of the County of Perth, the Inspector of Prisons for Scotland, the Crown Agent in Scotland, and one salaried manager appointed by the Queen. The General Prison was to detain prisoners sentenced in Scotland and was also for 'Reception and Detention of such Convicts under sentence of Order of Transportation or of Penal Servitude as her Majesty may please to direct to be removed to such General Prison, and sentences of 9 months and more were to be served in General Prison'.[3] Under the Act, twenty-one prisons were closed.

But it was not until the 1865 Prison Act (England) that many of the powers were taken from local authorities, though it still held that deterrence through severity was the chief aim of prisons, and upheld the silent system and the separation of prisoner from prisoner; hard bodily labour on the crank and treadwheel; the use of chains and irons, dark cells, bread and water, and flogging as necessary punishment. This Act divided hard labour into Class I, including treadwheel, shot drill (marching while carrying heavy cannon balls), crank, capstan, stonebreaking, or equally hard 'bodily labour', and Class II, other bodily labour. Only with the passing of the 1877 Prison Acts did the prison system become nationalised, bringing all local prisons in the UK under the full control of the central government. Thus began the modern British prison system.

Despite the volume of legislation, the busy activity of conflicting ideologies, the end of transportation, and the centralisation of prison authority, the period ended as it began to the extent that the same emphasis was placed on retribution and deterrence; useless hard labour of the crank and treadwheel, irons and flogging were still commonplace, while the public remained largely indifferent. On the other hand we had moved from the squalid, casual, promiscuous prisons of the congregate system to the rigid, inhuman, repressive silent system, with the accent implacably on the separation of prisoner from prisoner in the grim new fortresses where those immured slowly went mad.

6
Centralisation and Reform
1877-1908

We tore the tarry ropes to shreds
With blunt and bleeding nails;
. . .
We sewed the sacks, we broke the
stones,
. . .
We turn the crank, or tear the rope
Each in his separate Hell.
                    Oscar Wilde★

6

The Prison Acts of 1877 swept away the complicated system of locally-managed prisons, and brought them under the authority of the Home Secretary. Convict prisons such as Dartmoor and Portsmouth, where sentences of penal servitude were served, were already under the central authority. The structure lasted until the Criminal Justice Act of 1948. Since then there have been only slight changes in the legal machinery of imprisonment in general although the whole position of children and young persons has been fundamentally changed.

Until the formation of the Howard Association in 1866 (united in 1921 with the Penal Reform League to form the Howard League for Penal Reform) improvements in prisons were achieved by the efforts of a few individuals. Howard, through his inability to work with others, could be said to have sabotaged the effort to have new prisons built.[1] There was no organisation to implement Howard's plans, and prisons remained in the hands of local authorities despite the public sympathy he had roused. Nationalisation in 1877 ensured the enforcement of a common policy in all prisons. 'It also gave those who were trying to promote reform only one body to convince; previously, ideas had been touted from one uninterested county authority to another, usually meeting with an impassive obstinacy.'[2]

It must be remembered that Howard and other reformers had always stressed the physical conditions of the prisons, and that in Howard's time these were still mainly lodgings where prisoners were kept awaiting transportation or other punishments, and only debtors and political prisoners expected to be incarcerated for years. Howard was not primarily concerned with the purpose of imprisonment. But by the time the Prison Commissions for Scotland and England were appointed in 1877, the official view, as well as that of the general public, was that only by making jails places of harsh punishment could wrongdoers be deterred from returning to prison. The huge new prisons which shot up in the mid-nineteenth century to cope with the influx after the end of transportation were based on Howard's ideas in design. But it has not been properly understood that Howard never anticipated prisoners being shut up there for years or that such buildings might be needed to serve a remedial rather than a vengeful purpose. If Howard had been able to envisage social training in prisons, it is possible they might have been constructed quite differently.

Coupled with the trend towards harsher treatment as a deterrent to wrongdoers there was another factor contributing to the prisoner's sense of isolation from the rest of the community. Before 1877 and the takeover of control of all prisons by the Home Office, inspectors' reports had been published yearly. After that date these reports were no longer public, and so a valuable stimulus to public interest was lost. Despite the appointment of bodies of visitors, the prison system became a closed bureaucracy and so it has remained. Although since the early 1920s it has been the policy of the Commissioners to allow the public in, yet the unification brought about by the Prison Acts 1877 lessened the public interest and the sense of public responsibility.

To elaborate: once any organisation comes under bureaucratic control it tends to become much more rigid and conservative; civil servants are there to implement regulations. There is no interplay of ideas, no fresh thoughts are brought to bear on problems. Everything is done by the book therefore there tends to be very little development. Members of the public who may be interested are handicapped by the difficulty of getting access to the facts because civil service departments are notoriously secretive.

But the reverse of the coin shows a contrary tendency, for although prisons, even of the same class, still had great variations in regimes, yet on the whole the results of the 1877 Acts were good. Better organisation of prison labour and the ending of the worst scandals of some local jails[3] could only be brought about by a unified prison system. This ensured that standards laid down are adhered to, but the danger is that these standards tend neither to change nor to develop.

That not all were in favour of nationalisation of prisons can be seen from a letter of March 1870 to V. D. Broughton from Secretary Bruce saying, 'Many practical objections would be found to placing the General Prison at Perth under the Directors of English Convict Prisons, as well as to a withdrawal of the supervision now exercised by the managers over the local prisons'.[4]

By 1877 the number of prisons in Scotland had been reduced to fifty-six, their administration – by the Prisons (S) Act of that date – transferred from the local authorities to the State, and their maintenance provided for by Parliament. All local Prison Boards were abolished. The Act said that rules for the administration of prisons might be made at any time by the Secretary of State who was to be responsible for the appointment of prison officers and the control and safe custody of prisoners. Note that under previous legislation local authorities were the executive administering prisons, while the State controlled and inspected their administration. Now the State was to administer, while local authorities through the visiting committees were to inspect independently and report to the Secretary of State.

By the Act, provision was made for the appointment by the Crown of a body of not more than three Prison Commissioners of whom two might be salaried. The Sheriff of Perthshire and the Crown Agent of Scotland were also to be Commissioners ex officio. The general superintendence of prisons was vested in the Commissioners, subject to the control of the Secretary of State, and inspectors and officers were appointed to assist them. An annual report by the Prison Commissioners on every prisoner within their jurisdiction was to be laid before both Houses of Parliament; it was to include details of manufacturing processes carried on in each prison, and a list of all punishments inflicted. Every ordinary prison was to have an annually appointed visiting committee to report on any abuse, hear complaints, and observe conditions. Any sheriff or JP having jurisdiction in the place where the prison was, might enter the prison and examine the conditions of the prisoners (except those under sentence of death). All local obligation to maintain prisons was ended.

A serious defect in Scottish prison organisation until the 1877 Act was a lack of power 'in the arrangements for adjusting available accommodation to the fluctuations in population and crime'[5]

– such as when a prison became overcrowded while a few miles off one might be half empty. There were provisions in the Acts of 1839 and 1860 for counties contracting a union or partnership for prison purposes, but this was never done. And it was not in the power of the Board under the 1839 Act, nor of the Secretary of State under the 1860 Act, to close the only prison in a county though it might be subject to any limitation in classes of prisoners for which it remained open. Under the 1877 Act five prisons of this class were closed (Kinross, Stonehaven, Banff, Nairn and Peebles).[6]

The 1878–79 Report stressed that:

> 'It is desirable, on constitutional grounds, that the interior of prisons should be seen by others besides these who rule in them, and it is better that those who visit prisons should be responsible people with fixed privileges, than that they should come casually, – from the community at large.'[7]

As regards the important subject of the difference between English and Scottish prisons, the Report says, 'In the whole question of comparison between the prison service in England and in Scotland, consideration must be allowed for the influence of the English Act of 1865 – it had in a manner the advantage of being prepared under higher conditions of civilisation in prison treatment. By the revolution in penal management, drawing the convicts from the penal colonies, and decreeing that they should be treated at home under the penal servitude system, the English reformation was thus accomplished by the aid of experience in that class of penal discipline that is known to all practical people as the most difficult. As the prison service in both countries is now in the hands of one master, we may feel sure that any practice found effective and valuable in one of them will find its way to the other.'[8] The Report adds that 'In any comparisons between England and Scotland, involving the joint elements of efficiency and economy, account must be taken of the vast districts of waste and thinly peopled districts of the Highlands and Islands to the West and North'.[9]

By the Secretary for Scotland Acts 1885–89, powers over Scottish prisons were transferred from the Secretary of State for the Home Department to the Scottish Secretary.

Immediately after the 1877 Acts the five English Prison Commissioners under Sir Edward du Cane began to decide which prisons to close and to reorganise the local prisons with the object of uniformity in prison management, since there were gross disparities in the existing regimes. Du Cane, who had organised prison labour in Western Australia from 1851–56, set to work with determination. He held deterrence and strict discipline to be the dominant aim of punishment and he was convinced that the separate system was better than the silent; he strongly opposed association. In this latter attitude he had the support of the Secretary of the Howard Association. He was determined that all sentenced equally should undergo equal punishment. How different from the eighteenth and early nineteenth-centuries when money bought comfort, drink, food, and female companionship!

At this time the technique was to put the prisoner at once into bad conditions and to offer him better only if his industry and good conduct merited it. The modern rule is to give the prisoner from the outset most of the privileges which in the late nineteenth century had to be earned, and to use the threat of losing them to ensure good conduct and industry. The Penal Servitude Act of 1853[10] had introduced the Progressive Stage System. The sentence in a public works prison was divided into stages, each carrying with it increasing privileges. A convict could pass through four stages according to the number of marks awarded, and could forfeit privileges and sink to a lower stage. In the first stage the prisoner had to work ten hours daily in the first-class hard-labour, of which six to eight hours were on the crank or treadmill, he had to sleep on a bare plank board, and he earned no money. In the second stage the prisoner was employed as in stage one for a month, and was then put on second-class hard labour, sleeping on a bare plank bed two nights weekly and the rest of the week on a mattress; he could earn up to 1/- per week; he could be taught and have exercise on Sundays. In the third stage he was employed in second-class hard labour, he slept on a bare plank bed only one night weekly, earned not more than 1/6, had lessons and Sunday exercise and library books in his cell. In the fourth stage he always slept on a mattress, could earn up to 2/-, had the same privileges as in the third stage, could receive and send a letter and have a twenty-minute visit.

This system became characteristic of Penal Servitude and was to last until the Prison Act 1898. The Star Class system, introduced as a result of the Royal Commission of 1878, segregated first offenders from others. But with du Cane, all cells were made as comfortless and dreary as possible. 'Prisoners come out ... sometimes insane, often unemployable, nearly always bitter and resentful, with an average (at least for the three years preceding 1878) of 7d in their pockets ... undeterred and unreformed.'[11]

Then came the Gladstone Report in 1895. The committee which drew it up praised the strong centralisation of authority which had been entirely successful in terms of uniformity, discipline, and economy, but went on to point out that the danger of the highly-centralised system was that the prisoners had been treated too often as worthless members of the community, and the large number of recommittals gave cause for concern. The committee held that prison discipline should be designed 'wherever possible to turn them out of prison better men and women physically and morally than when they came in.'[12] This was clearly not being done, so the committee recommended that useless labour should be abolished; that confinement in cells should be limited; and that du Cane's severe regime should be relaxed.

The Gladstone Report is a landmark in the history of British penal reform chiefly for three reasons. The Committee gave consideration to the possibility of prison conditions designed to *reform* the criminal. It also recognised the need to improve conditions inside prison, and this included abolition of useless labour of crank and treadmill, reduction of solitary confinement, better food, more books and education, and work for prisoners in local prisons. 'Prison treatment should have as its primary and concurrent objects, deterrence and reform.'[13] This attitude was very different from the hard line taken by the 1863 House of Lords Committee. The equalling of deterrence and reform supplanted the hitherto prevailing belief that deterrence was the paramount aim of a prison sentence. This in itself was a great step forward. Thirdly the Committee recognised the problem of recidivism. Till the Gladstone Report there had been no serious attempt to treat the recidivist (a problem still unsolved today).

The Prison Act 1898 incorporated most of the Gladstone Committee's recommendations. It abolished unproductive hard labour of the first class – of crank and treadwheel – and ordered that the first twenty-eight days of hard labour must be done in separation; thereafter the hard-labour prisoners would work in association with ordinary prisoners, in reversion to the Silent System recommended by the Report. For the first month of a hard-labour sentence the convict had to sleep on a plank bed with no mattress. Section 6 of the Act empowered the Courts to order that a sentence of imprisonment without hard labour should be spent in the 1st, 2nd or 3rd divisions, and in the absence of any order, in the 3rd division. The Act also limited the power to order corporal punishment for serious breaches of prison discipline (a power which lasted until the Criminal Justice Act of 1967). Provision was made for remission of part of the sentence for industry and good conduct in cases of imprisonment as distinct from penal servitude.

The Act also contained provision for the Home Secretary to make rules for the government of local and convict prisons, with the result that further legislation concerning the conditions and organisation of prisons was made unnecessary until the 1952 Prison Act.

Sir Evelyn Ruggles-Brise succeeded du Cane as chairman of the Prison Commission the month the Gladstone Report was published. His years in office (1895–1921) saw a vast number of changes in prison conditions. Steps were taken to abolish the unproductive hard labour of the crank and treadwheel even before the abolition of first-class hard labour by the Act of 1898. After the first month of a hard labour prisoner's sentence, work was to be in association. The period of separate confinement which started penal servitude sentences was reduced. Prison diet was improved. Prisoners had weekly baths instead of fortnightly. There were more visits, letters and books, and an improved system of education.

Ruggles-Brise's period as chairman is important for witnessing a 'significant development in the avoidance of prison as a punishment and the evolution of alternative penal or corrective measures.'[14] He held too that prison should be regarded as the last rather than the first resort. He was largely responsible for the Probation of Offenders Act 1907, the first real probation statute in Britain. (There had been earlier examples in the USA, and in the 1820s in England magistrates had sentenced juveniles to a day's imprisonment on condition they returned to their parents or masters to be supervised.)[15]

Probation is the 'suspension of punishment conditional on there being no further offence for a period during which the offender is placed under personal supervision.'[16] Previous English statutes had permitted conditional suspension of punishment, but before 1907 no statutory provision was made for supervision. The Act allowed for the conditional release of old lags as well as first offenders.

In nineteenth-century Scotland and England one of the worst aspects of the penal system was the imprisonment of children. While reformatory and industrial schools had proved valuable as alternatives to imprisonment, it was not until the Children's Act 1908 that imprisonment of those under fourteen was prohibited, and imprisonment of those between fourteen and sixteen allowed only by special certificate of the court. At present those under twenty-one are not sent to prison but are dealt with in a variety of institutions which will be mentioned later.

But despite worthwhile advances there was still much hardship in the conditions under Ruggles-Brise. The convict's head was still cropped, his prison garb was still an 'ill-fitting dress of shame' covered in broad arrows, and although work was in association there was little recreation in association, and often more than seventeen out of the twenty-four hours were spent in the cell. And even though the rule of silence was no longer absolute it was an added misery.

Oscar Wilde, who served two years in Reading Gaol (1895–97), spoke for many inarticulate sufferers when he described the futile, meaningless 'work' the prisoners did:

> We tore the tarry rope to shreds
> With blunt and bleeding nails;
>
> ... ...
> We sewed the sacks, we broke the stones,
>
> ... ...
> We turn the crank, or tear the rope
> Each in his separate Hell.'[17]

Wilde, like many before and after him, comes to the conclusion that:

> 'The vilest deeds like poison weeds,
> Bloom well in prison-air;

It is only what is good in Man
That wastes and withers there.'[18]

He was appalled at the treatment meted out to young children
in prison – appalled that they were there at all. In a letter to the
Daily Chronicle, Wilde declared, 'The way that children are treated
at present is really an outrage on humanity and common sense'.[19]
Shut up in a dim cell for twenty-three hours a day, often terrified,
always hungry, and frequently unable to eat the 'coarse, horrible'
food offered to it, a child would sometimes rouse the pity of a
warder who might give it something edible and lose his job
because of his compassion. Wilde urged that no child under fourteen should be sent to prison, but if it must be there it should spend
its days in the schoolroom and its nights in a dormitory and have
far more exercise. In the same letter Wilde pleaded for the weak-
minded prisoners who became insane through ill-treatment,
although held by prison doctors to be shamming and consequently
often punished by brutal birching.

In another letter entitled *Prison Reform* Wilde writes on the
subject of the 1898 Prison Bill about to be read, and points out
what reforms in 'our present stupid and barbarous system are
urgently necessary'.[20] He declared that the suggested increase in
the number of inspectors and prison visitors would be useless as
such visitors only go to see prison regulations carried out, not to
help the prisoners. He stated that the necessary reforms were (1)
improvement of the food, which was revolting and 'just enough
to sustain, not life exactly, but existence'[21], and which 'in most
cases consists of weak gruel, suet and water',[22] leading to permanent diarrhoea in many prisoners. (2) Improvement of the appalling sanitary arrangements and especially the abolition of the disgusting custom of 'slopping out' (still prevailing). (3) Better
ventilation in the cells: for twenty-three hours a day the prisoners
breathed foul air. (4) 'The present prison system seems almost to
have for its aim the wrecking and the destruction of the mental
faculties ... Deprived of books, of all human intercourse ...
condemned to eternal silence ... brutalised below the level of any
of the brute creation',[23] is it any wonder, Wilde asked, that many
men go mad in prison? He pointed out that for the first three
months in prison no books were allowed except a Bible, prayer

book, and hymn book, and after that the books supplied from the prison library were of very poor quality. He wanted prisoners to be allowed more visits than the twenty minutes four times a year, more letters than the four a year permitted. He considered prison chaplains to be 'entirely useless . . . well-meaning, but foolish', and held an equally low opinion of prison doctors, calling them 'brutal in manner, coarse in temperament, and utterly indifferent to the health of the prisoners or their comfort'.[24]

The vast majority of prisoners through the ages have always been of low mentality, often illiterate, and quite incapable of describing their plight vividly or even coherently. So when a gifted writer like Wilde falls foul of the law and puts his experiences on paper either in prison or on release, his words have more effect, more influence, than those of prison staff, visitors, or politicians. The general public lend an ear. Wilde's strongly worded descriptions of the miseries of prison life near the turn of the century, coming as they did from one of the most brilliant literary figures of the day, himself just released, disgraced, from two years' imprisonment, must have made many readers of the *Daily Chronicle* ponder seriously.

Hard on his heels came W. B. Neville, a peer's son, sentenced in 1897 to five years' penal servitude for uttering promissory notes. He served three years and nine months in Parkhurst and Wormwood Scrubs and was released in November 1901 on a ticket-of-leave. Neville, a highly intelligent and articulate man, was another of the very few prisoners who could express themselves well on paper, and his picture of 'life inside' is a full and comprehensive one.

As regards governors and warders he considered them good on the whole (as did Wilde). 'It was a wonder to me that they got such a good class of men to join the prison service . . . Many . . . are old soldiers or old sailors, and the only thing that induces them to join the service, I suppose, is the prospect of retiring on a pension . . . Their work is incessant; their hours are very long; and their pay is decidedly not too high, . . . their responsibility is very great.'[25]

Neville felt that the half-hour, twice weekly given to teaching illiterate prisoners the three R's was far too little, and that a good opportunity was missed for making school a useful instrument of discipline and reform. He thought 'the perpetual silence is most infamous ... When I first went to Parkhurst no talking was allowed under any circumstances, but under the new regulations of April 1900, men who had reached the 'blue-collar' stage, that is, who have done three years in prison with good conduct, were allowed to walk and talk together for about three-quarters of an hour on Sunday afternoon'.[26] He hoped that this concession would extend in time to weekdays. (In local prisons also, talking was allowed only once weekly during exercise and that after six months in prison.)

Neville was as enraged as Wilde on the subject of prison diet. The total absence of all green vegetables from their diet induced such a craving in the prisoners that they would tear up and devour green weeds while on exercise. An enormous number of men suffered from skin diseases, boils, and rashes. Many were taken to hospital suffering from self-inflicted wounds in order to share in the better fare for the sick. The Home Secretary had said in 1891 that the ordinary prison diet was not to be regarded as an instrument of punishment, but that prison diet must not bear too favourable a comparison with the diet of free labourers in the outside world or of the inmates of workhouses. There was a constant fear lest prisoners were found to be better off than their counterparts outside.

Until 1898 the ordinary prison diet had indeed been regarded as an instrument of punishment. Thus the Committee of 1878, on whose recommendations all prison diets were based up to the partial adoption of the Report of 1899, laid down that to give a diet necessary to the maintenance of health during the longer terms would be to forego an opportunity of inflicting salutary punishment. Starvation was to be added to imprisonment and labour as an additional punishment. It was the diet based on this 1878 Report (the same as the old scale of 1864) that was in force during Neville's time at the Scrubs and Parkhurst until just before his discharge, and which Wilde endured during all his imprisonment. Neville found his food insufficient, often 'repellent' and bad, and never anything but 'an instrument of punishment'.[27] Too often contractors sent in rotten potatoes, bad flour, and sour bread. There was no redress and many men became wrecks. The new diet came in just before Neville left, but was only for hard-labour parties, so the printers, tailors, shoemakers were excluded and put on a new light-labour diet. Neville considered the 1899 Report on Prison Diet to be good. He gives tables of, first, the Old Dietary menus under which each convict was given 145–168 ozs. of bread weekly, and one pint of tea instead of gruel if he had served part of his sentence.[28] Neville then gives the New Dietary introduced in 1901; each convict had 168–196 ozs. of bread. Neville pointed out that the new dietary (although like the old, leaning heavily on bread and potatoes) meant that prisoners' health improved and violence decreased. 'Punishment by hunger, which prevailed from 1864 to 1901, was not only a crime, but a colossal blunder. It entailed . . . suffering and . . . injury on tens of thousands of helpless wretches.'[29]

William Sievwright, for thirty years a scripture reader in Perth General Prison, says in 1894 that the aim was 'to maintain the prisoners in ordinary health – that pampering may be avoided on the one hand and hurtful privation on the other. Many, no doubt, complain very unreasonably, I fancy, that such a vile class should be so well cared for. But it should be remembered that even criminal prisoners are not sentenced to be allowed to live in personal neglect and filth nor to be starved to death.'[30]

Sievwright describes the diet at Perth where persons under sentence of imprisonment not above three days had for breakfast a pint of oatmeal gruel, for dinner a pound of bread, for supper a pint of oatmeal gruel. Ordinary prisoners, females and juveniles, or convicts in the first or probationary period of discipline had for breakfast 8 ozs. of oatmeal made into porridge with $\frac{3}{4}$ of a pint of milk; for dinner 2 pints of barley broth with 8 ozs. of wheaten bread; or $2\frac{1}{2}$ lbs of potatoes with $\frac{3}{4}$ of a pint of milk and 4 ozs. of wheaten bread; for supper $1\frac{1}{2}$ lbs of potatoes with $\frac{1}{2}$ pint of milk or 4 ozs. of oatmeal made into porridge with $\frac{1}{2}$ pint of milk. These convicts past the first or probationary stage found their dietary somewhat improved. They got 8 ozs. of bread with $\frac{1}{2}$ pint of tea for breakfast and for dinner on four days of the week 6 ozs. of meat and 1 oz. of cheese and either 6 ozs. of bread and 1 lb of potatoes or 12 oz. wheaten bread. The menu of adult males who were ordinary prisoners consisted wholly of porridge, potatoes, bread, milk, and a little barley broth – no meat, cheese or tea. Male convicts not on probation got an additional bonus of 12 ozs. of fresh fish and $\frac{1}{2}$ pint of fish soup for one day's dinner, and $\frac{3}{4}$ pint of coffee nightly at supper. Male convicts on hard labour at public works had a rather better dietary.[31]

Neville gives a grim account of the dreary and wearisome prison routine. On weekdays, with the exception of Saturdays, the prisoners rose just after 5 a.m., slopped out, and breakfasted locked in their cells. Then came chapel, parade, search, work as cooks, blacksmiths, tailors, book binders, farm-labourers. At 11 a.m. they were searched again, worked till 5 p.m. and had supper in their cells. At 6.40 they were locked up for the night, but were not allowed to go to bed until 8 at lights out. On Saturdays there was no work in the afternoon, so when the men went to their cells for dinner at 11.10 they did not leave them till 9 a.m. on Sunday, a total of twenty-two hours solitary.

The prisoners had a weekly hot bath and shave, and every fortnight their hair was clipped down to an eighth of an inch. Only convicts sentenced to penal servitude had their heads shaved. The hair was allowed to grow again three months before release. Each man was given a pencil and slate in the cell, but as many were illiterate, Neville wondered how they could endure the hours. On discharge the prisoner was given a suit of clothes, hat, and boots, valued at £1.17.6, but even if he had served twenty years, the maximum he would find himself with was £6. As Neville points out, after a long stretch a man usually had no home or friends and it was often impossible to keep straight on £6. 'It would not involve a great outlay, ... if every prisoner were enabled to earn a small sum a year during the whole of his term, and would certainly keep many from coming back who do so now from sheer destitution.'[32]

Petty rules exacerbated the prisoners' outlook. When Neville arrived at Parkhurst, photographs of family could be sent but kept for only twenty-four hours. Later the prisoners were permitted to keep them. No toothbrushes were allowed until after at least a year!

As regards punishments, Neville did not think them excessive, consisting as they did of solitary confinement, loss of privileges or of remission, bread-and-water diet. Eighteen days was the maximum given for the latter, and was not continuous, being divided into intervals of three days alternating with equal intervals of low-labour diet. No labour was expected while a prisoner was on a bread-and-water diet. For very serious offences such as trying to escape, additional punishment of parti-coloured dress and chains was given; yellow and drab for attempting to escape and drab for assaulting officers. For the latter offence the birch or the cat could be inflicted. The possession of paper and pencil and letter-writing was punished by a long spell in solitary and a big loss of remission. Neville thought the cat was a big deterrent. 'I am well aware that the system sometimes makes good men bad, and bad men worse', but the worst must have been 'thoroughly vicious by nature, and beyond redemption before they came to prison'.[33] He knew of many suicides, by hanging, cutting the throat, starvation, and jumping off railings, and he wanted the 'balmies' or weakminded to be separated from the rest.

Many offences formerly punished by long terms of penal servitude were now punished by imprisonment only, with or without hard labour, for periods not exceeding two years; this was a great reform. A second reform was the segregation of first offenders, for up to 1879 there had been no separation of first offenders and habitual criminals. As a result the Commission could report in 1901 that since the formation of a star class in convict prisons, from 1879 up to March 1902 only 1.2 per cent of these discharged from the star class had returned to penal servitude. The star-class system was extended to local prisons in 1897–98. A third reform was the special treatment of young offenders from the age of sixteen to twenty-one, who were to be sent to Borstal – a penal reformatory, and in the words of the Prison Commissioners: 'it is becoming every day more evident that it is by prevention alone, i.e. by concentrating attention and care on those who are young enough to be amenable to good influences that this great problem can be satisfactorily handled'.[34]

The Prison Report of 1902 protested against the continuing imprisonment of young children, paupers unfit for work, and the dying. Many children were imprisoned for trivial offences like playing football in the street, or throwing snowballs. Some were imprisoned for a month before trial for an offence so trivial that its maximum sentence was fourteen days.[35] Prison governors frequently deplored the absurdity of short sentences given by too many magistrates – two days might be given, which meant in effect: bath, prison clothes issued, medical examination, and discharge next day! As each of these short imprisonments counted as previous convictions, thousands of boys were classed as criminals who should never have been imprisoned. In addition to the indefensible practice of convicting penniless children for the non-payment of a fine, there was the cruelty of sending the dying to prison – during 1901 thirty-five prisoners died after a week there. Sick paupers were sent to prison and sentenced to hard labour although too weak to work, the charge by the work house authorities being 'refusing their task'. The Commission of 1902 ordered magistrates to give paupers medical examinations before committing them to prison.

Sievwright in Perth substantiated Neville's description of the prisoner's dreary days: ten hours' work, one hour's exercise in silence, the strict routine, the hours of loneliness in cells, the longing to communicate. He too stressed the paucity of letters and visits. Ordinary prisoners (serving under two years) were not allowed to write a letter until they had served three months and then only if conduct and industry were satisfactory. Visits were allowed only after three months and at the end of each succeeding three months. But a convict, that is a prisoner doing penal servitude for three years and over, could exchange letters and a visit within one week of conviction and thereafter at intervals to be determined by conduct and industry.[36] The desperate desire for company led many prisoners to make pets of jackdaws, starlings, pigeons, even mice.

II

There are no descriptions of Scottish prison life at the turn of the century comparable to those by Wilde and Neville. Either there were no prisoners with a literary turn of mind, or they did not care to enlighten the world on such a subject, or failed to achieve publication. But as uniformity had been established in 1877 the conditions which Wilde and Neville describe may be taken as representative of Scottish prisons also. A composite picture of Scottish prison life emerges from the Reports of the Prison Commissioners (Scotland). Those consulted in detail are the Reports for 1878–84 and for 1898–1904.

The General Board of Directors of Prisons in Scotland closed

101 prisons between its inception in 1840 and its ending by the 1860 Prisons (Scotland) Act. The 1860 Act brought Perth General Prison under a body of Managers and closed 21 more. This left 56 of the 178 prisons which had originally come under the administration of the General Board.[1] The Commissioners held their first meeting in 1878 and closed 13 of the 56 local prisons transferred to them by the Act of 1877. The remaining prisons afforded between them cell accommodation for 1,938 males and 1,168 female criminal prisoners, making a total of 3,104. The average daily number of such prisoners during the year ending 31 March was 2,024 males and 1,028 females, making a total of 3,052.[2] By 1898 the number of prisons in Scotland had been reduced to 14.[3]

The Report of 1904 shows the average daily number of prisoners in custody since 1840. The population of Scotland in 1845 was 2,742,000 and in that year there were in custody 1,392 males and 774 females, a total of 2,166.[4] The population by 1880 had risen to 3,665,443 and there were in prison 2,043 males and 999 females, a total of 3,042.[5]

During most of 1878 all male convicts sentenced to penal servitude in Scotland were detained during their probationary period in the General Prison, and were later moved to a public works prison in England; but in January 1879, owing to the large increase in committals and limited accommodation for them in Scotland, it was necessary to remove them immediately to convict prisons in England. Thus 143 were removed to Pentonville leaving only 14 in confinement, all being either criminal lunatics or under observation for mental condition.

At the end of December 1898 convicts in confinement numbered 318 males and 9 females, and of these 12 males were sentenced to life, 1 male to 20 years, 10 males to 15 years, and 90 to 3 years. One female was given 3 years. The largest numbers were in the 25–30 and 30–35 age groups with 63 men in each. The numbers drop sharply in the group between 45 and 50, but rise again in the group over 50.[6] The chief crimes of which they were convicted were theft by housebreaking, theft, culpable homicide, rape, murder, incest, forgery, and horse- and cattle-stealing.

In 1878–79 there were no children under 12 in Perth General Prison, and only 15 male juveniles and 2 females between 12 and 16 years.[7] In 1898 in all Scottish prisons there were 30 children under 12 in custody and 381 between 12 and 16. These were kept apart and received 'special care' from warders.[8] In 1904 the Commissioners 'regret to add that' 191 boys and 15 girls under 16 were sent to prison.[9]

The phasing out of transportation in Scotland might have been expected to produce an increase in the numbers sentenced to penal servitude but other factors supervened. In 1851 the number of convicts sentenced to transportation was 362 men and 171 women. In 1857 the number transported had fallen to 47 men and 9 women, while 135 men and 60 women were sentenced to penal servitude. By 1867 when transportation was finally discontinued the numbers sent to penal servitude were 125 men and 51 women, dropping to 71 men and 4 women in 1904.[10] Penal servitude sentences were classified differently from transportation sentences, i.e. 4 years, 5 to 6 years, 7 to 8 years, 9 to 10 years, and life.

In the Preface to the 1898 Report the Commissioners noted with satisfaction that 'criminals sentenced to penal servitude continue to be comparatively few. The average yearly numbers during the last decade were 80 men and 6 women; while the numbers for the previous decade were 141 men and 22 women. The daily number of the convicts in custody the year before averaged 322 men and only 9 women. We believe the principal cause for the reduction in these numbers will be found to be the greater leniency shown by Judges on the bench in dealing with criminals.'[11] Thus, as in England, the average yearly number sentenced to penal servitude became less in the early 1900s.

At the same time the Preface to the 1898 Report for Scotland notes with misgiving that during the year there had been a large increase in the number of committals to prison. The average of the previous five years was exceeded by more than 5,000. The total receptions were 56,561 – 'a figure which has never before been reached in Scotland'.[12] There was an unparalleled rise in numbers during the last half of the year 1898. The Commission found this 'a very disappointing fact, having regard to the general improvement in the condition of the population . . . the rise in the commitments to prison has been proportionately more rapid than the increase in population'.[13] For a while in 1844 (the first year for which complete records were kept) there was one committal to prison for every 140 of the population, the 1898 numbers were one for every 75 of the population.[14] But the Commissioners were careful to point out that the high numbers did not indicate the prevalence of serious crime; rather were they indicative of the great increase in the number of new statutory offences, and the increased severity shown to drunkenness by the police during the previous 40 years. The committals of 1898 were 5,000 more than in 1897, many being assaults by husbands on wives, thefts and indecent conduct; but the main cause had been the rise of 3,800 under the head of drunkenness and breach of the peace. The increased number of committals for lesser offences rather than for serious crime is important, as it indicates a different type of prisoner, the petty offender rather than the hardened criminal, making up a bigger proportion of the prison population.

The year 1898 had seen in Scotland a great demand for labour of all kinds, and so the Commission concluded that more money was spent by wage-earners on excessive drinking, and added that 'the need for checking these offences, particularly in Scotland, by far more effective means than those afforded by a few days imprisonment, has at last been recognised'.[15] But a different picture was shown in 1904, the committals of ordinary prisoners having decreased by 5.9% below the last year's total. The average length of time that prisoners spent in custody had risen from 5.8 days to 16.5 days.[16] In contrast to the 1898 figures, the number of imprisonments for minor offences had gone down, but the more serious crimes had increased. Thus breaches of the peace and drunkenness showed large reductions below the average of the last five years. The Report says that it is 'very satisfactory to note a sensible decrease in the imprisonments for disorder, which have always been the controlling figures in the Scottish Prison Statistics'.[17] But on the other hand cruelty to children, intent to steal, thefts, frauds, and housebreaking had increased greatly; for example the average number of imprisonments for housebreaking with violence had risen 54% above the previous five years' average.[18]

The numbers daily in custody would have been higher but for the action of the Fine or Imprisonment (Scotland & Ireland) Act 1899 which led to the liberation of 7,433 prisoners before the end of their sentence – a step in the right direction. The total number of different individuals received into prisons during 1904 was

39,880. Some 2,386 had been in prison 20 times or more and there was little hope of improvement for them.[19]

It is apparent from the reports that, as at the present day, the majority of prisoners came from the labouring class. Thus in December 1898, among the male prisoners, the trades predominating were those of labourers and outdoor workers whose total of 1,944 far exceeded all others; 'iron-workers, riveters, etc.' accounted for 103, miners for 93, tailors for 82, pedlars and hawkers for 65.[20] It is interesting to note that there were only 6 professional men, 14 vagrants, 1 newsboy, and 1 servant among the prison population. In 1904 the agricultural and outdoor labourers were again the largest group with 988.

As for prison staff, in 1884 first-class prisons like Perth General and Glasgow had 100 male and female and 81 male and female respectively, while second-class prisons such as Barlinnie and Edinburgh had 46 males and 42 males and females respectively. Sixth-class prisons like Dingwall, Selkirk, Kirkwall, or Stornoway had only 5 prisoners each.[21] The total number of prison officers for Scotland was 429 including governors, chaplains, doctors, teachers, and warders. In the smaller prisons the chaplain, the governor, or even the matron would double as teacher. In 1904 the total number of prison officers was 454.[22]

The wide divergence of staff pay in the different prisons was a cause of disquiet and the Commissioners in 1878 advised a uniform scale. They also opposed many warders having a salary and free house *plus* coal and gas, and wanted all such allowances (save quarters) to be commuted into money payments and added to salaries. They advised the raising of the minimum age to 24 for males and 22 for females.[23] The Preface to the 1898 Report pays a mild tribute to the warders who 'have performed their duties with discretion and to our satisfaction'.[24]

The salaries and wages for a first-class prison like Perth in 1884 came to £9,201.15.9, while the gross expenditure (including uniforms, food, clothing, bedding, fuel, light, medical supplies, furniture, and gratuities to prisoners – not labouring materials or escorts of prisoners) amounted to £17,751.17.5. A sixth-class prison like Stornoway spent £146.3.8 on salaries and wages and £195.4.9 in gross expenditure.[25] The average annual cost per prisoner in prisons where annual daily number of prisoners in custody was 5 or more, came to £28.6.3 in Perth General for an average daily number of 627, and to £38.0.1 in Selkirk for an average daily number of 8.[26] The average cost per annum of different classes in custody was £21.13.7 for each ordinary prisoner, £43.12.8 for each convict, and £49.17.11 for criminal lunatics and inebriates.

The subject which next engages us is that of board, bed, and clothing for prisoners. Since 1839, local prisons in Scotland had been given uniform scales of dietary. These were subject to revision from time to time, the latest being 1874. The Report of 1899 on Prison Diet advocated a liberal one, and in 1901 a new and improved dietary was given to prisons.[27]

The clothing issued to both men and women prisoners sounds adequate and was probably much better than they were accustomed to outside. Male convicted prisoners were issued with cap, jacket, vest, braces, trousers, and a stock of moleskin; drawers of cotton in summer, serge in winter; shirt of unbleached cotton, pocket handkerchief, shoes – one pair leather, one pair canvas – stockings, grey with red rings, apron of plain sheeting. The untried male prisoners were supplied with the same as above, save that cap, jacket, vest, trousers and stock were to be made of corduroy and stockings to be dark grey with yellow rings.[28] The dress of their female counterparts was less drab in colour. Each was allowed a short green-striped gown, upper petticoat of red and black drugget, under petticoat of blue plaiding (two in winter), bodice of stout twilled cotton, shift of unbleached cotton, pocket handkerchief, neckerchief (in summer), shawl (in winter), shoes – one pair leather, one pair canvas – stockings, grey with red rings, cap of unbleached cotton, apron of bleached cotton. Untried female prisoners wore the same, save that their short gowns were scarlet-striped, their upper petticoat green and black drugget, and their stockings dark grey with yellow rings. Flannels were only to be supplied on the recommendation and authority of the medical officer. Prison dress was supplied to male and female untried prisoners only when their own clothes were not sufficiently clean and comfortable.[29]

With dress so with bedding, for at night the average prisoner would find himself sleeping in greater comfort than in the teeming hovel from which he came. Every prisoner except those required to sleep on a guard bed had to be supplied with a bedstead or hammock, a mattress and pillow, two single blankets in summer (three in winter), a bed rug, two sheets and a pillow case. When the bedstead was of iron, a strip of coir-matting was to be placed under the mattress. Those on guard beds got wooden pillows and everything on the list save mattress and pillow case.[30]

No doubt the generally adequate standard of bed, board, and clothing helped the prisoner to withstand ill-health. Despite this, numerous diseases were treated in Perth General Prison during 1869–78, the chief of these being phthisis, abscess, scabies, and ulcer.[31] The medical report on all prisoners in Scotland for the year ending 1898 states that of the 58,981 prisoners in custody during the year, only 1,865 or 3% suffered illness serious enough to warrant being on the sick register. There were 19 deaths in prison, excluding one by suicide and one by execution, which was equivalent to a mortality of 7.2 per thousand per annum (of the average daily prison population). Twelve out of the 19 deaths resulted from disease contracted before admission. (Of the 1,865 sick, 79 were due to zymotic (infectious) diseases – including influenza – 156 were from 'constitutional diseases', 205 from respiratory diseases, and 43 from heart disease.) There were no cases of typhus, enteric, diphtheria, or dysentery, and the phthisis cases also showed improvement over those of 1897. There were very few diseases such as anaemia, diarrhoea, and dyspepsia, which could be due to a faulty diet. Only bronchial diseases showed a material increase. It was 'satisfactory to observe that although admissions had increased by 9% and the average prison population by 7%, the total number of sicknesses acquired during imprisonment had decreased by 14%'.[32]

There were no serious epidemics in 1904, says the report on the health of the prison population in December of that year. There were only 10 deaths in prison including one suicide and one execution.[33] The chief diseases for which prisoners were treated in 1904 were abscesses, influenza, heart disease, D.T.s, insanity, ulcer, and wounds.[34]

At Perth General Prison during the 37 years from 1842 when the prison was opened, until 1878 the average rate of deaths per annum was about 1.5%. The chief diseases which proved fatal and the number of deaths from each were: phthisis (90), brain disease

(18), 'worn out' (18), heart disease (14), pneumonia (13), decay from insanity (10).[35]

As regards sickness in Glasgow Prison in 1882-83, the surgeon noted that there were fewer sick than in previous years and says a great proportion of complaints 'are closely connected with dissipation' in its various forms. 'Diseases which are the direct sequelae of intemperance and vice continue to bulk largely in the statistics of this prison and they are equally common among both sexes.'[36] The average death rate in the prison for the previous ten years was 9.52 per 1,000. The surgeon attributed this improvement to better nursing and more attention to cleanliness.[37] It would seem that the prisoner had a better chance of resisting disease inside the prison than outside.

Thus the prisoner is revealed as being at least as adequately fed, better clad and housed and receiving more medical care than his free brother. How were his days occupied? The common prison employments were carpentry; book-binding; making of mats, nets, mattresses and baskets; sock-sewing; stone-breaking; tinsmith work; weaving; winding; sewing; shirt and shoe making; tailoring; labouring; teasing of hair, hemp, flax, rope, and oakum (old tarred ropes which prisoners untwisted or teased out for caulking ships; those sentenced to hard labour had to pick 3 to 6 lbs of oakum a day).

The 2nd Annual Report of 1879-90 pointed out that in small prisons away from trade centres it was necessary to employ prisoners in cleaning the prison and in work like teasing oakum, wool or hair, and in local work. The great difficulty was the rule that prisoners sent to hard labour could 'only be employed at picking oakum dry, or the crank machine. The latter is wholly unproductive, whilst the former, owing to the difficulty of disposing of oakum, barely covered the cost of material when sold'.[38]

The Report of 1898 states that prisoners had been actively employed all year though it was often difficult to get suitable work as 'there is always in prison a residuum of so low a type – so deficient in intelligence and in physical strength – that it is well nigh impossible to provide any satisfactory occupation for such prisoners'.[39] The kind of work varied according to the general labour of the district and surroundings of the prison. Where land was available, prisoners were engaged in outdoor labour as far as possible and on building repairs too. The Report of 1904 pointed out that 'the restrictions on prison industries prevent the introduction of many of the forms of labour which would be best suited for obtaining willingly from the prisoner his best endeavours. We are, however, developing, where it can be done, associated work in preference to work done in separate cells.'[40]

In addition to work, the monotony of the prisoner's day was broken up by attempts to educate him. The most important alteration in the treatment of prisoners throughout 1883-84 was as regards education in prison.[41] Soon after the passing of the Prisons Acts 1877 a committee was appointed in England on this subject and a report made in 1883. Scotland was to be brought into 'harmony' with steps taken in England but certain modifications were agreed on. Education was to be given to all female convicts doing penal servitude, to prisoners serving over sixty days who were not over forty, and to juveniles under sixteen.[42]

The 1898-1904 Report states that illiterate prisoners under thirty-five with a sentence of over two months were taught, and affirmed that the chief causes of illiteracy were sending children to work too early, truancy, and careless parents.[43] In 1904 illiterates were to be taught in class rather than separately in cells. Weekly Sunday Schools, staffed by voluntary helpers, were held for men and women and there were lectures on 'interesting subjects'.

In addition to the discipline of order and regular work and in some cases of education, 'various moral forces are utilized with a view to the reform of prisoners, these being the influence of a minister of religion, visits by ladies, Sunday bible classes, Discharged Prisoners' Aid Societies, Salvation Army Officers who help with after care'.[44]

Notwithstanding more progressive attitudes in the realms of work and education, punishments or the threat of them continued to figure largely in the prisoner's life. For the year ending 1880 the most commonly awarded punishments were: (a) reduction of diet, which a total of 2,103 men and 575 females, in all the prisons, suffered. 685 men and 315 females were punished in Edinburgh alone, while Glasgow 'corrected' 297 men and 50 females; (b) sleeping on a wooden guard bed; (c) imprisonment in dark cells; (d) isolation at exercise; (e) restraint of limbs. No separate confinement or wearing of particoloured dress was given. The least-

awarded punishments were picking oakum, and forfeiture of gratuity.[45] The most common offences for which these punishments
were awarded were attempted communication (459 males, 43
females), deficiency in work (430 males, 158 females), damaging
prison property (448 males, 65 females).

In 1898 and 1904 the chief punishments were still the favourite
reduction of diet, sleeping on a wooden guard bed,[46] and in 1904
also forfeiture of marks. The least awarded punishments were
similar to those of previous years as were the offences punished.[47]

The attitude of the prisoners and their reaction to the treatment
meted out to them is important because of the conclusions that
may be drawn about the changing attitudes to penology. From
scanty quotations from chaplains, at times sanctimonious, a little
can be gleaned. Thus a Roman Catholic visiting priest at Perth
General Prison: 'I have found them as a rule quite happy and
content and frequently, and unasked, speaking with pleasure of
the kindness shown to them'. He adds, 'of course, exceptions are
always to be found in every possible condition of life, and it is
therefore not to be wondered at if a few professional and chronic
grumblers turn up, now and again, in the General Prison', and he
states that almost always when he was complained to, 'the cause
of the complaint was either unjust or trifling ... but most frequently the pure or impure outcome of loose passions'.[48]

The chaplain at Barlinnie says in March 1883 that library books
are much appreciated by prisoners and goes on to pontificate: 'But
some of them, I am sorry to say, prefer books that treat on secular
subjects, rather than those works which discuss religious topics'.[49]
The chaplain of Edinburgh Prison in 1883 shows resignation: 'It is
no easy matter to raise the fallen. Where intemperance has a strong
hold, where the character is much blemished, where the clothing
is bad, where imprisonments have been frequent, whatever advice
you may give you often cannot do much.'[50] In Extracts from the
Report by the Inspector of Prisons for 1898 there is an interesting
quote from Peterhead General Convict Prison. The resident chaplain, answering a question as to whether penal servitude did any
good to prisoners, stated, 'I think the reply on the whole must be
in the affirmative', and went on to say that quite often the first-
term penal-servitude men admitted that if they had got their
sentence years ago it would have made them different men. On

the other hand men were often confirmed in crime before being sent to penal servitude and so lapsed again when freed.[51]

We have seen during this period that the 1877 Acts resulted in a common policy for all prisons and a strong centralised authority. This centralisation was manifested by Du Cane's harsh, repressive policy which in turn led to the Gladstone Report in 1895 and the Prison Act of 1898 embodying many of that Report's progressive recommendations. The Probation of Offenders Act of 1907 and the Children's Act of 1908 were great steps on the road to reform.

The ending of transportation continued to have a profound impact. Before 1867 the whole aim of authority was to get rid of the wrongdoer. After that date, and throughout this period, a change in attitude is apparent. This does not mean that the public had become more enlightened in their ideas; simply that since transportation was no longer practicable prisoners now forced themselves on the attention of the public by being kept in the country. Imprisonment was now established along with capital and corporal punishment as a major sanction of criminal law.

During the period there were serious attempts to improve prison conditions, attempts influenced by the Gladstone Report and the 1898 Act. Concern was shown for the sick and prison diet was improved. There were sustained efforts to make work productive and regular. Some consideration was shown for the morale of the prisoners by promoting education instead of leaving them in a vacuum; by encouraging the use of library books, albeit with a strong religious flavour; and by lectures on 'interesting subjects'. In addition various moral forces were marshalled with a view to the reform of prisoners.

Thus a slow and painful trend can be traced towards the chief aim of twentieth-century penology – to rehabilitate the prisoner. It was now recognised that prisoners should be reformed, not just shut away and forgotten. The Edinburgh Prison chaplain said, 'It is no easy matter to raise the fallen ... you often cannot do much'. But it was now accepted that the attempt should at least be made.

But despite the improvements, much hardship continued in prison conditions. The prisoner, with shaven head, wearing his 'dress of shame' decorated with broad arrows, still spent many hours locked up alone in his cell. Sanitary conditions were deplorable; little recreation was allowed in association; the rule of silence was all too often stringently observed; letters and visits were few; punishments pressed hard on the weak, the chief one being the reduction of the still meagre diet.

III Prison Buildings

The Prison Act of 1877 and the nationalisation that followed had a profound effect on the actual prison buildings in Scotland. By the Act, fifty-six prisons under local management were transferred to the Prison Commissioners for Scotland. The closure under the Act of many small prisons, leading to increasing centralisation, meant pressure on accommodation in the larger prisons. This in its turn led to the need to build extensions or new buildings at the sites of the bigger prisons.

At Inverness the original prison in the Castle was one of the fifty-six transferred. The closure under the Act of the small prisons at Nairn, Portree, Fort William, Tain, Wick, and Dornoch, in the Inverness district, increased the prison population at the Castle beyond its capacity but owing to the difficulty of enlarging or disposing of the building nothing was done until 1886. At this date twelve cells were added, separating men and women, and providing bathroom and laundry facilities. This enabled the prisons at Elgin and Dingwall to be closed, and the concentration of the prison system in the North of Scotland to be effected. However, increased prosperity in trade and new industries led to a steep rise in the number of prisoners and necessitated frequent syphoning off of inmates to Perth Prison. The increase of the prison population at Inverness may be explained by the fact that previously this was a rural district with a close-knit community. Fathers and sons worked on the family crofts and parental authority was strong. But when the young people began to leave home to work in the new factories, parental ties loosened and authority lessened. Living in lodgings among strangers, frequently exploited by their employers – too often interested only in getting a hard day's work out of their employees – the new labour force experienced no sense of mutual trust or responsibility, and had no community of interest.

The opportunity to sell the Castle to the local authority for police use led to the erection of a new prison on ground off the Old Edinburgh Road near the Courts. Prison labour was used and the new building was fully occupied by 1903. It was intended as a place of detention for all descriptions of criminal and civil prisoners received from the northern counties of Scotland, exclusive of Orkney and Lewis. It had 49 cells for males and 10 for females, and 4 association rooms.[1]

At Aberdeen, a Charter of Robert III, 1394, sanctioned the building of a Tolbooth and Court House in the Castlegate. It consisted of the Laigh Tolbooth or Council Chamber and Council House, and the High Tolbooth which was Aberdeen's first prison. The Old Tolbooth was erected between 1616 and 1629 and part of it still remains. In 1636 a House of Correction was built to which were sent vagabonds, 'leud leivars', common scolds and 'incorrigible harlottis'. The inmates were employed in the manufacturing of broadclothes and kerseys (coarse woollen cloth). In 1809 a new Bridewell was opened and the *Aberdeen Journal* of October reported 'This highly necessary and important institution was publicly opened'. A great number of magistrates, clergy, police and 'most respected inhabitants', walked in procession escorted by a detachment of the 75th Regiment, to the new building. There the 'company were gratified with the attendance and approbation of James Neild Esq., formerly High Sheriff of Buckingham ... a gentleman who, for a great many years, had directed his attention and expended no small portion of his fortune in visiting the different prisons in Great Britain, with the benevolent intention of improving these receptacles of the criminal and unfortunate'.

In 1819 a new Court House was erected behind the Tolbooth with a jail, the 'East Prison', extending along Lodge Walk. In 1842 the Bridewell became the 'West Prison', but was closed in 1864 and pulled down in 1868. An Inspector of Prisons reporting in 1878 found the buildings of the East Prison badly situated and constructed, the cells being small, dark and ill-ventilated, and the cooking, washhouse and bathroom accommodation insufficient. The prison was accordingly declared unsuitable for modern discipline and a payment made by the local authorities towards provision of a new prison, which was not however finished till 1891. Again a reporter from the *Aberdeen Journal* was there: 'Yesterday morning the prisoners incarcerated in the old County jail were removed to the new prison at Craiginches ... The "Flitting" took place at three o'clock, the prisoners being conveyed to their new quarters in a 'bus with blinded windows, and on which the prison warders mounted guard ... The prisoners, who numbered in all 43, seemed to look upon the change as an agreeable break in their prison life.'

The original purpose of the new prison was to accommodate all prisoners received locally – that is, to be a general prison for the north and north-east. The original site, extending to four acres, was on the south bank of the Dee at Torry, a mile from the city centre. The buildings were made of Aberdeen granite and had, on three storeys, 61 cells for males, a hospital, a padded cell, and an associating cell, the female side had 21 cells, hospital, padded cell and associating cell. There were also male and female reception rooms, stores, chapel, baths, kitchen, laundry, and quarters for the female officers. In 1902 there was an extension of the male prison by 24 cells, built by prison labour. A further extension of 21 cells, and a hospital and bathrooms, was begun in 1902 and completed in 1904, again built mostly by prison labour.[2]

Started in 1840 and completed in 1859, the General Prison at Perth is now, as already stated, the oldest in Scotland. Originally, in addition to long-term prisoners, a separate building housed a few insane and some juvenile prisoners. Later, male convicts were received for probationary periods on solitary confinement, prior to transfer to public work prisons in England.[3] In 1886 when Peterhead Prison became operational their removal to Perth was discontinued and female convicts were received instead.

The original site at Perth comprised twenty-five acres. This included the prison of four halls, A, B, C, and D, constructed on the radiating plan, similar to that in prisons based on the separate system. Three of the four halls had cells used for solitary confinement, while the fourth was partitioned into smaller cells used as dormitories for convicts kept in association for much of the day. There were 580 ordinary cells, 16 punishment cells, and 108 cells for females. The Lunatic Department provided accommodation for 87 in rooms. In 1878-79 the Prison Commissioners acquired three and a half more acres for a new building to house all the female lunatics, leaving the existing building to the male lunatics.

The date of opening at Peterhead was much later than the other prisons. A committee on Employment of Convicts reported in

1881 that 'the most likely prospect for benefiting the shipping and fishery interest of the country at large and at the same time profitably employing convicts, is the construction of a harbour of refuge at Peterhead in Aberdeenshire'. The harbour was so called because it was one of the safest in Europe. Thus in 1886 the Peterhead Harbour of Refuge Act authorised the Prison Commissioners for Scotland to build a prison. This power enabled them legally to detain in Scotland on conviction all male prisoners sentenced by the Scottish Courts to penal servitude. As we have seen, previously these convicts had to be transferred to an English prison after their probationary period in Perth. The *Peterhead Sentinel and Buchan Journal* of 10 August 1888 described this result as 'part and parcel of a just and unanswerable claim on behalf of Scotland to the services of their own criminals'.

The prison opened in 1888 and by 1889 all the cells were nearly completed. The arrival of the first twenty prisoners caused great excitement in the town, and for days crowds occupied the railway station, avid for the first sight of the convicts. They travelled in a prison van, the only one in use in Scotland for railway purposes, the warders sitting in the middle of the van with ten convicts on each side. They were dressed in rough white sacking with broad arrows, and wore smart caps and shoes.[4] (The arrow-head placed on government stores and also on convict clothes had originated with Henry, Earl of Romney, who was Master General of the Ordnance 1693–1702, and employed his own cognisance of a pheon or broad arrow.) The convicts quarried the stone for the harbour, travelling daily by train to and from a quarry some miles away, guarded by warders armed with rifles. Cutlass and scabbard were worn by every warder at Peterhead from its opening until 1939. Rifles were carried until 1959 when all weapons were discontinued and batons substituted.

The 1886 Act stated that the whole building and grounds were to be a General Prison for the confinement of male prisoners sentenced to penal servitude, i.e. persons convicted of aggravated crimes for which, prior to 1891, the minimum period of detention was five years, thereafter reduced to three years. The original accommodation was for 208, but during the first years of this century the population fluctuated round an annual average of 350, reaching a peak figure of 455 in 1911.[5]

The prison at Dumfries, built in 1851-52, was one of the fifty-six prisons transferred to the Prison Commission in 1877. It was badly planned, cracked from defective foundations, in a filthy and dilapidated condition, and had not been heated for two or three years. In 1881 a site on the outskirts of Maxwellton was found for a new prison, to accommodate eighty prisoners and provide for officers' residences. It was finished in 1883, its initial purpose being to provide a place of detention for all descriptions of prisoners from the south-west of Scotland.

When the Prison Act 1839 was passed, there were eight prisons in the City and suburbs of Glasgow. By the end of 1840 all were discontinued except the bridewell in Duke Street, called the North Prison, and the Burgh Prison near Glasgow Green, called the South Prison; the latter ceased to be a prison in 1862. Increased pressure on accommodation at Duke Street, and at Hamilton, Lanark, and other local prisons in the Western District, led the County Prisons Board to recommend the erection of a new prison outside the city with cell accommodation for 1,000 prisoners and facilities for further extension. The building of the new prison at Barlinnie occupied the years 1880 to 1886, each block being brought into use on its completion. The purpose of the new prison was to relieve pressure elsewhere, thus allowing the closure of inadequate local prisons at Campbeltown, Rothesay, Airdrie, Hamilton and Lanark. Buildings at Barlinnie were to be a legal place of detention for all descriptions of criminal prisoners, and an Order in Council of July 1882 declared the prison to be a General Prison for Scotland. The buildings consisted of four-storey cell blocks with accommodation for 200 prisoners in each block. In 1890, corridors between cell blocks were opened up; in 1893 a new chapel was finished; and in 1894 a new cell block was built to meet the sudden rises in the number of short-term prisoners at certain times of the year, for example Christmas and New Year. In 1908 part of 'E' block was partitioned off to accommodate persons sentenced to detention under Part I of the Prevention of Crimes Act 1908.[6]

There are two strongly held opposing views on prison buildings today. One is that there should be no more prisons built and alternative ways of dealing with offenders found. The other is that not nearly enough money is being granted to modernise and maintain existing prisons or to build new ones. Shotts Prison in Lanarkshire, not yet completed, is designed to take the overspill from local prisons with outdated facilities such as Barlinnie, Perth and Saughton. It has only 60 inmates (1982), but when completed in 1986 (at a cost of £7.3 million) it will house 530, including long-term prisoners suitable for training in modern working conditions agreeable both to staff and inmates.

7
Lunatics in Prison

Nothing we can do for the comfort of our patients is too much to atone for the cruelty of past ages.

Dr Clouston★

7

The connection between lunatics and the development of prison theory and prison conditions may not be apparent at first sight, but in fact the earlier practice of confining lunatics in prison created problems which inevitably had a far-reaching effect on the development of prison reform.

The plight of lunatics in Scotland, as in Europe generally, had always been an unenviable one. 'In the criminal law of the Middle Ages very little notice was taken of the insane. Even raving lunatics were sometimes hanged and were, in any case, often treated as criminals whether they had committed an offence or not. They were frequently flogged, as criminals were, to drive the devils out of them.'[1]

Until the late eighteenth and early nineteenth centuries lunatics continued to be the responsibility of relatives or friends who looked after them – if they were so inclined – until the burden became too great when the unfortunates were often unloaded on to the town jails, although innocent of any crime. Those with no kith or kin suffered the same fate.

Howard deplored the pitiable state of lunatics in English and Irish prisons: 'in some few gaols are confined idiots and lunatics. These serve for sport to idle visitants at assizes, and other times of general resort. Many of the bridewells are crowded and offensive, because the rooms which were designed for prisoners are occupied by the insane. Where these are not kept separate, they disturb and terrify other prisoners. No care is taken of them, although it is probable that by medicines, and proper regimen, some of them might be restored to their senses, and to usefulness in life.'[2]

In 1818 Gurney had this to say about the plight of lunatics in Scottish prisons: 'A few lunatic asylums have of late years been erected in Scotland, but many more are required; ... At present

... insane persons are either required to roam at perfect liberty, or are immured ... in solitary dungeons. Thus there is preserved no medium between barbarity to the individual and injustice to the public.'

In Haddington, Perth, Kinghorn and Inverness, Gurney was particularly struck by the plight of lunatics. In Kinghorn, twenty years before Gurney's visit, a young laird had been confined for six years in such misery that he had ended his life by swallowing melted lead. In Haddington Gurney found a young lunatic who had been kept in an 'abominable dungeon ... in unvaried solitary confinement, for eighteen months'. In Inverness the prison was 'dirty and disgusting, but the cell of the poor convict [lunatic] was horribly loathsome ... hot sickly stench ... The poor creature had inhabited the cell six years.' In the old disused Perth jail in the High Street, he found two lunatics in solitary confinement: 'In these closets, which are far more like the dens of wild animals than the habitations of mankind, the poor men were lying ...' No one lived in to look after them; a man living in the town was appointed to feed them at certain hours. 'They were in fact treated exactly as if they had been beasts. A few days after our visit, one of these poor creatures was found dead in his bed. I suppose it to be in consequence of this event, that the other, ... again walks the streets of Perth without control.'³ There were numerous such incidents.

In 1812 Neild had written eloquently of 'the absurdity, the danger, and the cruelty, of admitting such unhappy objects into the association of a Gaol. It is hazardous to all, and capable of being made very injurious to the poor frantick wretch, exposed, as he or she must be, to various inconveniences. I sincerely hope this narrative may tend to do away entirely the sad Practice – I might call it justly the inhuman Custom, of sending Maniacs to common Gaols; where they have the worst chance of becoming, not furiously only but incurably mad; of endangering the Keepers, and destroying all order and decorum.'⁴

Neild's statement is illustrated by a letter in Perth Museum to the effect that in 1805 the Rev. James Scott, minister of the East Church, Perth, requested that Grissel Kelly, 'much deranged in her mind and so unmanageable that no private person will take charge of her', continue in detention in the tolbooth 'till she become more calm'. The Kirk Session provided for her maintenance. 'She has a daughter in the town who upon receiving some allowance of money would make meat and carry it to her mother.' But evidently only if she received 'some allowance'.

The insane roused even less public concern than did the ordinary prisoners and the general wish was for them to be kept out of the public eye. 'Until within these few years, this class of sufferers has met with little sympathy or compassion. It was very absurdly and unjustly supposed, that these unfortunate persons laboured under a disease that deprived them of feeling as well as of reason, and rendered them equally insensible to cold and heat, to foulness and want. The unhappy consequence of this fundamental error was not neglect only, but much actual ill-treatment ... One of the first steps towards the successful treatment of the insane was the establishment of Lunatic Asylums.'[5]

Towards the end of the eighteenth century new attitudes slowly began to take shape, products of the Age of Enlightenment. Gradually some people became aware of the paradox that as civilisation spread so did disease and mental illness. The Royal Edinburgh Hospital came into being in order to supply a great medical and social need which had become a matter of concern to such humanitarians. Its foundation in 1813 stemmed from two immediate unrelated incidents.

First Robert Fergusson, the poet, died in the Edinburgh Bedlam. He had become mentally sick and Dr Andrew Duncan (famous as the founder of the Edinburgh Public Dispensary), was called in to attend him. From a letter in the archives of the Royal Edinburgh Hospital, 'I found him in a very deplorable condition, subjected to furious insanity. He lived in the house of his Mother, an old Widow, in very narrow circumstances ... After several fruitless attempts to have him placed in a more desirable situation, he was at last removed to the Bedlam of the City of Edinburgh.' Another letter describes the unfortunate Fergusson's state. He had religious melancholia and suffered from profound depression. He 'became so atrocious that he required several men to keep him in bed'. He was removed to Bedlam in a sedan chair on the pretence of visiting a friend, but when he realised his position he 'set up the halloo of helpless misery and shouted hideously'. He was put in the usual stone cell with a bed of loose straw, and next morning the keeper found him 'pacing the floor with arms folded and in sullen sadness, uttering not a word'. Later, on being visited by his mother and sister, he complained of the extreme cold.

The compassionate Dr Duncan continued to visit Fergusson along with the doctor in charge of the Medical Department of the Edinburgh Poorhouse and of the Bedlam attached to it. But his condition worsened and after only two months in his gloomy prison he died in October 1774, aged twenty-four.

The Edinburgh Bedlam, the lunatic ward of the Edinburgh Charity Workhouse, known as the Cells or Schelles, was situated inside the old city wall which ran opposite the site of the present University Medical School. Even in 1817 conditions for pauper patients were appalling: 'Twenty cells, on the ground floor, are damp, and where the Patients in winter must suffer severely from cold. Part of these, attached to the old City Wall, have no fire-places or means of heating them ... They are lighted and aired solely by openings in the doors by which they are entered, and which doors open into the courtyard in which the patients walk.'[6] Stone floors, dirty straw, darkness, often chains, everywhere the lot of the mentally afflicted was an unhappy one. Even the 'dismal-looking' outside was enough to depress Hugh Miller as he relates in 'Recollections of Ferguson' from *Tales and Sketches*: 'I shuddered as I looked up to its blackened walls, thinly sprinkled with miserable-looking windows, barred with iron; and thought of it as a sort of burial place of dead minds. But it was a Golgotha which, with more than the horrors of the grave, had neither its rest nor its silence.'

Fergusson's tragic death in these wretched circumstances made such strong impression on Dr Duncan that eighteen years later, when President of the Royal College of Physicians in Edinburgh, he succeeded in persuading a number of influential citizens to find ways and means of establishing a 'Lunatic Asylum' in the neigh-bourhood of Edinburgh, where the mentally ill could be assured of enlightenment and humanitarian treatment. Another letter tells us that Fergusson's case had afforded Duncan 'an opportunity of witnessing the deplorable situation of Pauper Lunatics even in the opulent, flourishing and charitable Metropolis of Scotland. The loss of Reason is perhaps the most deplorable disease to which a rational being can be subjected; and in my opinion it is impossible to conceive a more interesting object of charity than the Man of

Genius when a Pauper Lunatic. Since that period I have mentioned, my feeble endeavours have been steadily directed to the
erection of a well constructed Lunatic Asylum at Edinburgh; and
it is with some satisfaction I can say that these endeavours have
been attended with at least some benefit to unfortunate Manics in
Edinburgh.'

But although Duncan's appeal was so sponsored, funds were
slow in coming in. There was a general dislike of the subject, even
among the most benevolent and humane. So the second incident
leading to the founding of the Asylum occurred in 1806 when
Henry Erskine, Lord Advocate, and Archibald Sinclair managed
to prevail on the Government to give a grant from Scottish estates
forfeited after the Forty-Five. Ground at Morningside was bought,
a Royal Charter was granted, and the Asylum was put under the
control of a body of trustees. It was opened in 1813, a grim grey
building in four acres surrounded by high walls.

Everywhere the dawn of a new epoch was signalled. Asylums
had been opened in Montrose in 1782 and Aberdeen in 1800, while
in Paris in 1792 Philipe Penel inaugurated a more humane era in
the treatment of the insane when he abolished the chains of the
inmates of the Bicêtre Hospital; and in 1796 Tuke, the Yorkshire
Quaker, founded the Retreat at York. Duncan was influenced by
these experiences and when the Asylum opened, ordered Tuke's
book to be read there so that all in charge 'should understand the
need and the purpose of kindness in their treatment of the
patients'.[7] At the time this was a revolutionary approach, as it was
a complete reversal of the former policy of custody and restraint.

In its first days the Edinburgh Asylum took no pauper patients
and the managers were severely criticised as the lack of accommodation prevented them from taking in patients whose relatives
could not afford to pay for their maintenance. By 1840 however
there was a large increase in the number of patients as many
parochial authorities negotiated with the hospital to admit paupers. In 1840 the Queen became patron of the hospital, which
became known as the Royal Edinburgh Lunatic Asylum. (To
cope with increased numbers a new building went up in 1842
called Western Department or West House, while the original
building was thereafter called the Eastern Department or East
House and was reserved for paying patients.) In 1873 Dr Clouston

persuaded the Board of Managers to buy the estate of Craig House which was opened in 1894 as Craig House Hospital. His aim, a very modern one, was to provide every possible amenity to help recovery, saying: 'Nothing we can do for the comfort of our patients is too much to atone for the cruelty of past ages'.[8]

Other Scottish towns followed the example of Aberdeen, Montrose and Edinburgh. They founded asylums which at first were chiefly private madhouses, and gradually extended their scope to cater for 'pauper lunatics' and to remove these from jails, bedlams and the, not always loving, care of relations. Aberdeen had been opened in 1800, instituted by the managers of Aberdeen Infirmary for the accommodation of lunatics of Aberdeen and neighbouring counties, the cost defrayed by voluntary contribution. In Glasgow, Robert McNaire, a merchant, saw the neglected state of the insane of all ranks, who for want of proper accommodation were placed in damp and dismal cells, and by industriously collecting subscriptions he succeeded in founding an asylum which opened in 1814. In 1824, chiefly with the view of placing the title to the property of the Institution on a better footing, a royal charter was applied for and obtained. At Dundee an asylum had been established by public contributions and opened in 1820 through the efforts (started as early as 1798) of Dundee Royal Infirmary.

Everywhere new sensitivity was shown towards lunatics. The regulations of the Dundee Royal Lunatic Asylum urged: 'Their own good sense will prevent the visitors from teasing the patients by idleness or improper questions, or by any expression of ridicule or contempt', and 'Every asylum ought especially to keep in view great gentleness and considerable liberty and comfort combined with the fullest security'. The regulations of Glasgow Asylum were to the same effect: 'The Keepers shall use the Patients with the greatest mildness and gentleness ... No Keeper shall at any time attempt to deceive or to terrify a Patient, nor to irritate the Patient by mockery, or mimicry'. The Second Report of the Dundee Directors 1822 could claim: 'Severity and corporal punishment are here unknown ... Several who had known only chains and solitary confinement for many years, have experienced in this house immunity from all restraints' and had greatly improved. One elderly man, confined for fifteen years in a prison in the north of Scotland (being a criminal maniac), and 'whom

continued violence and furious outrage had condemned to perpetual chains', improved in a very short time. At Perth, Murray's
Royal Asylum for Lunatics had been established by the will of
James Murray in 1822 and opened in 1827. 'While all is sufficiently
secure to prevent injury or escape, all is free from the gloomy
aspect of confinement, and there is an air of quiet comfort',
approved Peacock,[9] and Penny waxed enthusiastic: 'The meanest
patient is well fed and clothed, and those from among the higher
classes who can pay for it, are as well lodged and cared for as they
could be in a palace – No coercion is used; everything is mild and
soothing to their feelings . . . Each person has a separate room. To
frustrate any attempt on their lives the curtains of the beds are
hung from the roof in such a way, that if eight pounds weight
were attached to them, the whole would come down.'[10]

At Inverness however in 1855 the insane were still housed in the
lunatic wards of the Infirmary. The Scottish Lunacy Commission
reported in 1857 that these were 'stone vaults, which have no
means of being warmed', with little air or light. Bedsteads 'are
fixed wooden troughs, with a bottom sloping towards the foot
where a tray is introduced. At the head and foot, are chains for the
purpose of fastening the arms and legs of the patient. This precaution is said to be specially necessary in winter, to keep the
patients in bed, and to guard against their throwing off their
coverlets and being killed by the cold.' No means of washing was
provided. The unfortunate lunatics were supposed to be there
until 'they can be sent to the chartered asylums in the south', that
is only for three weeks or so, but sometimes they were thus
immured for six months, all the time in a cell, with no exercise as
there were no enclosed airing-grounds and no attendants. One
man 'is styled keeper of the lunatics; but he is at the same time
gardener, barber, and porter, and has neither the means nor the
time to attend to the patients'. When lunatics were sent south to
the chartered asylums they went by 'steamboat, or outside the
coach,' with a policeman and no female attendants.

Scotland was ahead of some countries in the treatment of paupers in hospital. For example the Massachusetts General Hospital,
which had two departments, a hospital for the sick in Boston and
an asylum for the insane in Charlestown, took no free patients in
the latter because the 'protracted nature of mental disease renders

it impracticable', and further, the Report of the Massachusetts General Hospital, 1836, states, 'the painful necessity of rejecting applications of persons of color has sometimes arisen from the unwillingness of the ward patients to admit among them individuals of that description'.

In addition there appears to be no record of Scots visiting the lunatic wards or the prisons for the purpose of tormenting the insane as the English were wont to do. In the eighteenth century men took their families to the London Bedlam, encouraging their children to join in the sport of poking the lunatics with long poles to stir them to rage or feeble antics. Twopence was paid for this privilege. The name Bedlam was corrupted from the Hospital of St Mary's of Bethlehem which was transferred to Moorfields in 1676 and is the subject of one of Hogarth's pictures. In Switzerland, Germany, and France jeering at lunatics seems also to have been customary, while in America they were apparently treated with less inhumanity.[11]

The Criminal Lunatics Act 1880, being 'an Act for the safe custody of Insane Persons charged with Offences', ordered that if anyone charged with treason, murder, or felony is found to have been insane at the time of the offence and is acquitted, that person must be 'kept in strict custody, in such place and in such manner as to the court shall seem fit, until His Majesty's pleasure shall be known'.

The only place known to the law of Scotland for the confinement of a criminal or dangerous pauper lunatic was the common jail, thus making it difficult for magistrates making committals. Sir William Rae waged war in Parliament on behalf of criminal and pauper lunatics, and in 1816 reported to the High Court of Justiciary 'There is at present no provision for the custody of criminal lunatics, the inconvenience of which is felt to a great degree. Such persons must either be left in jail or entrusted to the uncertain care of friends and the freedom which many of those enjoy has often had effect on deranged persons in the commission of crimes ... There ought certainly to be one department in Scotland appropriated to Criminal lunatics to which they should all be sent and from whence they ought never to be allowed to depart while in life.'

In 1826 Rae, now Lord Advocate, again drew the attention of

Parliament to the state of the prisons in Scotland. A committee was appointed and reported that the 'state of the prisons is very defective in point of security, accommodation and management'. Nothing was done. The Act of 1829 'directing reports to be made respecting gaols in Scotland' only repeated well-known facts. But Mr Hall, Inspector of Prisons, in 1836 reported in detail the circumstances of the prisons and urged that 'A lunatic asylum be created for the reception of all lunatic prisoners in Scotland'.

The Prisons (Scotland) Act 1839 laid down that provisions must be made for criminal lunatics, and the Report for Prisons in Scotland 1840 ordered part of the General Prison at Perth to be fitted up for insane prisoners. In the earlier part of the century it will be noted that all the Scottish asylums and private madhouses were built by private enterprise and voluntary subscription. Now the Government at last shared the burden.

Although great advances had thus been made in the more humane treatment of lunatics, yet the conditions in which criminal lunatics lived left much to be desired. When the General Prison at Perth was opened in 1842, in addition to long-term prisoners it was also decided to house in a separate building a few insane, epileptic, and juvenile prisoners, and in October 1846 the old part of the prison, known as the French depot, was fitted up as a 'Lunatic Department' and admitted ten prisoners (seven male, three female). It was converted to that use in consequence of an expressed, or supposed desire, on the part of the Managers of the chartered asylums, to be relieved of the care of criminal lunatics. In 1855 there was accommodation for thirty-five males and thirteen females, and there were twenty-one males and six females living in very gloomy flagged cells with barred windows and one to four beds in each. The cold was intense and baths were allowed only once a month. The whole arrangements were made principally with a view to the security of the patients, and scarcely, if at all, with reference to their treatment as sufferers from disease. For example 1856 found three patients under restraint: 'One had an iron chain placed round his waist, to which one hand was fastened; another had a hand fastened in a similar way and his legs were hobbled by rings placed round the ankles, and connected together by an iron chain. The legs of the third were restrained in the same fashion'.

The building continued to house the insane until 1867 when it was handed over to the Deputy-Governor and Officers, and the insane were moved to a building which had been a juvenile prison since 1859. Later, in 1879-81, the Prison Commissioners for Scotland built a new building for female lunatics, leaving the male lunatics in the existing building, and placed both under the charge of the Medical Officer of the Prison.

A General Register of patients in asylums from 1805 to December 1862 has a list of asylums and patients, private or pauper, when admitted and when discharged. Sometimes pauper lunatics were removed speedily to the Poorhouse. An entry for 1827 shows a pauper female admitted to Dundee Royal Asylum and removed the same day to Dundee Poorhouse, where she was discharged or died in 1865. Sometimes relatives were not above getting rid of unwanted 'unfortunates' to pauper asylums, and the Madhouses (Scotland) Bill 1841 tried to stop this: 'Anyone who sends without licence any furious or fatuous person, or any lunatic, or any person as such, to the custody or keeping of any person having or keeping a house for the reception of furious or fatuous persons ... shall pay a penalty of £200'; and persons convicted of receiving lunatics without a licence could be imprisoned for three months; thirdly, a sheriff on application by the Procurator Fiscal could commit dangerous lunatics into safe custody, 'where any furious or fatuous person or lunatic shall have been apprehended, charged with assault or other offence inferring danger to the lieges ... or shall be found at large.'

The Lord Advocate, moving the second reading of the Lunatic Asylum (Scotland) Bill, May 1847, reported 'the most startling facts relating to want of accommodation for pauper lunatics in Scotland'. In no less than 24 counties in Scotland, including Argyle, Ayr, Clackmannan, Kincardine, and Peebles, there was absolutely no accommodation for lunatics in the shape of public asylums; and where they did exist their accommodations were generally very inadequate. There exist in Scotland 3,410 pauper lunatics supported in whole or in part by parish relief; of these 1,619 paupers were accommodated in asylums in different parts of the country; for the remaining 1,791 of these unfortunate persons there was not a cell in any asylum, public or private, in any part of Scotland; and it was to the way in which they were maintained in the dwellings of their relations and friends that he now wished to call the attention of the House.

From a table to Scottish counties the Lord Advocate showed eight public and twenty-five private establishments for lunatics, and the total number of patients was 2,417, the number of pauper patients being 1,619. The rate per head for the maintenance of pauper lunatics in each establishment varied between £26 and £14, while those pauper lunatics living with their families had a yearly sum allocated varying from £3 or £4 to the princely sum of 14/3d. 'Was it possible', asked the Lord Advocate, that those 'who had such a miserable pittance could exist in any state but that of the greatest misery and degradation painful to contemplate?' He had found out 'the most distressing particulars ... Many of these poor creatures were confined in dungeons chained on their beds of straw and lived on little better than garbage'. In fact it was impossible to feed them on wholesome food at a rate of £3 or £4 a head. A few cases taken from the report of the Poor Law Commission Enquiry for Scotland would show how pitiable was the lot of the latter class of lunatics, and he quotes: 'John Livingston, a violent maniac, lying upon straw on a wooden floor in a loft above his brother-in-law's smithy. He is very ill just now ... has been a lunatic for eight years ... He is obliged to be constantly chained.' Another, Betty Fraser, aged 40, an unmarried maniac, taken charge of by her parents, 'was kept in constant confinement in a garret over the room in which they lived ... £4 a year was allowed for Betty Fraser's support. She had been kept for many years confined. She generally lay in bed with a blanket ... She was very violent if anyone went into the room and would attempt to escape when the door was opened ... She was never washed and her food was put in for her at a hole in the wall.' Alec Anderson, aged 25, was described as 'fatuous and sometimes violent'. He lived with his widowed mother and sister and was 'confined in a bed which is boarded up so that he cannot get out. He has been kept in this way for nearly six years. He sometimes gets out of his box-bed and is with difficulty got back. He is outrageous at times and threatens his mother and sister. They wouldn't object to his being sent to any asylum. His food was put through the door.'

It is hardly surprising that these unfortunate men and women *were* violent and tried desperately to escape from their coffin-like prisons. The Lord Advocate had many other similar cases to cite, and he referred to Dr Browne of the Crichton Asylum, Dumfries, who reported on the state in which pauper lunatics had been brought to his asylum. The mode in which they had been treated at home was 'entirely inconsistent with their comfort and care and with the dictates of common humanity. They were generally brought bound, galled, in a state of shocking filth, crouching, with their limbs contracted, showing that they had been long confined or had been long in bed.' The Lord Advocate made an impassioned plea to the House, deploring that 'such a state of things should have existed up to the present moment in a country like Scotland', and expecting the House to end such evils. If the Bill was passed it 'would remove a great reproach and gangrene from the social system of Scotland'.

Many doctors, however, angrily opposed the Bill on the grounds that the powers given to the sheriff to enquire into the 'conduct' of the superintendents, medical persons etc., 'are painfully inquisitorial', and that powers conferred upon the Inspector General reduced doctors to the 'position of attendants and clerks'. The heritors too were full of ire. At a special General Meeting of the Commissioners of Supply for the Stewartry of Kirkcudbright and other heritors of the Stewartry, all agreed that the Bill should be opposed as unnecessary, and that 'by the Poor Law Statute for Scotland the Board of Supervision of the Poor is entrusted with the duty of providing for due accommodation and treatment of insane and fatuous poor ...' The heritors declared 'altogether uncalled for' the provisions in the Bill for transferring the superintendence of the Lunatic Poor from the Board of Supervision to a central Lunatic Board in Edinburgh.

Independent efforts were also made on behalf of lunatics. 'The Alleged Lunatics' Friendly Society', founded in 1845 and supported by voluntary contributions, declared: 'This Society is formed for the protection of British subjects from unjust confinement on the grounds of mental derangement, and for the redress of persons so confined; also for the protection of all persons confined as Lunatic Persons from cruel and improper treatment'.

The Lord Advocate, Sir George Grey, brought in the Lunatic (Scotland) Act 1857, for regulation of the care and treatment of

lunatics and for the provision, maintenance and regulation of
Lunatic Asylums in Scotland. It set up a General Board of Commissioners in Lunacy for Scotland, with offices in Edinburgh. Two
commissioners were to inspect, at least twice yearly, all public,
private and district asylums and any house in which a lunatic was
detained. These paid commissioners 'may once or oftener in each
year ... visit any Prison where a Lunatic is and inquire into
conditions. Also all Poor-houses which house Lunatics, and inquire
into food and conditions'. Sheriffs and JPs were to inspect and
report back to the Board, all private asylums were now to be
licensed by the Board, and lunatics were to be admitted by two
doctors and a sheriff's order. With regard to District Asylums for
pauper lunatics Scotland was to be divided into eight districts and
every pauper lunatic was held to belong to the Parish of his
settlement at the time the order of his reception to the Asylum
was made, and the expense of his maintenance in the District
Asylum was to be defrayed by his parish. Dangerous and criminal
lunatics could be committed by the sheriff with a medical certificate to a 'place of Safe Custody either in the county or in the
adjoining county. If insanity stands in bar of trial', the lunatic must
be kept in strict custody.

The following statistics applied to Scotland in 1857:

Private lunatics residing with relatives:	1453
with strangers:	297
alone:	50
total:	1800
Pauper lunatics residing with relatives:	1217
with strangers:	640
alone:	141
total:	1998
Total:	3798.[12]

An 1859 Memorandum of the General Board of Prisons stated:

'Criminal lunatics or those lunatics who pass through the
prisons may so far as respects legal method of disposing of
them be classified as follows:

1. Proved to be insane in bar of trial.

2. Proved to be insane in bar of punishment.
3. On trial acquitted on the ground of insanity when the act was committed'.

These three classes were to be kept in strict custody until her Majesty's pleasure be known. The usual practice was to commit to the County Prison. The next classes of cases cited were:

4. In prison charged with an offence and certified on medical authority to be insane.
5. In prison under sentence, supervening insanity certified on medical authority.

The Prisons Board had power to remove Class 4 prisoners either to an asylum or to the General Prison. In Class 5 the lunatic might be in a local or general prison. If the former, he was removed on statutory certificate by two medical men; if the latter, he was transferred from the prison proper to the Lunatic Department on the certificate of medical officers. When sentences expired and the lunatics were to be liberated, the Procurator Fiscal was told that 'he may provide for public safety as liable to be affected by the liberation of a madman'. But 'Dr Malcolm, the visiting physician of the General Prison ... questions whether in the general case, anything is done for the public safety and believes that the prisoners are thrown loose upon society'.

There was a dubiety in methods of legally disposing of criminal lunatics which naturally meant much delay. The expense of their maintenance when disposed of was also subject to variations. Removals ordered by the Prisons Board might be either to asylums or to the General Prison. The Board had no power to enforce reception in an asylum, their authority was to contract 'for the close and safe custody and maintenance of such insane or lunatic prisoners'. It was pointed out that there was a natural desire on the part of the local authorities to have criminal lunatics removed to the General Prison rather than to asylums. The managers of asylums had great objections to the terms 'close and safe custody' as a condition.

There was no law for the removal of a criminal lunatic across the Border except in the case of convicts sent to transportation or penal servitude. The Secretary of State had power to remove convicts to any prison in Britain. In one instance where it was desirable that an insane male convict should not remain in the General Prison, the Secretary of State at the desire of the Board, granted a warrant for his removal to a prison in England, that he might be thence transferred to Bethlehem.[13]

The *Daily Courant* of April 1860, referring to the second Report of the Scottish Lunacy Board, recalls, 'the frightful state of matters, disgraceful to a Christian land, revealed several years ago as to the condition of a large portion of the pauper insane population of Scotland, and what righteous indignation it excited at the time'. The writer pointed out that many districts had not obeyed the Lunacy Act and the Lunacy Commissioners had no powers to enforce it. The Commission's report estimated that asylum accommodation was then required in Scotland for 4,353 persons, while the number estimated on 1 January 1860 as accommodated in asylums and poorhouse lunatic wards was only 3,424, leaving 929 patients unprovided for. 'A very considerable number of pauper lunatics amounting last year to nearly 800, are still accommodated in poor-houses.' 'This poor-house lunatic ward system is kept up partly from lack of accommodation elsewhere, but partly also from the idea which the Parochial Boards have that it is an economical arrangement.' The *Courant* maintained that despite the Commissioners' conscientious visiting of public and private asylums, poorhouse lunatic wards, and private houses, there were still glaring abuses, and it gave the example of a private patient at Banff, 'chained by the ankle to a corner of the chimney', and of an unfortunate woman in Caithness, existing in a straitjacket roped to her bed: 'for several years she is said, without intermission, to have been subject to this inhuman treatment'. The *Courant* deplored 'the melancholy fact that insanity is greatly on the increase in Scotland', as in France and England. In 1843 the number of Pauper lunatics in England and Wales was 16,764, rising in 1859 to 30,318. In Scotland in 1847 the number was 2,650, rising in 1858 to 5,564, and in 1859 the number of insane, pauper and private, was 7,878. The increase was at a much greater ratio than the increase of population. 'Patients labouring under insanity increase upon our hands faster than we can provide accommodation and means of treatment for them.' The increase in numbers may have been caused partly by earlier diagnosis and treatment.

In 1861 the Dangerous and Criminal Lunatics (Scotland) Bill, to amend the Law relating to the Apprehension and Custody of Dangerous and Criminal Lunatics declared that when any lunatic was charged with an offence dangerous to the lieges, it was lawful for the sheriff, with a medical certificate, to commit him to an asylum in or outside his jurisdiction. Also if a prisoner 'within 60 days of the expiration of his sentence in the General Prison, be found insane, and that Insanity of a kind which renders it advisable that he should be detained in the Lunatic Department of the General Prison rather than in a Lunatic Asylum, then the Secretary of State will authorise him to be detained; ... if two doctors find a prisoner in a Local Prison to be insane, although his sentence is less than nine months, yet he shall go to the General Prison'. Also the term 'Lunatic' was now to include 'every Prisoner of unsound mind and every Person being an Idiot'.

By the 1866 Lunacy (Scotland) Amendment Act, if a lunatic escaped, the order for his reception remained in force, 'provided always that such Lunatic ... shall return or be brought back to such Asylum or House within a Period not exceeding Twenty-Eight Days from the day on which he left'; and by clause VII the order for detention of a lunatic was to expire in three years and to be renewed yearly unless the asylum superintendent granted a certificate saying that his detention was necessary for the safety of the public.

Later many medical superintendents of asylums in Scotland asked for the repeal of this clause, but the General Board of Lunacy refused, saying that the difficulties resulted not from its carrying out but from its non-observance.

A printed pamphlet on dangerous lunatics of April 1871 (in West Register House) has a table showing the number sent to asylums at the instance of the Procurator Fiscal as dangerous lunatics from 1861–70. In 1861 the number was 27, falling to 10 in 1865, and rising to 36 in 1868 and 30 in 1870. Of the last, 23 came from Lanarkshire, Renfrewshire, and Dunbartonshire. It is noted that persons falling into the statutory category of 'dangerous lunatics, do so mainly from having been arrested by police and by no one coming forward to undertake their being placed in asylums. Where it is not clear that they will become chargeable to their parish, inspectors of the poor hesitate to interfere lest they should exceed their duty and be made liable for damages in an action at law.'

'As a rule, persons who are dangerous lunatics in the statutory sense are maintained at the expense of their parishes. They thus become pauper lunatics who ... should be sent to the asylum of the district in which the parish, charged with their maintenance, is situated.' Frequently a lunatic was taken up by the police outside his own district and therefore sent to some other asylum.

During 1870, nine patients were admitted into the Lunatic Wards of the General Prison, Perth. Those nine were guilty of murder, violent assault, or were thieves by habit and repute. Six were discharged not recovered and were transferred to local prisons from which four were sent to ordinary asylums, one was handed over to the superintendent of police, and one to the care of parochial authorities. Thus the manner of dealing with criminal lunatics in Scotland does not seem to rest on any very fixed rules but to depend very much on the views taken by local county authorities as was noted some years earlier.

With regard to alien lunatics during 1870, twenty-eight pauper lunatics were removed from Scotland because they had no settlement there – seven to England and twenty-one to Ireland. There were seven private patients removed, namely six from asylums and one from a private dwelling. Of these, four were sent to England, one to Ireland, one to France, and one to Jamaica.

Correspondence from the Prison Managers in Castle Terrace, Edinburgh, to the Home Office in 1872 concerns the disposal of inmates of the lunatic department of the General Prison, under the Criminal and Dangerous Lunatics Act 1872 and suggests that 'it is desirable that all criminal lunatics disposed of by tribunals of Scotland should be detained in Scotland, both because the native establishments are likely to be better adapted to their habits, and because the means of an accurate comparison of the relative amount of insanity among criminals and the cost of the treatment of Criminal Lunatics in the two countries is apt to be lost, if the Criminal Lunatics of the one country are detained in the other'.

The 10th Annual Report on Prisons states that the daily average number of lunatics in detention in the General Prison in 1868 was 48, in 1869 was 50, and the total expense of the lunatic department was £1,250. The cost of a lunatic at the English Broadmoor was £67.4.9 in 1868 and £64.8 – in 1869.

The 11th Annual Report on Prisons states that because of overcrowding it is a relief that the 1871 Criminal and Dangerous Lunatics Amendment Act allowed for the release of those no longer insane (from drink, puerperal fever or violent mania). But they were to be in the charge of friends or relatives; and this conditional liberation by the Secretary of State had to be inspected by doctors periodically, and the Secretary of State could take them in again.

A letter from Whitehall to the Lord Advocate in 1874 included a list of twelve inmates of Broadmoor Criminal Lunatic Asylum whose sentences had expired. 'These persons who were all convicted in Scotland, were removed to Broadmoor from places of confinement in England – and would, had they been convicted in England have been removed under 30 and 31 Victoria c. 125 to lunatic asylums of the Counties in which the offences were committed. But as neither of these statutes apply to Scotland, Mr Cross is doubtful whether he can avail himself of further of their provisions in dealing with these persons whose continual detention at Broadmoor is not only a heavy charge to the State but excludes from the asylum other patients for whom accommodation there is urgently required'; and the letter goes on to ask 'whether there are any means by which these insane persons can be legally removed to Scotland or otherwise disposed of'. A scribbled note at the foot of the page by the Lord Advocate says that, 'without further legislation it appears to me that the Criminal Lunatics in question cannot be removed from Broadmoor to Scotland. I think it is well deserving of the consideration of Mr. Cross whether, as Mr. Walker suggests, the maintenance of all criminal lunatics should not be made a charge on the Imperial Exchequer.'[14]

In 1884 a letter from a Dr Mill described the Lunatic Department of the General Prison as very overcrowded. The Commissioners in Lunacy were pressing for a great increase in accommodation, 'in fact for a recasting and enlargement of the whole arrangement. Such a project would cause a great, immediate expense in building and perhaps it would be found incompatible with the present economic arrangement by which what is virtually a national establishment for criminal lunatics is kept up as a men's department of the General Prison. The first arrangement is to provide for these 'quasi-lunatics' as they are called who are not insane. These are the most dangerous inmates of the establishment as they can plot and combine, while the insane are hardly ever known to act together. There is always danger, of course, of a relapse, and in handing any one of them over to relations, conditions would be required for periodic medical report or otherwise according to circumstances. Such a measure has now been in force in England for some years.'[15]

The Report of the Prison Commissioners for 1896–1904 states: 'The Lunatic Departments attached to Perth General Prison are legal places of detention for all descriptions of criminal lunatics.' The Preface says that 'The Commissioners are satisfied that there remains nothing in the present system of prison discipline to disturb the mental balance of any one in confinement, but there are many who come into prison suffering from mental debility'.

The Lunacy Commissioner's Report for 1898 states: 'The establishment [Criminal Lunatic Department] was found in excellent order: the inmates are suitably provided for, and the way in which they are treated is in every way suitable and satisfactory'. During the previous year a system had been introduced under which 'by earning marks, the lunatics may be able to purchase small adjuncts to their regular diet such as jam and biscuits as well as tobacco'. Some of the lunatics who had been longest in the Department were transferred to ordinary asylums, as they were found no longer to require the special treatment of a Criminal Lunatic Asylum.

The Annual Report of the Prison Commissioners for 1904 has a report by the Medical Superintendent on the Criminal Lunatic Department. He was glad to report that 'mechanical restraint has not been found necessary in their treatment'. Dances and concerts were given at intervals during the year. There were sixty-four lunatics in the Department in 1904, fifty-two males and twelve females. Insanity was found in forty-four cases on admission in 1904, and thirteen more were found insane during sentence. They were transferred to asylums. Thirty-nine more were so mentally feeble that although they could be treated in prison they were unfit to look after themselves when discharged. Therefore they had to report to the Inspector of the Poor so that he might take charge of them when freed. At the end of 1904 there were forty-six male and four female criminal lunatics of whom the majority were charged with murder. 'The separation, lately effected, of the troublesome and violent lunatics from the others has had excellent results.'

By the Prisons Act 1904 the distinction between the General Prisons and the Ordinary Prisons was abolished. The Royal Commission 1908 on the Care and Control of the Feebleminded recommended that the General Board of Lunacy in Scotland be designated the Board of Control and should undertake the supervision of all (i.e. idiots, imbeciles, epileptics) and that the word 'lunatic' should be discontinued and 'hospital' be substituted for 'asylum'. The Board of Commissioners in Lunacy survived as a separate organisation until 1913 when, by the Mental Deficiency and Lunacy (Scotland) Act, it was renamed the General Board of Control for Scotland. Its composition was slightly altered under the Reorganisation of Offices (Scotland) Act 1939, and since then its organisation has been more closely integrated with that of the Scottish Home and Health Department.

The mention of 'dances and concerts' is significant as illustrating the fact that criminal lunatics were also benefiting from the more humanitarian climate of the time. There were annual balls, games of all kinds, lectures, concerts, and even the 'cinematograph' shown for the first time in 1902, all aimed at relieving the monotony of the lunatics' daily routine.

Important changes were taking place in Scotland in the care and treatment of lunatics. From 1881 the trend of public and scientific opinion laid greater stress on the mental state of the criminal and its scientific treatment rather than on the punishment of his crime. Real efforts were being made to discontinue the practice of locking all the doors all the time, and to present the attendants in the guise of nurses rather than of jailers. 'Needless to relate the new ideas did not meet with unqualified approval. It required courage to adopt the system in the face of public prejudice, and adverse public criticism. A number of superintendents preferred to continue with the strait jacket, manacles and chains. With such means no blame for any incidents could be attached to the person in charge.'[16] A medical superintendent had been appointed to the Criminal Lunatic Department at Perth in 1878 and 'it was at this point that it began to develop as a forensic psychiatric hospital'.[17]

Before the First World War, Parliament had discussed the possibility of a separate State Asylum, but it was not until the mid-1930s that the ideas crystallised and a site was selected at Lampits Farm, Carstairs. In 1935 Parliament approved the creation of a Criminal Lunatic Asylum and State Institution for Defectives as a joint establishment aiming at rehabilitation and security. The State Institution housed mental defectives of dangerous, violent and vicious propensities, and the Criminal Lunatic Asylum persons of unsound mind detained during His Majesty's Pleasure. The buildings were finished in 1939 but as the war intervened they were used as a military hospital until 1948. It was decided that a State Institution for defectives should be built separately from the State Asylum, and this was finished in 1957.

About a hundred patients, the great majority men, were in Perth Criminal Lunatic Department from 1948 to 1957. With slatted wooden beds fixed to the floor, narrow windows high in the walls, a general air of gloom and decay brooded over the place. 'I was ashamed to bring folk into the Admission Block', said one officer.[18] By the 1952 Rules for Prisons the inmates of the Criminal Lunatic Department were not to be subjected to penal discipline, but to be 'treated as patients under curative and alleviative treatment'. In October 1957 Section 63 of the Criminal Justice (Scotland) Act 1949 came into operation, by which the care and custody of criminal lunatics, now called 'State Mental Patients', was taken over from the Scottish Home Department by the General Board of Control. Ninety-nine male patients were transferred from Perth to the State Mental Hospital at Carstairs in a fleet of buses, accompanied by doctors, nurses, and a police escort, the Chief Constable of every town en route being advised of their approach. The female State Mental Patients continued at Perth, now designated 'a ward of the State Mental Hospital'.

The Annual Report of the General Board of Control for Scotland in 1960 remarked that there were far more mentally ill in 1960 because of the increasing stress and strain of modern life, but that higher numbers could be partly accounted for by earlier diagnosis.

By the Mental Health Act 1960 the General Board of Control was replaced by the Mental Welfare Commission for Scotland. It abolished the State Mental Hospital and the State Institution for

Defectives and set up the State Hospital under a management committee responsible to the Secretary of State.

At Carstairs all patients have single rooms. Accommodation is composed of sixteen villa-type wards with no distinction, other than for treatment purposes, between the mentally-defective patients and the mentally ill. Admission to the hospital may be from the Courts, from the Prison Service, or from ordinary mental or mental deficiency hospitals.[19]

Authority for detention of patients falls into two categories. First, State patients, those admitted from the Courts as a result of criminal proceedings under orders restricting discharge, may not be discharged, transferred, or given leave of absence without the Secretary of State's consent. Patients transferred from prison are also State patients during the currency of their sentence. Second, Non-State patients (those admitted (a) following criminal proceedings but without an order restricting discharge; or (b) ordinary detained hospital patients – usually on transfer from a National Health Service hospital where they have proved unmanageable) may not be discharged by the consultant without the consent of the Management Committee. These patients have a regular right of appeal to the Sheriff against their detention. The Mental Welfare Commission may also order the discharge of such a patient (and has done so).

Patients are not normally discharged from hospital direct to the community but are transferred in the first instance to a National Health Service Hospital, and the responsibility for future disposal then passes to that hospital. In the first full-scale study of the workings of the 1960 Mental Health Act, Nigel Walker and Sarah McCabe in *Crime and Insanity in England* 'question whether this process of unloading people from prisons into hospitals has now gone far enough ... Psychopaths ... may be released from hospital sooner than they would be from prison ... only to commit more crimes'.[20] At the present (1980) public unease over this problem is increasing. In this context mention should be made of the disturbing breakout from the State Mental Hospital in November 1976 when two patients murdered a male nurse, a patient, and a policeman during their escape. They were arrested, subsequently charged with murder, found fit to plead, and are now serving life sentences in prison. The affair led to great concern about security

at the hospital. Sergeant Joe Black, secretary of the Scottish Police
Federation, attacked the psychiatrists involved, saying 'We have
gone overboard for treatment rather than the protection of the
public. We must restore the balance'.[21]

The average age of patients is thirty-two and, based on statistics
over three years, the average length of stay is about six and a half
years. All the usual forms of psychiatric treatment are provided,
and crafts of woodwork, printing, rug-making, maintenance of
grounds and gardens are carried out by patients. The Education
Department was established in 1969, and classes in basic education
began with the high-grade mental defectives, and in 1971 the
mentally-ill patients were given higher education, mostly by correspondence. The local education authority also give classes. There
are monthly dances, regular cinema shows and concerts, football
and other sports. Personal clothing is allowed only to a limited
extent. The patients also earn incentive payments for work though
they may not handle cash.

The Management Committee of fifteen members manages
the hospital in accordance with the 1960 Mental Health
Act. The Physician Superintendent, who is also the Professor
of Forensic Psychiatry at Edinburgh University, is responsible
for the day-to-day running of the hospital. 'The Physician
Superintendent, Professor Kenneth Macrae [since retired] agrees
that, in all probability, the hospital has more murderers under
its roof than even the toughest of Scotland's prisons, and "as time
goes on, with the abolition of capital punishment there will be
many, many more long-term patients who have been on a murder
charge". Professor Macrae emphasised the word "patients".
"This is a hospital"; he adds. "It is not a prison, we have nurses,
not warders".'[22]

That is a good and helpful note on which to end this chapter.
The path of the mentally afflicted has been an arduous one through
the centuries, days of lying in chains on straw, in chill darkness;
from the miserable neglect and starvation of the mid-nineteenth
century through the Acts of the later-nineteenth and early-twen-
tieth centuries, each clearly demonstrating the strenuous efforts
being made to protect the lunatic and aiming at his well-being and
better treatment. So to the present, and the pleasant single rooms,
bright colours, education, crafts, games, dances, concerts. The

trend is clear, and the modern attitude to those no longer called 'lunatics' is best expressed by Professor Macrae in his emphasis of the word 'patients' and his statement 'This is a hospital; it is not a prison'.

8
The Twentieth Century

Punishments are inflicted, that crime may be prevented,
and crime is prevented by the reformation of the criminal.
                                        T. Fowell Buxton★

Men come to prison as a punishment, not for a punishment.
                                        Alexander Paterson†

8

Penal practice and attitudes tend to develop by way of haphazard reaction to particular problems which may persist indefinitely, or become either more or less demanding, or later disappear altogether to be replaced by new ones. Neither practice nor attitudes will necessarily keep abreast of these changing considerations, and indeed some time lag is usually inevitable so that, more particularly in a rapidly changing society, the penal system may be said to be continually out of date.

On 10 July 1910 the House of Commons heard the Home Secretary, Mr Winston Churchill, say that 'the mood and temper of the public with regard to the treatment of crime and criminals is one of the most unfailing tests of the civilisation of any country'.[1] What then is the 'mood and temper' of the twentieth century public towards the treatment of crime and criminals? It is undoubtedly reform-orientated, emphasising rehabilitation as opposed to punishment. This attitude has only gradually emerged. After 1877, when all power over prisons was centralised, the result was uniformity of routine and treatment in all prisons, but it is questionable to what extent that was a gain. It certainly meant more economic administration but it made experiment in reform very difficult. A system which discourages independent thought is not likely to lead to rapid progress. But official complacency towards the repressive nineteenth-century jails was shaken by the Gladstone Report in 1895, and again by the reaction of the more intelligent and better-educated of the conscientious objectors in the First World War. The nineteenth-century aim to make prison life so unpleasant that offenders would be deterred from committing fresh crimes clearly did not succeed, so that it was for practical as well as humanitarian reasons that increased emphasis came to be put on the rehabilitation of offenders.

Thus on the eve of the First World War, prison life and conditions were still harsh and the buildings themselves the same dismal, forbidding fortresses of the era in which they were built. The medical officer at Glasgow Prison, J. Devon, described life there in 1912. The convict's bed was a wooden shutter hinged to the wall so that it could be folded up during the day; males under sixty were given no mattress for the first thirty days; the untried were clad in brown corduroy and if convicted exchanged these garments for white moleskin. The rule of silence was still enforced, though now less rigidly, work being done sometimes in association but without speaking. Devon considered that instead of conversation leading to corruption, as was widely believed, the rule of silence could lead to gradual, steady mental deterioration over a period of time. Silent exercise lasted for an hour, with the older and physically feeble prisoners walking round a slower ring. Swedish drill had been introduced for the female prisoners, which they called the 'daft hour' but evidently enjoyed. Untried prisoners could get newspapers and books sent in, and a pint of wine or beer daily, but no cigarettes. There was a library – of poor quality – and occasional lectures and concerts. Every prisoner was given a Bible and Prayer Book and the three recognised religions were Presbyterian, Episcopalian, and Roman Catholic. Convicted prisoners were allowed only one letter and one visit in three months. Punishments were meted out by the Governor, but if the offender's diet was to be changed or physical discomfort was involved the Medical Officer's approval was required.

Even with those grim conditions prevailing many still asserted that prison was too comfortable. Devon found that the public in general was quite uninterested in prison conditions but, ahead of his time, he pointed out that people should realise that the treatment of criminals was as much a matter of public health as the treatment of the sick and that it was to the interest of the community that it should be undertaken in such a way as to lead to their reform. He held that prison had a bad effect on prisoners and that when they were turned loose on the community it was advisable to prevent them being liberated in a condition that would make them more dangerous than before conviction. He stated that the prisons had never been designed to reform – their declared purpose was to detain and punish criminals, and the extent to which they did punish varied greatly with the background of the prisoners.[2]

Two authors not indifferent to prison conditions were Galsworthy and Shaw, who both abhorred solitary confinement. Galsworthy's play *Justice* (1910) roused consciences in some quarters, and Shaw wrote passionately against the state of the prisons in *The Crime of Imprisonment* (1922).

Although Glasgow Prison was a dreary cheerless place, an English prison like Dartmoor was much worse. The death rate there was the highest of all the prisons (as it had been in the time of the French P.O.W.s). Conditions were very dirty and harsh punishments, including floggings, common. Gross overcrowding had eased somewhat by 1931, but late in that year the Governor was aware of prison unrest and in 1932 a mutiny broke out, 'the greatest crisis which the Commissioners, staff, and reformers had ever faced'.[3] Yet between 1908 and 1949 the trend towards reform grew stronger. In England the prison scene was dominated by Alexander Paterson and ideals similar to his were pursued in Scotland. Reform within began with Paterson's appointment to the Prison Commission in 1922. He had begun work on the Borstal system and started the 'open' Borstal camp. Borstal was instituted in 1908 by the Criminal Justice Act of that year and took its name from the village of Borstal in Kent. Girls and boys between sixteen and twenty-one years were sent to reformatories for periods of up to three years. Paterson applied his new ideas to the treatment of 'star class' prisoners (adults in prison for a first offence) and the new 'minimum security' prison was introduced.

In 1909 Churchill had asked Paterson to undertake the first attempt to organise state assistance to the discharged convict. Paterson's often quoted aphorism that 'Men come to prison *as* a punishment, not *for* punishment'[4] exemplified his strongly-felt conviction that deterrence and retribution are achieved by the mere deprivation of liberty. He held that the best way to use imprisonment was to try to turn out the prisoner a better citizen than when he came in. Although society should be protected permanently by the reform of the offender, yet he agreed with Devon that under the existing system 'a man is not primarily sent to prison in order that he may be reformed'.[5] Neither staff nor buildings were shaped to that end and 'If the institution [Borstal] is to train lads for freedom, it cannot train them in an atmosphere of captivity or repression'.[6] As long as prisons were built to hold 5,000 or more men it was impossible for the staff to know them all, and Paterson urged that 500 should be the limit if the smallest attempt was to be made to reform.

Paterson's impact on prison life was incalculable. His ideals and achievements shaped the trend of future developments in prison reform and many modern reformers are still seeking to reach his objectives. In particular he sought to counteract the apathy which eventually overcomes most prisoners by advocating for all a very active life, physically and mentally. He held classification to be essential and urged that the word 'prison' or 'penitentiary' be abandoned and replaced by different categories of institution, each with a different function and regime. He considered very short sentences worse than useless, and thought six months should be the minimum. He accepted that some men were incorrigible and that society must be given maximum protection from them; the clauses in the Criminal Justice Act 1948 relating to preventive detention were largely inspired by him. For the incorrigibles he wanted the indeterminate sentence as the only safeguard for society, though he believed that a man definitely deteriorated after ten years in prison, and thought twenty years or more to be worse than death. 'There are cases where it is kinder to break a man's neck in a second than to spend twenty years in breaking his heart.'[7] He thought that confinement in dark punishment cells was worse than corporal punishment and he was against solitary confinement. Like Howard, Paterson visited many foreign prisons, and some of these visits confirmed his views on the squalor and degrading conditions of many British prisons, which he considered medieval by comparison with America where, by federal law, no citizen may be confined without a flush toilet and running hot and cold water day and night.

But even before Paterson's appointment in 1922 there had been agitation for reform by the conscientious objectors of the First World War. Those who found themselves in prison became ardent reformers, insisting that prevailing conditions were more likely to encourage crime than reform. The majority of C.O.s served between 28 and 112 days in a military detention barracks. There they were subject to tough rules and scales of punishment. Since many

C.O.s set out to create as much trouble as possible by hooliganism or strike action they often found themselves in close confinement on punishment diet. In May 1916 the Cabinet agreed that C.O.s who were court-martialled should be transferred to civil control.

Those unwilling to undertake any form of service at all were known as Absolutists and numbered one in every 12 C.O.s. Up to 30 November 1917 there were 44 Absolutist exemptions in Scotland. As the Absolutists (the majority of whom were members of the Independent Labour Party) were still classed as soldiers, on completing their prison sentences they were sent back to their units, only to be court-martialled again and returned to prison. No C.O. was ever shot. Like ordinary criminals, they were subject to the prison rules of the 3rd Division. The 1st and 2nd Divisions were generally reserved for civil offenders, and the 1st Division suffered little more than loss of freedom, since they lived in cells cleaned by prisoners of lower divisions, had their own food and books, and did no work. The 2nd Division was a modified version of the 1st. The 3rd Division meant for the C.O.s strict separation for the first 28 days, visits and letters only after two months, and hard labour in the form of sewing mail bags in silence for six to ten hours daily. They declared they were 'repelled by the degradation of the individual'.

Some went on hunger strike and had to be forcibly fed. Many were of poor physique and some deliberately courted ill health by discarding overcoats in cold weather and refusing to see the prison doctor.[8] When their health deteriorated they were released for a time under the Prisons (Temporary Discharge for ill-Health) Act 1913.[9] Nine of them died from natural causes and were raised to instant martyrdom by their sympathisers although nine deaths in three years in a population of 1,200 C.O.s represented a lower death rate than for prisoners as a whole, and the decimating influenza epidemic of 1918 was a contributing factor. Despite Philip Snowdon's inflammatory pamphlet *British Prussianism: the scandal of the Tribunals* alleging ill-treatment, very few such cases were authenticated.

Although numerically insignificant the C.O.s were a great nuisance to the Government. In addition, there were subversive agitators to be dealt with. On Clydeside, left-wing extremists

included John Maclean preaching revolutionary Marxist doc-
trines, the vociferous James Maxton, and William Gallacher. They
violently opposed the Munitions Act of 1915 and conscription.
The 'Red Clydesiders', including David Kirkwood, an engineering shop steward, were arrested in Glasgow in March 1916 for
sedition under D.O.R.A. (Defence of the Realm Act). Kirkwood
was deported to Edinburgh and confined to a five mile radius of
the city. Maclean, Maxton and Gallacher were put on trial and
sentenced to imprisonment in the Calton, Maclean for three years,
Maxton for a year and Gallacher for six months.[10] The various
accounts of their prison experiences do not tally. Maxton himself
said the prison officers had been kind, and his cell became the
centre of socialist propaganda – he succeeded in persuading some
warders to join the Independent Labour Party. Other writers have
chosen to give dramatic and highly-coloured accounts of their
sojourn in jail, declaring the Calton Jail to be 'a terrible place
calculated to depress the spirit of the strongest ... The full story of
the sufferings of the prisoners during that period will probably
never be revealed,' adding mysteriously, 'Many of the details are
too harrowing for publication'.[11]

After nine months of idleness in Edinburgh, Kirkwood defied
authority and returned to Glasgow in 1917. He was arrested at
Crieff Hydro and again deported, this time to a vault in Edinburgh
Castle. He gives a curiously self-pitying account of his brief fourteen days imprisonment.

'My new habitation was a vault, far below the ground, into
which the only light entered from a small grated window high up
near the roof ... I was a done man. My mind refused to think ...
Hours passed in utter loneliness ... I was alone in the darkness ...
I seemed the most helpless of mortals. I was very near to breaking
point ... the tears quietly came to my eyes.' His bedding
was 'filthy' and 'the food gied me a scunner [disgusted] ... For 14
days that vault was my home. I had no letters and no friendly
callers.'[12]

Kirkwood then joined Maxton and Gallacher at Moffat Hydro
where they were relaxing after their Calton experience. Later he
became pledged to the cause of the war and enthusiastically increased production at a Glasgow shell factory. Maclean was released after serving only half his sentence and in 1917 continued to

pose a serious threat to industry and political peace. He was appointed first Soviet Consul for Great Britain by Litvinov. Again arrested for sedition April 1918 and sentenced to five years' imprisonment, he went on a continuous hunger strike all the rest of the year until released in December 1918, a sick man subject to depression and persecution mania. In 1919 a strike was called by the Clydesiders, wild scenes in Glasgow resulted in the leaders being arrested for 'inciting to riot'. Soldiers and tanks appeared in the streets. The strike collapsed and the militant wing was broken. The Communist Party of Great Britain was formed after the war but gradually its membership and influence fell in the 1920s.

C.O.s, although only a small segment of the prison population, were more than typically articulate but their accounts are not necessarily therefore more reliable. Many prisoners feel that they are unjustly convicted and others are by nature at war with society. But the C.O.s had a particular quarrel with society in that as a group they felt they should not be imprisoned at all. They saw themselves as victims of persecution of a purely topical public mood, insisted they had committed no crime and that it was because of their consciences, which were clear, that they were in prison. Therefore their views were likely to be more biased than those of ordinary convicts. This intransigence made them particularly awkward to deal with and at the same time perhaps lent their accounts more plausibility than they deserved. But these accounts did at least have the result of stimulating public concern about prison conditions and contributed to the setting up of the Prison System Inquiry Committee in 1919, whose report was published in 1922 as 'English Prisons Today'. This was edited by S. Hobhouse and F. Brockway, former C.O.s. They declared, 'The most manifestly dehumanising prison rule is that which demands silence on the part of the prisoners ... The labour is mostly mechanical and largely wasteful ... The sanitary arrrangements are degrading and filthy, and the dress is hideous, slovenly and humiliating'.[13]

When we come to consider prison structure and policy at the beginning of this modern period we find that little or no change had taken place since 1877. Control remained the primary organisational task with the consequent mutual hostility between staff and prisoners. There was criticism of the 'para-military' structure and the recruitment of ex-servicemen as officers. (In 1922 the term 'prison officer' superseded 'warder'.) It was argued that neither the training nor the calibre of these men fitted them for anything other than custodial duties. When custody and control are the primary concern of the prison authorities the treatment of prisoners is bound to become a secondary consideration, and this dilemma is difficult to resolve. Escape attempts raise an immediate public outcry; the prison authorities' job is to protect the public from these dangerous men; why are they not doing it properly?

In 1912 no specific qualifications were laid down for the posts of governor and assistant governor. At that time and subsequently, they were usually retired officers of H.M. Forces, of the rank of say lieutenant-colonel or its equivalent. More recently the pattern has changed and there have been governors who have risen from the lowest ranks of the prison service with no professional qualifications, but who have made their way by zealousness and force of personality. Today the pattern is changing yet again and those with university qualifications either in sociology or psychiatry are being promoted over the heads of the 'ranker' officers and will secure the top posts to the resentment of the latter.

Early in the century warders' wages were low, their terms of service poor, and discipline, by their militarily-conditioned superiors, severe. Working hours were long and even a trivial breach of discipline was punished by a fine, anything more serious by dismissal. Paterson summed up the situation thus: 'Every country gets the prison service for which it is prepared to pay'.[14] He felt that the quality of the staff was very important; they should be men of personality and character. There was no single career which prepared a man for prison service. If the salary of a prison officer 'is so low that it can only attract men incapable of finding any other work, the prisons will have a staff consisting of men without character, without intelligence, and without much interest in their job ... if you want to exert an influence on human beings, you must call upon men capable of exerting that influence'.[15] Yet in 1955 Wildeblood, a prisoner in Wormwood Scrubs, could write, 'it is not, by its very nature, the kind of occupation likely to attract the best type of man. Promotion is slow, and leads only to the position of Chief Officer ... If, as has so often been stated, the twin objects of imprisonment are deterrence and reform, the role of the warder is uniquely concerned with deterrence'.[16]

More recently still, in 1968, 'Zeno', another intelligent, articulate prisoner, who served nine years in Wormwood Scrubs and other English prisons, took an objective look at the officers. 'Most of them should never be in the service, unless they are employed solely as custodians, and the Home Office has announced so many times that this is only one part of the prison officer's job. Unfortunately it is the only part most of them are equipped to carry out'.[17] Zeno allows that 'there are a few warders of courage and common sense though not particularly intelligent ... on the faces of the majority of them a look of complete indifference born of an apathetic acceptance of the narrow limitations of the job they do and of their surroundings; on the faces of a few of them, a very few, traces of occasional compassion. These are the men who could change the whole prison service, for they have an empathetic understanding of what it feels like to be imprisoned.'[18] But all too often, he asserts, there is 'the apathy of second-rate men muddling through a job, perhaps the most difficult in human relations'.[19]

What sort of man then does the modern prison service aim to recruit? The official attitude is expressed thus: 'While today's Prison Officer needs qualities of humanity, leadership and control, equal importance is attached to maturity, patience, understanding, and a sense of humour. Not everyone, of course, can match up to these exacting requirements or indeed to the service's standards of fitness and education'.[20] The candidate must be over twenty-two and under thirty-five (unless with long service in the Forces), over 5 feet 7 inches (5 feet 6 inches in England), British, and must not wear spectacles. The notice to applicants says, 'Much of his work is routine, including locking and unlocking, supervising meals, work and exercise, but he also has opportunities for assisting in the rehabilitation of his charges by his bearing, example and advice'.[21] Many prisoners and staff would question the optimism of the last words. Conditions of entry include: 'Candidates must be of unexceptionable moral character and of undoubted sobriety, and free from pecuniary embarrassment',[22] and 'Preference is given to candidates who have served in H.M. Regular Forces and to those with special trade or nursing qualifications',[23] bricklayers, carpenters, painters, plumbers, caterers, clerical workers, 'instructors in physical training or gymnastics, or who have had any kind of experience in the control of lads or young men'.[24] The applicant has to perform certain written tests but of a very basic standard, which suggests that he requires to prove only that he is not entirely illiterate.[25] If he passes these he is interviewed by the Board, submits to medical examination, and if approved does seven weeks' training, usually at an establishment near his home. He is then appointed a Prison Officer for twelve months on probation. Just after the Second World War, the Officers' Training School at Wakefield turned out fully-fledged prison officers in only three weeks. 'We just taught them how to turn the key', said one senior officer laconically.[26] Officers at prisons and young offenders' institutions wear uniforms; in borstals, detention centres and open prisons, they wear plain clothes. They get free quarters (though not immediately); they work a forty-hour week, with some weekend work and some night duty. An ordinary prison officer gets £60–£72 weekly plus free house and uniform (1979)[27] with extra allowances for a special job. Retirement is at 55, with gratuity and pension.[28] There are no overtime agreements in Scotland, and only about six to eight hours overtime weekly is worked. In England and Wales there is an agreement under which uniform grades may be required to do about twelve hours overtime weekly, in practice much more. Officers maintain that without overtime they would be hard put to make ends meet.

It is hardly surprising that there are many grievances felt by officers and difficulties in attracting recruits. As with the armed forces, tied housing remains a feature of prison service. John Renton, spokesman of Scotland's 2,602 prison officers since 1971, has said that members are discontented with this situation, the standards of houses are low and officers anxious to get out of the established 'prison village' (dating from the nineteenth century), where they feel isolated from the community. Irregular hours of work, including some evenings and weekends, tend to make social life centre within the quarters, leading to a greater feeling of isolation. In the U.S.A. the authorities are evidently alive to the disadvantages of the system and the trend is now away from housing staff on the site. But in Britain the practice of building new prisons in the middle of nowhere aggravates this isolation and perpetuates the problem. The constant mobility expected from staff is also a drawback to recruitment; traditionally governors have been 'nomadic', with the interruption to children's education and wives' careers which that entails. Working conditions for staff are often very poor and vary greatly from prison to prison. For example there is a strong contrast between conditions at Cornton Vale, the only women's prison in Scotland, and those at Barlinnie or Peterhead. However the *Prisons in Scotland Report* for 1980 observes that for almost the first time since the Second World War the Department stopped recruiting. The number of staff rose to the highest ever level - 2,748 - probably owing to the rise in unemployment elsewhere.

Officers also suffer from a strong feeling that public opinion is unfair to them and out of sympathy with them and their task. One officer writes, 'With the present day tendency to view even the most violent and dangerous prisoner as a wayward boy and the hard-dying Victorian tradition of the 'screw' as hard, brutal and totally devoid of human feeling, it is far too easy to pass off demonstrations as expressions of frustration over unsuitable staff and repressive regimes'.[29] While the public is so ready to criticise the prison service as reactionary and inimical to all change, it might be salutary to consider the immense burdens prison officers have to shoulder. The relationship between keeper and kept is by definition an uneasy one. Basic-grade prison officers and their charges are almost always of working-class background and probably with some experience of poverty, and both are of limited education. But the former represent the law, the latter the opposite, and the officers therefore instinctively try to stress their superiority, reinforced by the knowledge that they are members, however lowly, of the uniformed hierarchy, an attitude which must intensify the prisoners' sense of humiliation and personal insignificance. Moreover social workers are being recruited in increasing numbers, and with (in the view of the ordinary officer) 'half-baked' ideas, are leap-frogging over his head in the promotion race. The average prison officer feels that he is still only a turnkey, playing a purely negative role and doing a job where boredom alternates with tension, 'a job with many frustrations and few rewards'.[30] If he is to be under continual fire from liberal reformers the numbers in the service will thin still more.

In a television programme several prison officers tried to answer the question, 'Why do men become prison officers?' and what do they hope to achieve? What motivates a man to spend all his working life among those who have cut themselves off from normal society? An officer at Lincoln Prison, asked why he joined the service, said, 'Well, I've always been in uniform. I was seven years in the Navy'; he felt that he could not settle to life 'outside'. He added, 'I'm doing twenty-three years' service, and I think we all get institutionalised'. To the same question another gave the answer, 'Security. I was made redundant in the engineering works. That's all I came in for, security.' The comment was made that the numbers of ex-servicemen now joining are fewer and one officer said he resented civilian workers, such as welfare officers, in prison. He complained that the officers' work is 'only custodial' and 'as far as doing anything constructive, there is no scope whatsoever, for psychiatrists and so on take over'.[31] Walter Davidson, second-in-command of Barlinnie's Special Unit, said on retirement in May 1980, 'I think I joined the service mainly for security and I think the reasons are the same today, housing and security, because no one knows a thing about the service until they go into it'. Of the training to become prison officers he said, 'The seven weeks basic training is excellent but it only provides the nuts and bolts. There is no man-management, no study of behavioural patterns'.[32]

There is an obvious need for better educational standards among the uniformed staff and wider and more intensive training after recruitment, the more so since many governors are still appointed from their ranks. But it is difficult to see how this is to be achieved when at the same time, even with the present rudimentary educational requirements, the recruitment position gives cause for concern. Renton said (1978), 'Unless we start recruiting people who have the ability and the chance to become governors, then we are never going to attract the right kind of person. If you recruit with the intention of hiring a guard then that is what you will get'. He added, 'It is a fact that the prison service is one of those institutions which only come to the notice of the public when things are going wrong. The prison officers have some justification when they claim that they, as much as their charges, are society's forgotten men.'

It is worth noting that many problems bedevil the prison system in America. One of the crucial facts is that while the convicts are predominantly black, young, unemployed, and from large cities, the vast majority of guards are white, middle-aged (many in their late sixties), and from small rural towns. The latter feature is accounted for by prisons usually being located in isolated areas, where they tend to become vital to the economy of the district and draw on the local population for their personnel. Some are near army bases, and in these most of the guards are ex-service-men.[33] An ex-prisoner, Nathan Leopold, argues that penal administration needs to be upgraded as a professional career carrying enough social prestige and salary to attract good men, both at warden (governor) and guard level. A very similar situation to our own. 'Often in the States completely illiterate men are warders – almost anyone will do. The acceptance of such very low standards is not rehabilitative, for the prisoner spends most of his time in the custody of those who are mostly just turnkeys'.[34]

Another major problem facing the authorities in the U.K. as elsewhere has long been the employment of those in custody. Work often means only the making of paper sacks and paper boxes for eight hours a day five days a week, or the sewing of mailbags. 'The value of this particular work is nil', asserted an officer, 'a waste of time, boring and repetitive, and they have no interest in it whatsoever'.[35] Devon, writing in 1912, said few could earn their living outside by the work they did in prison. It consisted of the lowest kind of unskilled labour, on account of the objections of the Trade Unions to unfair competition. The pay was very low and not conducive to hard work; if the sentence was over fourteen days and the prisoner not on hard labour, he could earn four marks daily, and for every six marks earned, he got 1d. when freed. If on hard labour, he got 1/- a month if his conduct and work were satisfactory. The situation has not changed markedly since then.

Writing over forty years later, in 1955, Wildeblood found in the tailoring shop that work 'was a maddening, useless task, sitting there in the dull glow of a forty watt bulb screwed up high in the ceiling, eternally stitching away at the tough canvas, eight stitches to the inch'.[36]

Zeno in his turn spent months sewing mailbags in Wormwood Scrubs, then made denim overalls for prisoners, and could earn, in 1968, 6/- weekly if he worked flat out for thirty-three hours.[37] In fact he managed to earn only 3/6d. He gravitated to the library, as the most intelligent prisoners usually do. He thought the worst aspect of imprisonment is the complete and utter waste of time which is all that a long prison sentence offers.

The Home Department is fully alive to the fact that prisoners often make up an unwilling and unskilled work force and that 'any proposal to pay prisoners substantially higher amounts than at present is justifiable only if it is established that the value of the prisoners' work would support such payments'.[38] 'Nothing is more demoralising than idleness in an overcrowded prison.'[39] There should be improved workshop accommodation and work should 'be obviously purposeful, efficiently organised, and carried out so far as possible in conditions similar to those in outside workshops'.[40] Contracts for government departments are the main source of work in prisons, apart from manufacturing of equipment for prisons and borstals, their domestic services, and maintenance of their buildings and grounds.

The normal system on the Continent is the use of prison labour on contracts from outside industries. At one time in the U.K. considerable numbers were employed outside the walls on such useful projects as agriculture, land drainage, forestry, and road works, but in recent years this work has dwindled, partly because of opposition from the Trade Unions and partly through unemployment in some areas. Problems of work in prisons 'will never be solved until society as a whole accepts that prisons do not work in an economic vacuum, and that prisoners are members of the working community, temporarily segregated, and not economic outcasts.'[41] Once this was accepted, more realistic pay would result. In 1939 payments or 'earnings' started 'related to the price of cigarettes at that time. The wages ranged from 3d. to 1/- per week with an average of 7d.,'[42] increasing to an average of 2/8d. a week in 1959. Weekly pay varies now (1981) between 80 pence and £3 depending on the type of employment and how hard the inmate works. The amount is very low, especially compared with France and some other prison systems abroad. The suggestion is often made that prisoners should be paid 'the economic rate for the job', i.e. the same wages as workers outside, which would be applied towards the prisoner's keep, the maintenance of his family, social insurance contributions and saving for release. The balance he could keep for spending in prison. This would mean greater self-respect for the prisoner and more security on release. It would also make it easier for prison industry to be accepted as a normal part of the national economy, as prisoners would then be employed in conditions similar to those of free industries.

In 1972 a start was made on remodelling Scottish prison industries and new staff were recruited for the purpose. The list of agreed objectives included keeping prisoners occupied, providing training to enable them to obtain suitable jobs after release, allowing them to earn money as a motivation for work, and making economic use of a potential labour force. The Report for Prisons in Scotland for 1977 gives statistics of those engaged in various occupations. Textile work shows the biggest percentage, and other types of employment include woodworking, engineering, farms and gardens, laundry services, domestic cooking and baking. It is always stressed that prisons must not seek to gain a competitive advantage over outside manufacturers from the use of cheap labour, that their market share of any product must not be so large as to create undue concern to private industry, and their activities must not unduly worsen unemployment problems. In the past the prison industries have depended too heavily on the custom provided by other departments (Department of the Environment, the Ministry of Defence, and, no longer a government department, the Post Office), the amount provided by the private sector being negligible. Most of this work has been unskilled, repetitive, and boring, often too little of it available so that for instance the making and repairing of mailbags has been done by hand while machines stand idle to make the limited orders last out.

America faces similar problems. Incentives are lacking as wages are low and most jobs are monotonous and unskilled. Work 'tends to be uninteresting, soul-deadening drudgery, with no application to modern methods of manufacturing',[43] and therefore with no rehabilitative effect. In this context Sweden has proved to be very progressive. There prison wages are divided into savings and spendings; wages of those working on free labour permits (working outside under private individuals) are higher and divided into three parts: cost of keep in prison, for dependants and for indemnities, to spend and to save.[44]

Impressive claims are made in British official reports for the prison education service, its broad aim being to encourage new interests and widen horizons among inmates. Education is given under the heads of remedial education for illiterates (received by 25% of inmates in young offenders' establishments); higher education by evening classes and correspondence courses; recreational with art, music, handcrafts, drama, physical recreation; and vocational. This is all provided by the local education authorities. The programme in Scotland is under the control of two full-time education officers assisted by prison officers who undertake teaching duties and also by part-time professional and other staff and guest speakers for evening classes. There are compulsory classes for inmates under twenty-one, but for others everything is optional. The Prisons in Scotland Report for 1978 stated that prison education ranged from the specialism of teaching illiterates to the supervision of those taking courses for the Open University, and that inmates gained passes in the Scottish Certificate of Education examinations at 'O' and 'H' levels. Officials claim there is no doubt that these activities are rehabilitative and that the programme should be further developed, especially by the appointment of a greater number of full time qualified teachers. There is satisfaction at the progress made by hitherto illiterate prisoners, many of whom had their first experience of writing letters home and reading their incoming mail themselves.

The reports on health in Scottish prisons highlight certain types of illness, such as respiratory and dysentery-type disorders which we may assume are caused in part by overcrowding. There has been in the last few years an encouraging fall in the number of inmates suffering from pulmonary tuberculosis, from 150 in 1973 to 55 in 1980.[45] Infections like pediculosis (lice) and scabies and various forms of venereal disease are all prevalent. More significant however are three classes which probably have a linking factor – mental disorders, drug dependence and alcoholism, and self-inflicted injuries including attempted suicide, all of which have increased in recent years.

In 1977 there were eight deaths, all male; three were suicides, two were accidental (one the result of glue-sniffing, one from drug overdose) and three from natural causes. In 1978 there were again eight deaths (male), four from natural causes, and four by suicide including one who jumped over an upper gallery. In 1980 there was only one death, again a suicide by jumping from a gallery.[46] The statistics however make no attempt to correlate the prison figures with those for the population as a whole and it is therefore difficult to draw any definite conclusions from them. It is generally accepted that the incidence of neurosis and alcoholism is much higher in Scotland than in the rest of the U.K. Cause and effect are difficult to distinguish but it seems reasonable to assume that many admitted to prison are already suffering from mental disorders and the escape mechanisms which follow them (which may indeed be a cause of their committing offences), though the traumas of imprisonment and of prison conditions may aggravate the disorders. It must also be taken into account that growing awareness of psychiatric problems, more sophisticated medical techniques, and more effective diagnosis may affect the figures. It is at any rate clear that mental disorders, alcoholism, and drug addiction are receiving increasing attention from the prison medical service.

An English prison report claims that as a result of the National Health Service and changing social conditions prisoners on admission are generally in better health than twenty years ago,[47] Given that prisoners on admission are fitter than those of twenty years ago, the authorities aim to keep them in good shape once they are inside. The weekly dietary offered to prisoners has greatly improved even since 1948 when there was still a disproportionate amount of 'Bread and Marg.' and the nightly pint of cocoa would not do much to allay hunger pangs from teatime until next morning.[48] It is now claimed to be wholesome and adequate and that the 'general standard of prison catering now compares favourably with that in hospitals and other institutions'.[49]

It is 200 years since Howard wrote his *State of the Prisons*. Have we made the progress he envisaged? In the sphere of health, education and employment, improvements have been made, but overcrowding in many Scottish prisons today means pressures and strain on prisoners and officers. It is even worse in England and Wales, where the prison population (including those on remand) was 44,223 in March 1980, and 40% of the total prison population had to share single cells. In 1978 according to the May Report (1979), 5,082 prisoners were jammed 3 in a cell, 11,016 were 2 in a cell. The figures for Scotland were respectively 217 and 1,268. Officially Scottish prisons are not overcrowded; on 4th April 1980 there were 5,116 in Scottish prisons designed to hold 5,200. But these statistics conceal the fact that untried (on remand) prisoners live 23 hours a day in a cell 13' by 8' shared perhaps with two others – 'trebled up' for days or months in conditions worse than when the nineteenth-century prison fortresses were built. Those accused of non-payment of fines or violent assault may be penned up together. In D Hall of Saughton prison in Edinburgh (completed after the First World War to replace the Calton), men are trebled up in cells designed for one, with a double bed, a single bunk, and three chamber pots. Conditions in the mornings when the cells are unlocked are overwhelming. In such squalor, tempers fray easily and explosive tensions can build up. Many inmates prefer cell-sharing for companionship, but three to a cell is intolerable for prison officers too. In some prisons the pressure on the bathing places by the hordes of inmates make it difficult to keep up reasonable standards of hygiene, and the ancient heating pipes ensure that prisoners are often half suffocated or nearly frozen.

In Scotland, unlike England or Wales, all accused must be brought to trial within 110 days of a custodial remand provided the whole period has been spent in custody. Emergency legislation was introduced to suspend this requirement because of a strike by the Scottish courts' staffs during the winter of 1978-79.

Charles Hills, Governor of Saughton, says, 'There is no indication that the overcrowding problem will diminish since there is no indication that the numbers in custody will decrease and some that it will increase. There is no new building being undertaken to provide for an increase in capacity.'[50] The prison system's last resort would be to increase remission but the Home Secretary, Mr Whitelaw, has rejected large scale remission. (For all sentences of more than a month a prisoner is allowed a third remission.)

Inmate population at 30th June 1979:

England and Wales	Males	40,885
	Females	1,434
	Total	42,319

Scotland   Males   4,439
                         Females   172
                         Total   4,611

In England and Wales the average population is 12% greater than design capacity, in Scotland only 1%. In 1978 in England and Wales 16,098 inmates were two or three in a cell, in Scotland 1,485.[51] In Scotland the average daily population in 1945 was 1,955: 5,062 in 1978; 4,585 in 1979; 4,860 in 1980. Because of the exceptional reduction in reception and average daily population figures in early 1979 (due to the court staff strikes), it is difficult to assess whether the figures for 1978 mean a continual upward trend.

Despite the serious difficulties in recent years caused by a rising prison population and consequent overcrowding, shortages of staff, work and funds (it now costs £6,000 a year to keep a prisoner), these must be set against the legislative and other steps taken towards penal reform during this century. In this book it is possible only to summarise the more important changes. The Criminal Justice Act 1948 (in its limited application to Scotland) and the Criminal Justice (Scotland) Act 1949 abolished sentences of penal servitude and hard labour, sentences to particular prison divisions, sentences of whipping, prisoners' 'ticket-of-leave', and substituted the term 'inmate' for 'convict'. In 1948, Peterhead prison was 'the only Scottish prison in which flogging can be given and none of the evidence which we have received has convinced us that it is necessary'.[52] Despite great pressure to bring back corporal punishment the Advisory Council on the Treatment of Offenders 1959 resisted this in its 1960 report. In the Prison Service College Museum at Polmont there is evidence of cruel punishments inflicted until 1948. Here is the triangle to which offenders were tied by wrists and ankles before being flogged, the canvas belt and canvas collar to protect the prisoner's neck and loins, and the canvas waistcoat to protect his chest and ribs. The cat and the birch are also shown. Only those over twenty-one (there was no upper age limit) suffered from the cat and the maximum number of lashes was eighteen. The cat weighs 9 ozs. and comprises a cloth covered wooden handle $19\frac{1}{2}''$ long with 9 lashes of whipcord. Each lash is about $\frac{1}{8}''$ thick and 33″ long.

The Murder (Abolition of Death Penalty) Act 1965 abolished

the death penalty for murder for a trial period of five years, which was subsequently extended on a permanent basis. The Criminal Justice Act 1967 introduced a system of parole for selected prisoners and young offenders. All prisoners serving over eighteen months are eligible for release on parole after serving one-third of sentence or twelve months whichever is the longer. Parole always entails a licence and is not something to which the prisoner is entitled as of right. He must apply for it. Parole is far from popular with many inmates, who find the anxiety of hopes being raised only, too often, to be dashed, an added strain in their imprisonment. Some refuse to have their names put forward as they dislike the idea of social enquiries into their home backgrounds, others because they resent any 'favour', as they see it, from authority. However, opting out by prisoners remains fairly low, self-rejects being high in a prison like Peterhead with a large number of 'hard men'. Local Review Committees are appointed for each establishment holding inmates with sentences which make them eligible to be considered for parole or for release on licence from a life sentence. It is the duty of these committees to consider each case and to make recommendations to the Secretary of State on their suitability for release. Each inmate is interviewed by a member of the committee. During 1980 a total of 729 determinate sentence cases were considered by the ten local review committees and 269 of these were recommended for release. In addition a number of life and H.M.P. cases together with those of Children and Young Persons were considered. From the introduction of the parole system in 1968 to the end of 1980, 138 persons serving life sentences or detained during Her Majesty's pleasure have been released. Of these, 20 have been recalled to custody including two who have been recalled more than once, although 5 have been subsequently re-released.

By the Children and Young Persons (Scotland) Act 1937 children under eight cannot be punished for crime. A number of statutory provisions regulate the sentencing and treatment of young offenders, most of them codified in this 1937 Act and the Criminal Justice (Scotland) Act 1963. A subsequent amendment by the Social Work (Scotland) Act 1968, effective from 1971, reduced from seventeen to sixteen the minimum age for committal on a sentence of detention in a young offenders' institution, with the effect that some offenders who would previously have gone to approved schools outside the penal system are now committed to prison-service institutions. The Act resulted too in Children's Hearings by which children under sixteen (in some cases up to eighteen) were to be dealt with according to their needs and not with regard to the offences they had committed.

The basis of classification has been radically changed and new types of prisons with diversified functions have been developed to meet a variety of training needs – open prisons, Training for Freedom schemes and pre-release courses. In 1966 the Mountbatten Report to improve prison security after spectacular prison escapes in 1964–66 (including that of George Blake, sentenced to 42 years for spying) recommended the concentration of the worst security risks into one establishment. But the recommendations by the Radzinowicz Committee for seven dispersal prisons were adopted instead. Thus the high-risk men were scattered around the country. Mountbatten introduced a system of different categories of prisoner, top security being category A. His report ushered in an era in which concern with security became and has remained, central to large parts of the system.

The courts have been given power to make hospital or guardianship orders for mentally-abnormal offenders. Progress has been made in the psychiatric treatment of prisoners, and the aftercare and probation services have been re-organised.

The suspended sentence introduced by the Criminal Justice Act 1967 is a prison sentence whose operation is held over on certain prescribed conditions with the object of keeping first offenders, especially the young, out of prison. It has been under attack for resulting in more prison sentences and a move away from probation and fines. Scottish courts have no power to suspend sentences but for a long time have had power to defer sentence. This power was confirmed in 1963 and the provision was repeated in the consolidated Criminal Procedure (Scotland) Act 1975. Preventive detention and corrective training for the treatment of persistent offenders are often considered to be experiments which have failed, 'the one aimed at the humane isolation, the other at the reform, of the persistent offender, and each was unsuccessful'.[53] Borstal and detention centres are failures if the aims were rehabilitative.

We now come to a question increasingly and insistently postulated today, are prisons effective in their declared purpose, do they in fact 'work'? What we are discussing here is of course the secondary purpose of imprisonment. There would probably be general agreement that its primary purpose is deterrent – the threat of deprivation of liberty directed towards those who may contemplate committing offences. Its effectiveness in this primary purpose (as regards those who have never been in prison) is of course unquantifiable; even an opinion poll incorporating a direct question such as 'Would you have committed crimes if you had not been deterred by the risk of being sent to prison?' would be unlikely to elicit many objective answers.

What then is the twentieth-century attitude towards those already in prison? It is officially expressed in the 1972 Report on Prisons in Scotland thus: 'The purposes of training and treatment of convicted prisoners shall be to establish in them the will to lead a good and useful life on discharge, and to fit them to do so'.[54] Is this highly-laudable purpose being achieved, or does the existing system work in the direction of the prisoner's deterioration rather than his rehabilitation? The short answer seems to be that in most cases rehabilitation is not achieved, as prison officers agree that over 75% of prisoners are recidivists. This is hardly surprising in the light of what we have learned about the calibre of staff and the conditions in which they work, as well as the antiquated buildings still in use but designed for a different theory of penology – 'to serve the purposes of solitary confinement, treadmill hard labour and brutal repression. They stand as a monumental denial of the principles to which we are committed'.[55]

For further explanation of the failure of the system we have to look to the opinions expressed by two main groups, those who have studied or experienced prison and its consequences from 'the right side' of the bars (prison officers, probation officers, social workers, sociologists, etc.), and those who have themselves been convicts. Neither group gives an entirely reliable account, the former because of prejudice, incomplete information, an over-developed taste for polemics and so on, the latter because of bitterness and resentment at real or imagined injustices and a desire to get their own back on the system. But both groups are virtually unanimous that the system has largely failed in its purpose.

Though even the more articulate prisoners are not necessarily objective, some of their opinions are worth quoting. A Gorbals man who served a term in Dartmoor and Parkhurst in 1927 when the rule of silence was still in force has written, 'The *real* punishment begins *after* a man leaves prison ... the human flotsam spewed out daily from our prisons who drift back into crime as inevitably as night follows day solely, in the vast majority of cases, merely to exist[56] ... You may call our prisons institutions or hotels, or sanatoria, anything you like, but, in terms of reformation, these names mean nothing at all ... The walls are still there. The bars, the bells, the yells, the smells – particularly the smells. Call a cell a 'room' by all means but Jim Lag will not be impressed – he knows it is still a cell – with no handle or keyhole *inside* the door.'[57]

Wildeblood, already quoted, says, 'We are always being told that the purpose of imprisonment is not so much retribution as reform – it is useless to put a man away for a long period, do nothing to change or improve him, and piously hope that by the time he is released he will have magically transformed himself into a good citizen[58] ... Men in prison ... do not merely remain as bad as they were when they came in; by a visible process of moral erosion ... they become worse.'[59]

Zeno, also quoted previously, maintains (and this is borne out by all prison officers), that the effect of a long term in prison is to render a man incapable of making decisions. 'For nine years I was not able, not permitted, to make a decision of any consequence, and now I have lost the will to decide'.[60] And he talks of having to 'attempt to prove to myself that the British penal system has not altered me irrevocably in any way, and that I can still mix easily with my fellow men'.[61]

John McVicar, at one time the 'most wanted man in Britain', during his two years of freedom after escaping from Durham top-security jail, had a sentence of twenty-six years to serve for robbery with violence when the additional years for escaping were added. In 1979, freed on parole, he was studying for a post-graduate degree at Leicester University. He tells how by the age of twenty-one he 'had spent four years in institutions which were meant to correct criminals yet not one moment of that time had been directed to treating my criminality – my criminal attitudes

and values were being strengthened'.[62] On a television programme McVicar said, 'So many guys who serve a long time
either end up bitter lemons or old women. Even when you serve
it easy, long-term imprisonment is a cruel punishment ... The
method I chose to counteract the corrosive effect of serving so
long was studying'.

Jimmy Boyle, at one time labelled by the media 'Scotland's
Most Violent Man', had a record of violent crime in Glasgow
which ultimately resulted in 1967 in a life sentence for murder
with fifteen years the recommended minimum. To this were
gradually added twelve years, incurred for serious assaults on
prison staff in Barlinnie, Peterhead, and Inverness. This formidable
total obviously left Boyle with nothing to lose. On the futility of
prison he says, 'But every time I went into prison I broadened my
criminal horizons by making more and more connections in different areas. These were people who knew what the nick was all
about, would go into prison, do their time and go out again to
take up where they left off'. And on its effect, 'The fact is that
prison eats your insides out, and ties your stomach in knots, leaving
your heart very heavy'. On leaving Inverness Prison for Barlinnie
Special Unit, he affirms (thus supporting Zeno), 'I had come from
a world where decision-making was taken out of my hands. If I
had wanted a cup of water, the toilet, soap, etc. etc., then I had
had to ask for it. Now I was having to cope with not only these
decisions but to think in terms of other people and it was pretty
frightening'.[63] While in the Special Unit, Boyle discovered an
unexpected talent for sculpture and exhibited during the Edinburgh Festival.

One must, of course, guard against the danger of leaning too
heavily on 'critical descriptions of the way in which penal measures
– usually institutional measures – are administered, some written
by penal reformers, others by offenders with a talent for autobio-
graphy ... Since the number of people who can gain first-hand
experience of prison or probation is limited, [and their integrity
and bona fides is ipso facto suspect] this kind of literature is
valuable but it must not be mistaken for scientific description'.[64]
It is interesting to note that 'Prison officials have not, for the most
part, been very prolific in their writings' – the lower echelons of
staff have written nothing, and prison governors have confined

themselves to reports.[65]

From the prison staff, social reformers and others the story is much the same. As long ago as 1818 Buxton quoted a London jailer as saying that in nine years 'he had never known an instance of reformation; he thought the prisoners grew worse'.[66] In add-ition we have the words of David Haggart written in the Iron Room of Edinburgh Jail where he lay condemned to death in July 1822: 'A prison is the blackest and wickedest place in the world. Many a poor boy is brought to the gallows at last, because his first offence is punished by imprisonment ... I cannot say that my bad habits were learned in jail, but I am sure they were confirmed there'.[67]

In our own time 'Every prisoner becomes so institutionalised that he ceases to be an asset and becomes a burden on society'.[68] A prison officer says, 'They're on about rehabilitation all the time. But it's no use. More crime is planned in prison than outside, for they've nothing else to think about in perhaps ten years'. And another says, 'there is an invisible line between him [prison officer] and the prisoners, so many men don't *want* help, they are happy the way they are'.[69] Renton confirms this last statement, 'Many criminals do not *want* to be helped. They just want to pay their debt to society and then get out'.[70] He stresses the difficulties in the way of attempts at rehabilitation – the unacceptable ratio of staff to inmates at about 1 to 20, or 1 to 40 in the more crowded prisons, the enormous mental and physical demands on low-cal-ibre recruits and their sense of insecurity in the face of increasing assaults in prison. (They carry no weapon except the traditional baton.) Professor Radzinowicz set up the first Institute of Crimin-ology in Britain at Cambridge in 1959. He refers in the *Spectator* of July 1977 to his *Growth of Crime*, saying, 'My book is pessimistic in a sense: I cannot see many prisoners being reformed, nor can I see a falling crime rate'.

It seems then that there is general agreement that today's prisons fail in their task of rehabilitation and reform, and the incidence of recidivism argues that they do not deter many convicts from further crimes. (We do not of course know how many the prospect of prison has deterred from committing their first crime.) What then do prisons achieve, if anything? Do they punish? Is the loss of liberty a punishment in itself? Most reformers today take the view that not only is the loss of liberty itself a punishment but that it constitutes the main element in punishment. Some, including John Renton, go further and maintain that the loss of freedom is sufficient punishment and is the utmost which a convicted person ought to suffer. In this they follow Buxton who expressed the same opinion, 'Where the law, therefore, condemns a man simply to be committed to jail, the suspension of his personal liberty is the utmost which he ought to suffer ... This is the whole of his sentence and ought therefore to be the whole of his suffering.'[71] This is possibly a somewhat naïve opinion, since 'The loss of liberty is a considerable punishment for some men but for others, such as the socially inadequate, it is no hardship for it is a protection from the cruel world outside. Thus, in reality, one man's punishment may be another man's refuge'.[72] And the converse may apply; it is arguable that a professional man who values his reputation highly is sufficiently punished by a conviction which deprives him of that reputation, without the added ordeal of imprisonment. There is sometimes a danger in slavish adherence to abstract principles however worthy, such as that of 'equality before the law.' To make the punishment fit the crime may be less practical than to make it fit the criminal.

The conclusion that prisons in their present form are failing in their declared purpose automatically raises further questions. Should they be abolished altogether? If not, what alternatives should be introduced for the treatment of certain categories of offenders? What improvements should be made in the treatment of those for whom there is no suitable alternative to custody?

The first question can be disposed of fairly briefly. Only a handful of extremists would seriously suggest that it would be practicable to do without prisons altogether, and it is significant that no large modern state has achieved this ideal. It is generally accepted that, human nature being what it is, there will always be a hard core of violent or otherwise dangerous criminals who must for the security of society and sometimes for their own sakes, be kept in detention for long periods. This has become ever more necessary with the progressive abolition of capital punishment for the more serious categories of crimes. Thus the number of prisoners on very long sentences, though still small, shows a big increase. In Scotland between 1968 and 1977 receptions of prisoners serving three years and over increased by 46%, reflecting the rise in violent crime and the longer sentences being imposed as a result. 'To devise a regime for those men which must both be consistent with maximum security and not make the prison rule that imprisonment should "encourage and assist the prisoner to lead a good and useful life" look like a cynical joke – this is indeed a herculean task.'[73]

Experience in every country shows that there are some offenders who just will not make friends with society ever. Paterson agrees: 'If, however, a man is never likely to be a useful citizen, then a completely indeterminate sentence is the only safeguard that the courts can offer to society'.[74] Radzinowicz supports him: 'Imprisonment will always be with us, and detention for possibly long periods, even permanently, will always be necessary'.[75] 'Such evil-doers must be kept apart for long periods; in the exceptional case for life . . . But to prevent the progressive deterioration which often results from long confinement in prison . . . their conditions in confinement must be humane and tolerable . . . Many are disturbed, unstable and immature.'[76] 'There will be a residue of irreversibly violent criminals . . . They have to be outlawed from the community, literally life-imprisonment.'[77]

The second question is a much less academic one. Serious efforts are in fact being made to find alternatives to custodial sentences for such offences as prostitution, alcoholism, vagrancy, drug addiction (though not drug-peddling), gambling, psychotic and aberrant crimes, motoring offences, and non-payment of fines. In order to avoid the cost of keeping these offenders (most of them on short sentences) in prison, and their own loss of earning capacity which involves payment of social security to their families, it is suggested that hostels be set up to house them and that they remain within the community subject to intensive counselling and treatment. It is hoped that hostels 'for homeless offenders not merely as a means of preventing their return to prison but also as a "possible alternative to imprisonment" for offenders of various kinds'[78] may be increased.

The following statistics are of interest as illustrating the types of offences bringing people to prison in Scotland today and the extent to which the pattern has changed since early in the century. It is also interesting to note the differences between the present and earlier centuries, especially the sixteenth and seventeenth when 'crimes' against religion and morality loomed so large. The pattern is not necessarily representative of the incidence of particular crimes; the picture may be distorted by other factors such as the ratio between offences and convictions, and the imposition of other penalties such as fines as alternatives to imprisonment. The figures are for receptions.

Crimes (Men)	1913	1938	1971	1972
Crimes of violence	1,257	684	1,133	1,157
Theft	2,823	1,173	3,448	3,174
Housebreaking	585	981	4,071	3,596
Offences				
Breach of the peace	11,195	2,728	5,571	5,485
Drunkenness	9,532	2,623	1,286	1,333
Road Traffic Acts Offences	52	285	1,844	1,582
Crimes (Women)				
Crimes of violence	42	29	18	19
Theft	702	145	115	218
Housebreaking	24	17	43	33
Offences				
Breach of the peace	4,214	525	283	299
Drunkenness	5,542	1,109	139	142
Prostitution	1,270	99	61	85

Even in the light of the reservations mentioned above some of these figures give cause for concern[79].

The following two tables are even more alarming. Both represent average daily numbers in prison. The first is for Scotland alone:

	Total Population	Total in Prison	Proportion per 100,000
1909–13	4,809,152	2,817	58.3
1928–37	4,914,575	1,698	34.7
1962	5,196,600	3,238	61.9
1971	5,217,400	5,338	101.9
1972	5,210,400	5,220	100.0[80]

The second, correct to mid-1973, shows figures on the same basis for West European countries, including Scotland:

	Total Population	Total in Prison	Proportion per 100,000
Holland	13,119,000	2,540	19.6
France	51,004,000	29,553	59.9
Norway	3,866,468	1,432	37.1
Sweden	8,092,693	4,977	61.4
Denmark	4,800,000	3,350	69.8
W Germany	61,194,600	51,175	83.6
England & Wales	55,534,000	40,178	72.4
Scotland	5,300,000	5,000	94.3[81]

It is difficult to escape certain conclusions as to the criminal propensities of the Scots compared with people in England and Wales and in other European countries.[82] There has been an increase in crimes of violence such as serious assaults against police while resisting arrest, and robbery with violence. In Lothian and Borders assaults on the police increased from 5 in 1977 to 66 in 1978.[83] Police would like more serious penalties, not tiny fines, for their broken noses and arms. There is an increased use of offensive weapons, particularly knives. Most disturbing is the increase in crimes of violence and cruelty to children, often committed by their own parents. There has been a 209% increase in murder convictions from 1955 to 1975,[84] and prison staff are united in their wish to restore capital punishment for certain categories of murder such as terrorism and the killing of police and prison officers, and some would be in favour of all murders being so punished. Mr Black, Secretary of the Scottish Police Federation, said 'Scotland is the most violent country in Europe right now. It is disheartening.'[85]

Alcoholism is much more serious in Scotland than elsewhere in Britain and violence is also proportionately much more so. The high Scottish figures could mean that we have more convicted offenders than any of the countries cited in the table above, but it could also mean that we send people to prison for offences which other countries, for example Holland, do not. 'The chance of being assaulted, murdered or robbed is much greater here than in any other part of the country. The picture of the Scot as drunken and quarrelsome and with scant respect for the law seems to be all too true.'[86] The Chief Constable of Aberdeen, Mr Alex Murrison, in 1974 supported this view. 'Almost every murder in Scotland is drink-related, and remember that you have at least four times as much chance of being murdered in Scotland as you have in England.' Many prison staff accept without argument the statement of one high-ranking officer that 'We Scots are a very violent, savage, quarrelsome, difficult people. "No prisons" simply would not be the answer.' The great bulk of crime in Scotland today is committed by a small section of the population – men in their teens and early twenties. In 1978 the average daily prison population was 5,062 of whom 4,893 were males and 169 were females. Over a third of that population (36.2 per cent) were under twenty-one, and more than half were aged less than twenty-five.[87]

The Lord Advocate, Lord Mackay, revealed that in the six months from May to November 1979, 255 serious cases of violent crime had been indicted, including fifty-one cases of murder or culpable homicide, twenty more than for the whole of 1969. The average age of the accused was sixteen to twenty years. He pointed out that these statistics represented only the number of crimes actually reported to the police. Referring to the link between alcohol and crime, Lord Mackay said that Scotland still suffered from a serious problem of alcohol misuse. 'The problem of violent crime in our society has reached disturbing proportions and nothing will be achieved by ignoring it ... So many factors have contributed to the pattern of violent crime in Scotland today: the pace of social change, the growth of affluence, the decline in religious belief, and the loosening of discipline both in the home and in school. There is no short-term solution.'[88] The *Prisons in Scotland* Reports show that the number of convictions for assaults has soared from 1,228 in 1977 to 1,831 in 1980 although those for rape and other offences against females has dropped from 94 to 78.

Despite this mindless violence, the new militancy and prison protest rapidly growing in America has not yet gained ground here. But strikes and demonstrations by prisoners and counterpressure by officers have increased tensions, particularly in some high-security prisons such as Peterhead. The 'Sixties in America were marked by the growth of the civil-rights movement, from peaceful 'sit-ins' to bloody urban riots and the formation of black revolutionary groups like the Black Panthers. George Jackson, an articulate, black, political militant, stated the belief of this new breed of prisoner unequivocally. 'Very few men imprisoned for economic crimes or even crimes of passion against the oppressor feel that they are really guilty.' He described the police as 'gun-slinging pigs from the outside enemy culture',[89] and substituted 'capture' for imprisonment for wrongdoing. Such men argue they are victims of class and ethnic oppression and that their imprison-ment represents political repression rather than punishment for crime[90] (a tenet held firmly by the I.R.A.). After Jackson's death and after the bloody riot at Attica Prison, penologists wondered if any reforms within the current prison framework would mollify such prisoners. The new militancy is widespread in the prison system and affects white inmates as well. President Nixon devoted more money and attention to the problem than any previous President, calling the prisons 'Universities of Crime', urging the need for humane prison reform. With gulfs between black and white, poor and very rich, the U.S. has special problems not affecting Sweden, Denmark or ourselves in Britain, although here in recent months there has flared up the problem of offenders claiming to be justified by political or patriotic motives, differing from the ordinary criminal in openly admitting that they are at war with the society they are attacking and regarding themselves as above the law. Prison officers here agree that this new wave has added to their difficulties. Members of the I.R.A. and U.D.A. are held in various Scottish prisons.

Nothing could better illustrate the absence of a consensus on the treatment of criminals than the debates in Parliament and the correspondence in *The Times* and other journals about the Re-habilitation of Offenders Act 1974. While there is general agree-ment with the humanitarian motive behind the Act: that a con-victed person who has paid the penalty for his crime, 'tholed his assize' in Scottish legal parlance, should in the absence of further offences suffer no further penalty, the methods proposed for the achievement of this worthy end have aroused the bitterest contro-

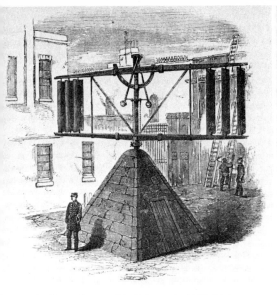

The treadmill was first used in Brixton in 1817. Male and female prisoners worked up to six hours daily merely to turn the fan pictured above. *National Library of Scotland*

David Haggart in the Iron Room of Edinburgh Prison while under sentence of death in 1821. *National Library of Scotland*

A prisoner at crank labour in his cell. The crank turned a blade set in a container of gravel. Over 1,000 turns were required daily and severe penalties were imposed for deficient performance. Both crank and treadmill were abolished in 1898. *National Library of Scotland*

Robert Fergusson, whose wretched death in Edinburgh Bedlam in 1774 had great influence on Andrew Duncan. *National Gallery of Scotland*

Dr Andrew Duncan, founder of an insane asylum in Edinburgh in 1813. *By permission of the University of Edinburgh*

The Bedlam Wing of the Edinburgh Charity Workhouse. *By Courtesy of Edinburgh Central Libraries*

…dburgh Jail (*right*), …oxburghshire, was built in …23. Note the fortress-like …pearance. *Royal Commission on …e Ancient and Historical …onuments of Scotland*

…alton Jail (*below*), on Calton …ll, Edinburgh, was begun in …08 to replace the Old …olbooth. *Reproduced by gracious …rmission of Her Majesty the …ueen*

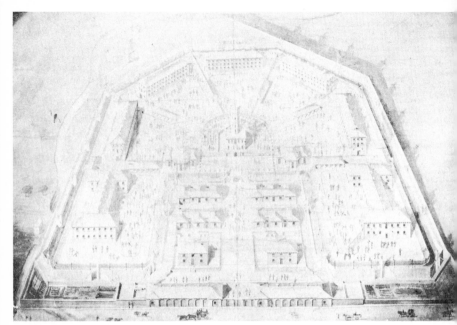

A plan of Perth Prison built in 1812 for the detention of French prisoners of war. *Royal Commission on the Ancient and Historical Monuments of Scotland*

Perth Prison showing the original octagonal tower. This is the oldest prison in Scotland still in use. *Royal Commission on the Ancient and Historical Monuments of Scotland*

ners exercising in the yard of Perth Prison, c. 1900. This yard is still in use. *Royal Commission* *e Ancient and Historical Monuments of Scotland*

warders of Greenock Prison, 1910. *Prison Service College, Polmont*

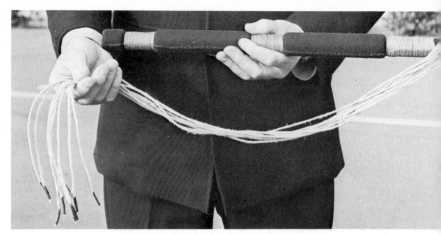

In 1948 Peterhead was the only Scottish prison where the cat might still have been used. Adul offenders received a maximum of twenty-one lashes. *Police Service College, Polmont*

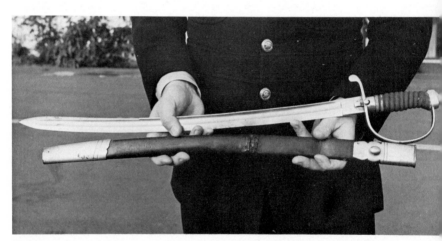

Cutlasses were carried by every warder at Peterhead Prison from its opening in 1888 until the were replaced by batons in 1939. Rifles were carried until 1959. *Police Service College, Polmont*

Peterhead Prison, 1950s. *The Scotsman*

Interior view and plan of a room in Cornton Vale, Scotland's only women's prison. Near Stirling and opened 1975–76, it is more reminiscent of a university campus than a prison.

hton Prison, Edinburgh, built after World War I. *The Scotsman*

The controversial cages at Inverness Prison. *The Scotsman*

The rose garden at Barlinnie Prison. *Glasgow Herald*

versy even among the most intelligent, reflective, and responsible individuals.

A Departmental Committee under the chairmanship of Lord Dunpark was set up to consider whether the Scottish courts should (as the English courts have been since 1972) be empowered after conviction to order the making of restitution by the offender to the victim of his crime. Their report was presented to the Secretary of State in July 1977.[91] The Committee saw no objection in principle to the introduction of an element of compensation into Scottish criminal procedure, and indeed they saw it as a reintroduction of an historical Scottish remedy which had existed until the late eighteenth century. In recommending its adoption they did not think it a valid objection that the majority of criminals are of small means and therefore incapable of making adequate reparation. It seemed proper that the courts should have discretion to order the criminal to pay according to his means, with the result that some victims would receive full restitution and many at least partial recompense. The trend in magistrates' courts in England and Wales was towards ordering compensation to be paid by every offender who could afford to pay something. An order for compensation could be imposed with or without a fine or sentence of imprisonment, but if with a fine and if the offender could not afford to pay both, then compensation should take precedence over the fine. Imprisonment should be the ultimate sanction for default in payment of compensation. It is clear that these discretionary powers, if given to the courts, could have the effect of reducing the prison population.

The Committee had however further considerations in mind, as evidenced by this paragraph in their Report:

'It seemed to us from evidence which we received that there may be some loss of public confidence in law enforcement, which is in part due to victims of crime being ignored by the criminal law. There has been a substantial increase in criminal prosecutions in recent years, with consequent increase in the number of offenders and victims involved in the criminal process. These prosecutions and the disposal of offenders receive much attention from the media. There is frequent suggestion that official attention and resources are bestowed exclusively, and in ever increasing amount, upon offenders. There is a view that offenders, whether in or out of prison, are maintained in comparative comfort by the state, and that little or nothing is being done for victims. Some victims may experience retributive satisfaction in the punishment of their offenders, but this does not make good the loss suffered. With crime at a high level the victim is unlikely to be confident that the penalty imposed on the offender will deter future offenders and protect him from further criminal activity. Thus, in our opinion and in the light of evidence received, it is important that the law should be seen to do something effective for the victims of crime.'[92]

More than 100,000 comparative orders were made in England in 1979, and about 71% of those found guilty of criminal damage were ordered to pay. In June 1980 Scots M.P.s approved the provision in the Criminal Justice (Scotland) Bill giving courts powers to enforce payment of compensation by offenders to their victims.

The Howard League for Penal Reform, with an optimism which seems hardly justified in the case of Scotland, claims that Britain's prison population is declining and that the Home Office should now start pulling down the old fortress prisons and replacing them by purpose-built remand centres, observation centres, and secure institutions, and that these should not be sited in remote areas which create difficulties as regards visiting, employment for prisoners, and recruitment of staff. The League also proposes a ceiling of ten years on any sentence except life imprisonment, and a programme of alternatives including adult probation hostels, bail hostels, non-custodial measures, fewer remands in custody before trial. Here they are attempting to answer our third question (improvements in the treatment of those in custody) at the same time as the second; and indeed the two questions are really inseparable since the so-called 'open prison' is open only in the sense that the prisoner is allowed freedom of movement within defined limits, and should he go beyond these permitted limits he will immediately be sent back to a closed prison; some such sanctions must obviously operate in whatever conditions the offender is controlled. Even the substitution of community service orders (England 1972, Scotland 1978) and day training centres (not yet in Scotland) for prisons with or without bars would need sanctions for those who refused to cooperate. 'Control in the community is

... certainly less costly than imprisonment; but is it practicable and can it ever be effective as a protective measure?'[93] The Home Office Research Unit, commenting on the newest form of non-custodial disposal, community service orders, observed that, 'There was no evidence of any reduction in re-conviction rates following community service'.[94] The new bail law, which no longer requires payment of bail as a guarantee of release from prison, came into effect on 1 April 1980. It is too early to tell whether it will effectively reduce the remand population. The controversial Criminal Justice (Scotland) Bill (1980) introduces police powers to stop and search, to detain for six hours and to interrogate.

The reformers make various suggestions for improving conditions for those who must be kept in custody in the prisons proper. The size of the prisons is criticised on the ground that it makes classification and individual treatment impossible; so it is urged that the number of staff be increased and that they be paid higher salaries to attract a better calibre of recruit; also that modern scientific methods of treatment be adopted. Certain punishments should be abolished, in particular solitary confinement, which is sometimes imposed for periods of several months upon very disturbed, aggressive men and which, it is argued, may actually aggravate paranoid conditions and therefore should be replaced by individual psychological treatment or group therapy.[95] Dietary punishments too come under attack,[96] together with the stopping of letters and visits, which punishes not only the offender himself but also his innocent family. And it is argued that forfeiture of earnings and the loss of association and of remission can only have a detrimental effect on the prisoner's morale. (One might reply that it is one thing to propose treatment in place of punishment for those in need of it, but as regards those who do not need it but are incorrigible troublemakers we are not told what sanctions are to be substituted for existing forms of punishment.) It is suggested that prisoners be allowed more visits and more letters, the latter uncensored. Few would quarrel with the complaint that the time awaiting trial is too long, but the remedy is not in the hands of the prison authorities, the trouble arising from under-manned police forces, under-staffed Procurator Fiscal services and overlong court lists.

There is great concern about the problems arising after release; it is felt that there are too few open prisons, part of whose function it is to prepare prisoners for release; the discharge grant of a few pounds, recently raised, should be increased further, more hostels should be built to provide accommodation, and there should be greatly improved probation and aftercare services. The purpose of the Training for Freedom (T.F.F.) scheme is to provide conditions in which an inmate's ability to live in the community can be tested while he is under sentence, and to ease his transition to normal life on release. Selected inmates live in hostels attached to penal establishments and go out daily, unescorted, to work with outside employers. Their sentences must be more than four years in length.

The result of an enquiry into the United Kingdom prison service, ordered by the Home Secretary, was published in October 1979. It covered pay, conditions, financial resources, and industrial relations. The May Committee's Report declared that an extension of the prison-building programme to replace Britain's antiquated jails, reduce serious overcrowding, and improve conditions for staff and inmates is urgently required. The Report also called for reductions in the prison population by keeping out the mentally disordered, petty offenders, fine and maintenance defaulters, alcoholics, and the socially inadequate. It stressed that the worst prison buildings were very bad indeed and recommended that Dartmoor should be closed. 'What was permissible in a convict prison for the rigours of penal servitude on the reoccupied Napoleonic site of the 1850s is nowadays simply against nature'.[97] Peterhead Prison, scene of much recent unrest and riots, should be 'substantially redeveloped', and it was urged that new prison building should eliminate cell-sharing other than in dormitories or special enlarged cells and that integral sanitation and washrooms should be the aim. The disgusting practice of 'slopping out' is still the custom in many British prisons. It was fully realised what all these reforms would cost but they were felt to be essential. However, we have comfortably accepted decades of neglect of prison building and in the present grave economic climate in Britain there is not much hope that Government or local authorities will have money to invest in new non-custodial facilities for offenders.

Prison staff still feel that they are underpaid and overworked, and trapped in a forgotten backwater. But governments have always been loath to spend public funds on the prison service. Radzinowicz says (*Spectator* 1977) 'I'm afraid that penal reform will always occupy the last place in the long queue of social priorities'.

The May Report praised the dedication of prison staff to their frequently very difficult tasks, carried out in most cases in very poor working conditions; it supported the claims by officers that facilities for staff were 'very poor indeed' [98] when compared with those for prisoners; advocated that ideally there should be no overtime; and sympathised with their complaint of many years standing that their role was that of mere turnkeys.

It remains to be seen how many of these plans and suggestions will be adopted and how long it will be before they are implemented.

Conclusion

In the words of the May Report, 'It has been clear to us that the prison system has not moved in any single and consistent direction during its history, but that its form and ethos have passed through a number of distinct and separate phases'.[1]

Before the nineteenth century the general attitude of society and of the authorities was to discard offenders, to regard them as beyond redemption, or to be indifferent to that possibility; to get them out of sight as swiftly and permanently as possible by execution, banishment or transportation, or to mete out brutal punishments (such as mutilation or public humiliation), which it was hoped would act as effective deterrents. Alternatively, in certain cases crimes were regarded not as against society but as against the victim, and the offender was allowed to pay his debt by monetary or other compensation (assythment) to the victim or his relations. The function of prison was purely custodial.

With the abolition of heritable jurisdictions and with the gradual development of more civilised and more humane attitudes, the ending of transportation, and the growing centralisation of authority, savage physical punishments or banishment from the parish, or from the country by transportation, became either unacceptable to public opinion or no longer practicable. Capital punishment then became restricted to the gravest crimes – murder or treason which directly threatened the central authority – and the existence of prison buildings previously used to house French prisoners of war, and much more effective than the old insecure jails, provided a more obvious solution in the shape of custodial sentences. Imprisonment then moved into first place as the major sanction of British criminal law.

Thus the central authority was forced to take the responsibility for the treatment of all offenders; and this was a novel problem on which it could not draw from accumulated experience.

Since the end of transportation there has been a slow but continuing trend towards the mitigation of prison conditions; this trend quickened in the first half of the twentieth century and has further accelerated in the last twenty years with an increasing emphasis on the rehabilitation of the offender and on efforts to treat him in the community rather than behind prison walls.

So we come, after a 'pattern of "progress" from the capricious cruelty of the eighteenth century, through the cold barbarity of the nineteenth, to the enlightened policies of the twentieth'.[2] But in this century, the tendency has been to forget the victim and the damage done to society, and to concentrate all efforts on ameliorating conditions for the offender and rehabilitating him, with the result that one of the primary or logical purposes of imprisonment, i.e. deterrence, has been apt to become overlooked or at any rate given less than due consideration.

In this 'progressive' age much interest is shown in the aftermath of imprisonment and the problems of recidivism, and the endeavour to rehabilitate offenders in the community is regarded as supremely important.[3] But 'This attempt to combine the incompatible philosophies of punishment and reformation still divides penologists and confuses the public'.[4] Public opinion still lags behind reformers' ideas of criminals' 'proper treatment' and remains emotional and inconsistent. Despite the uneasy atmosphere in prisons today, and the organisations proliferating to improve the conditions of inmates, the general public remains largely unmoved and uninterested unless some particularly sensational event seizes its attention. It is still true to say that 'Society couldn't care less once the man has gone down the steps from the dock'.[5] Meanwhile the incidence of crimes of violence soars, the public is no safer, recidivism increases.[6]

The law defines what is a crime and reflects the values of society as a whole. Our tomorrow's judgement may be different from today's, we may 'come to tolerate a certain amount of nonconformity. Already, male homosexual acts between consenting adults are no longer a crime. Nor is attempted suicide.[7] Abortion is increasingly legalised and censorship is eased. Perhaps a lot of people who are criminals today would no longer be regarded as criminals tomorrow'.[8] Acts called 'crimes' in one age become permissible in another or frankly disbelieved (for instance, witchcraft), and punishments fitted to an affluent society will not do for a poorer one. Inevitably new crimes are created and some abolished as society grows more sophisticated.

The present trend towards amelioration of prison conditions may be an over-reaction to the unduly harsh treatment of prisoners in the past. Has it gone too far? A positive conclusion cannot be drawn except that we know 70% to 80% of ex-prisoners are not deterred from offending further. All we can say is that prison does not seem to have been an effective reformatory influence or a deterrent to those who have already been offenders. We are in the realm of pure speculation when we ask whether improved or harsher prison conditions would lessen or increase recidivism. It does however seem reasonable to hazard a guess that if the process of amelioration were to go too far recidivism would increase: while if conditions were too severe the prisoner might become brutalised to the point of being driven to further crime. Somehow a balance must be struck.

'The Law Society in England have produced proposals for reforms in legal punishment; the S.N.P. have a programme of measures for the treatment of criminals and delinquents; the judges' *obiter*, the bodies, the parliamentarians, the party machines and the man-in-the-street, all make pronouncements on individual aspects, or over the whole field of criminal punishment. Every man his own penologist. This is an embattled area. There is no cosy consensus ... There is neither consensus nor clear thinking, nor research nor surveys, on which to base firm conclusions.'⁹

Postscript

In the course of visits to the Scottish prisons, what struck me was the seeming sincerity of all ranks of prison staff, their concern for the welfare of the prisoners in their charge; their progressive and at the same time realistic, unsentimental, and open-minded outlook; and their comments, pertinent and apposite.

The opinion prevailed that capital punishment, appalling as it might be, was a lesser evil than the increasingly long sentences now being meted out, which have the effect of reducing men to mere vegetables. They would not have disagreed with Paterson's ideas on this subject, nor with the comment by Radzinowicz, 'The time limit, in a good prison, to reform a man, not to destroy him, is about 3 years. If after 3 years he is not reformed – not influenced for the better – his chances are very slender and after 5 years he becomes a real liability.'[1]

Probation and community training should be greatly extended, and this could reduce prison population by half. But the feeling generally was that public opinion was not yet fully in support. There should be higher wages for prison work, and the opinion was that the Trade Unions as well as the Treasury were at fault here. There was a general feeling among prison officers that successive governments, while lavish in their spending of public money on other objectives, are too reluctant to allocate funds for prevention of crime and the rehabilitation of prisoners. Almost all were in favour of more visits and letters but opinion varied on home leaves and conjugal visits. It was considered that the latter are unnatural in the prison environment and create too many tensions in both parties. One particularly clear-sighted officer advocated home leaves every three months, to be increased thereafter. These should be given from the very beginning of a long-term sentence, not just in the last four years, and he stressed that leaves should be given this way or not at all as otherwise they 'are worse than useless'. Such schemes have been successfully pioneered in California and Toronto. In this way marriages would have a much better chance of survival and families' long, exhausting journeys to prisons for brief visits would be ended.

Staff have special problems with prisoners 'under protection' for their own safety, for example on account of epilepsy, or because of their being guilty of cruelty to or molestation of children (the latter class hated and harried by all other prisoners). Often they have to be kept in single cells on the ground floor near the offices. At one prison, one such inmate refuses ever to come out of his cell without the protection of an officer.

There are comparatively few of the professional classes in prison. The majority of prisoners in Scotland, as in most countries, are emotionally immature, come predominantly from the lower economic and social strata of society; many are almost illiterate and many have an I.Q. of 80–85. A great number are undersized and stunted (although the 'tough customers' in top security are often strong, well built and intelligent). A member of a visiting committee remarked that you have 'to fight against a feeling of pity all the time, otherwise you would never be able to discipline them when they come up before you'.

Punishment cells in closed prisons (sometimes underground with only a stone bed and a Bible of which 'we are not allowed to deprive the prisoner') are seen by some as serving a useful purpose, a 'cooling off process'. Immured here for forty-eight hours or 'whatever Governor orders', those endeavouring 'to beat the system' by insolence, disobedience, or fighting other inmates are brought under control. Solitary confinement cells, of which Peterhead, for example, has fifteen, serve the same purpose.

The controversial five segregation cells known as the 'cages' at Inverness Prison are in a different category as punishment. They are intended for occupation by very violent prisoners with previous convictions, transferred from various prisons and guilty of grievous bodily harm to prison officers. They were not used from March 1973 until December 1978 when an inmate who attacked a prison officer with a razor and inflicted serious injury was sent there. He had seventeen previous convictions and had been involved in four prison assaults. Each barred 'cage' is inside an ordinary prison cell. The bed is a fixed wooden platform some three inches off the floor. Apart from the bedding the only movable item is a plastic chamber-pot. There is a fixed triangular table top in one corner against the bars, and a 'rounded seat of concrete growing, just like a mushroom stalk without a head, out of the floor'. One man spent nineteen months in a cage. The only people the prisoner sees are those guarding him. Exercise (alone) is one hour daily under guard in a segregated yard surrounded by an eighteen-foot fence. The prisoners eat alone in their cells and if conditions permit, work there alone, thus twenty-three out of twenty-four hours are spent in isolation.

The experiment of the Barlinnie Special Unit, a jail within a jail, has created world-wide interest. Seventeen men have been through the Special Unit since its inception in 1973. When capital punishment ended, a new type of prisoner appeared, young, ruthlessly violent, and with nothing to lose because society had nothing to punish him with except an even more indeterminate sentence. To make matters worse, such men proved they could trigger off extreme violence and become the heroes of a prison sub-culture. There are also now large numbers imprisoned for offences connected with terrorism. In the 1960s there were forty serious incidents in Scottish prisons, already struggling with the problems of overcrowding and under-staffing. The Scottish Prison Officers Association demanded a change - many of them were in real danger and under intolerable pressure - so the Special Unit was opened in the former women's wing of Barlinnie. Unique in Europe, it isolated the most violent and disruptive members of the Scottish prison population. In April 1980 five inmates were serving life sentences for murder, including Boyle, two other had six sentences between them for violent assault. Inmates do not wear uniform, have a say in how the Unit should be run, pursue a variety of hobbies and enjoy relaxed visiting rules. The scheme remains an experiment and has aroused much controversy. One often-heard criticism is that the really 'bad boys' are being given all the advantages of special treatment, but it is a brave experiment and one that deserves to be studied carefully.

To add to the modern prison officer's many problems of control is the fact that now psychiatric hospitals can take mentally disordered offenders only with a degree of security which the courts feel offers insufficient protection to the public. But their presence adds to the control problems in prisons and can be as disturbing to inmates as to staff – back to 'lunatics in prison'?

The general atmosphere of the prisons varies enormously, from the cheerfulness of Penninghame Open Prison and the flower-filled 'rooms' with gay curtains and bedspreads of Cornton Vale to the grey gloom and dinginess of Barlinnie, where the over-crowding is daunting. Here prisoners are often 'threed-up' in a cell, and the huge number of young men on remand, wandering aimlessly around, has as depressing an effect as the purposelessness of the occupants of the 'hall of the inadequates'.

Peterhead has its own distinctive atmosphere. This prison can accommodate 330 men, with a top-security wing housing some thirty really 'hard cases'. The doubly-secured perimeter is con-stantly patrolled, but the prison area is too large for effective supervision. The dreary environment and the grim climate have a bad effect on prisoners and officers alike and from October morale deteriorates in the face of the winter ahead. Gale-force winds come howling in from the North Sea, the men have to cross a great stretch of concrete to the work-shops; they get soaked going there and soaked coming back. 'Peterhead is a terrible place. Conditions are bad', is the comment one hears in every prison. Sufficient money has not been allocated for improvements. The buildings, dating from 1886, are antiquated, the cells primitive and some so tiny that there is hardly room to turn round, there are heating problems from the ancient pipes so that the cells can be stifling hot or freezing cold. There are no facilities for rehabil-itation or recreation proper, no dining hall, so that all must eat in cells, and work facilities are inadequate although two new build-ings for educational purposes have been built. So frustration, boredom and resentment are fostered and increase, a fact which unrest and many roof demonstrations illustrate all too clearly. Here as in all prisons sex offenders must be segregated to protect them from the wrath of the other inmates. So some twenty-one 'inadequates' live and eat together in a twilight world.

Cornton Vale, replacing Gateside in Greenock as the only women's prison in Scotland, was built by Borstal labour in 1975. It was envisaged as a move away from the punitive concept of prison and is described in a Scottish Home and Health Department pamphlet as a 'Vale of Hope'. As in women's prisons generally in the U.K. it is not nearly full and there is no shortage of work. Designed to hold 220 prisoners including adults, young offenders, Borstal inmates and those on remand, Cornton Vale has only about 117 inmates including 30 on remand (1982). Entirely new in concept and design it consists of a complex of buildings in which the hard fact of confinement is skilfully camouflaged by ornamental wrought iron-work in place of merely functional bars, by landscaped gardens with carefully-tended flowerbeds, and a charming pond for good measure. Instead of galleries of cells in large central blocks, the institution – the word 'prison' is avoided – is dispersed into small 'cottage' units, each holding seven inmates with their own comfortable 'rooms', not cells, a kitchen, a large communal sitting-room with armchairs and T.V. and a mother and baby unit. The inmates occupy their time with domestic work, laundry, baking, gardening, making of soft toys and other crafts. The whole emphasis is on brightness and cheerfulness – the women are clad in differently-coloured dresses of their own choice – and determined efforts are made to encourage the wrongdoer to think of the future rather than to contemplate her crimes.

Penninghame Open Prison near Newton Stewart was opened in 1954 in a nineteenth-century mansion standing in spacious grounds. It has accommodation for seventy-five men, housed in dormitories. More than half are employed in the gardens and in outside work in village and surrounding farms, and the rest on maintenance on the premises. They enter into the life of the outside community, help with building and gardening projects and give extremely popular concerts and plays. A number are allowed home for Christmas for five days, all returning at the required hour. Many more such excellent open prisons are needed.

The work inspected at the different prisons varied considerably. After watching (at Perth, Saughton, Barlinnie) the half-hearted, dispirited sewing of mailbags, making of fishing nets, breaking up of old PO cables, fashioning of suits for anti-biological warfare, one understood the futility of so many prisoners' days. But hearing the hum of the excellently-equipped joiner's shop at Perth where men worked busily, intently, and seeing the bright, gay colours in the painter's shop where the inmates obviously enjoy their work on all kinds of children's toys, made it obvious that employment and prison industry could become less soul-destroying. The prisoners, clad in pink-striped shirts and shapeless brown serge trousers, are eager to work in the laundry as thus they always contrive to look smart. 'You can pick out the laundry workers at exercise.' The shoe shop at Perth produces the shoes for all the Scottish prisons, dozens of boots and smaller shoes for 'the ladies of Cornton Vale'.

Aberdeen prisoners work at nets for fishing and oilrigs, machine-knit sweaters and socks (120 pairs a day), and repair shoes for all the Scottish prisons. Peterhead makes nets too, turns out denim overalls, and had a good joiner's shop which the prisoners destroyed themselves. (At Aberdeen, an 'evil core' of some twelve men consistently destroyed a pool table which had given a great deal of pleasure to many prisoners. As fast as it was mended it was again destroyed. Lacking weapons, the vandals used their bare hands. This posed yet another problem for the burdened staff.) Saughton has book-binding and printing; and from time to time in the different prisons there are exhibitions of prisoners' work, including paintings, and boxes made with hundreds of matches, recalling those of French prisoners of war.

Visits to prisons on the Continent and in America are of value in revealing similarities and differences between the British and foreign attitude to prisons; we can learn from them. The earliest part of the prison at Rothenburg in the state of Baden-Württemberg was built in 1810; Germany had no transportation facilities and so her prisons were built earlier than ours. Part of the building dates from 1906 and with its galleries and cells is almost identical to those of Britain and the U.S.A. The prison should house 420 but has 550 serving short sentences of up to a year, often longer if under interrogation or appeal. Category A prisoners have one man to a cell, others two or three. Out of a population of eight million Baden-Württemberg has 7,000 prisoners. The vast majority are manual workers with low IQs and over 75% are recidivists. There is only one women's prison in the state, with about 90 to 100 inmates (roughly the same ratio as in Scotland). Rothenburg resembled British prisons save that all cells had flush toilets, and the young assistant Governor who showed us round (in 1978) expressed surprise when told of conditions in the U.K. In the modern block are no galleries but ordinary corridors and the 'rooms' have curtains, carpets, and wash-hand basins. Inmates can earn up to 60-70 marks a month (£15-£16). The yearly un-supervised leave of eighteen days is a right not a privilege, and cannot be lost through misbehaviour; it is not granted to danger-ous offenders. Over 90% return when due. Visits every two weeks are also a right and cannot be forfeited.

In 1949 the Federal constitution of West Germany abolished capital punishment. The assistant Governor of Rothenburg said 'I don't believe in revenge but I think it a very bad thing to have abandoned capital punishment.' He went on to say that he thought death was too easy for terrorists (the Baader-Meinhof gang are centred in the state), who should be imprisoned for life under very stringent conditions. The problem of placing terrorists has not been solved - it is too dangerous to put them all in one prison. A life sentence in Germany usually *means* life, but some domestic murderers are released after 20-22 years! No parole system as we know it exists, but remission is usually granted after two-thirds of sentence is served. This does not depend entirely on good be-haviour as in Britain but on condition of approval of the Governor and the State Attorney. There is not much chance of alternative treatment for fine-evaders, vagrants, drug addicts and so on, as 'they have broken the law of the constitution of 1949 and therefore *must* go to prison'.

West Germany has none of our problems with Trade Unions in regard to prison labour, but there is difficulty in getting work for prisoners as the quality produced is poor and so commercial firms show little interest in it. Recreation in the prison presents difficulties owing to shortage of staff, and as there is no dining hall all meals are taken in cells.

An immensely high wall surrounds the prison, yet thirty-five escaped in 1973 (not all at once!), though in time all were recap-tured. 'These escapes caused us much sorrow and much paper-work' was the rueful comment. As in Britain there is reluctance on the part of the Government to spend money on prisons.

The prison at Fleury-Mérôgis near Paris received its first inmates in 1968 and is designed as a remand centre (Maison d'Arrêt) to replace the Santé and Fresnes. It is a vast complex on a 50-acre site and has cell accommodation for 3,112 men, 430 women, and 560 young offenders aged eighteen to twenty-one. About 40% are convicted of lesser crimes and serve up to three years at Fleury. The rest are on remand, many accused of serious crimes and if convicted are sent elsewhere. Bail in France is very rare and people can spend years on remand. They are allowed visitors daily. There is no work for them as not enough is available. From a catwalk 12 feet above the ground officers can observe the convicted engaged in skilled work – the manufacture of automobile parts, for example, for which they can earn £300 a month. 'Libération conditionelle' (parole) may be granted after serving half the sentence. France still has the guillotine but seldom uses it.

In this ultramodern prison all cells have lavatories and wash-hand basins. In the exercise yard men play football, run races. 'We can have 1,000 men at exercise at any one time.' When inmates have to be moved any distance they are taken in an electrically driven minibus which moves within the building. Four tried to escape recently (1979), pulling guns, but were shot down at once.

There is an alarmingly high suicide rate at Fleury-Mérôgis. The prison is so huge and so clinical that it creates neurosis, especially among those used to the squalor of the slums. They feel isolated, lost. One formed the impression there (1979) that even Peterhead was somehow more homely and human. Its sheer scale seems to dwarf and diminish the ordinary human being to an intolerable extent (there is a lesson here for our future planning) as do the mechanics of the place – electronic controls separate each of the five 'trepales' or cell units. Each trepale has three sections with accommodation for 600 inmates. The same percentage as in Britain and Germany return to prison; rehabilitation was not mentioned.

In the U.S., to quote Radzinowicz, there is a climate of crime far more extreme than our own. There is more of it and it is more violent. There are as many murders in Manhattan each year as in the whole of England and Wales and the crime rate is rising. According to the *U.S. Report on Corrections 1973* over half the adult prisoners in American State institutions are in maximum security prisons, some of which are 'dark, dingy, depressing dungeons'. Many local jails, especially in large cities, are dangerously over-crowded and conditions are often gruesome with violence en-demic. I have visited none of these places. The only American prison I have seen was the nineteenth-century Charles Street Jail (Suffolk county), Boston, Massachusetts, where 200 prisoners, the majority untried, are held sometimes for months. It proved an astonishing contrast to Scottish prisons. A free-and-easy atmosphere prevailed. Above the prison entrance the surprising notice 'All persons entering the jail must surrender fire-arms'.

There are both men and women at Charles Street. The women prison officers, clad in white uniforms, are middle-aged or elderly, plump and cosy, reminiscent of smiling matrons in a pleasant British preparatory school. On arrival inmates are told reassuringly that they are entitled to be treated as human beings.[2] The majority of the prisoners are black; forty were being accused of first-degree murder. The felonies represented are chiefly armed robbery, second-degree murder, unarmed robbery and rape. If convicted, felons are transferred to State Prisons; those guilty of misdemeanours to Houses of Correction. There is no death penalty in Massachusetts, but life means what it says, though convicts become eligible for parole after fifteen years.

In the euphemistically named 'Boys' Town', that part of Charles Street Prison for those under eighteen, the inmates are locked in their cells from 4 pm for sixteen hours. There is nothing for them to do, no work unless they choose. All prisoners are allowed T.V. and radio in cells, bringing in their own sets. 'Lights out' is not till 11 pm and listening in on earphones may continue indefinitely. There are never three in a cell. Flush toilets are taken for granted; on hearing of the sanitary conditions common to many British prisons, the officials professed total disbelief. Confinement in solitary cells may be imposed as punishment, but writing and reading materials and daily exercise are permitted while there. Prisoners are allowed any number of uncensored letters, and any sentenced inmate, doing thirty days or more, is eligible for remission of five days for each pint of blood donated to an approved agency, the limit being five donations yearly. Basketball, pool, checkers, and chess are played in rotation. Men and women used to be in chapel together, but their behaviour resulted in the chaplain refusing to preach and the sexes are now separated.

The Director of Education and Rehabilitation (an attorney at law and lecturer at Boston University), was refreshingly free from cant. To the question 'Do you find you are getting anywhere with rehabilitation?' he replied honestly, without hesitation, 'Nowhere at all. Nowhere at all.'

As well as the growing racial problem, the prison officers 'have every problem there is. But nothing bothers me any more. Murder in America means nothing. Coping with such conditions you either go insane or you adjust to them.'

On the women's side of the prison an even freer atmosphere was apparent, the inmates addressing the staff with insolent familiarity and demands to air their grievances. I was introduced to a young black woman who had been involved in a murder. She had been returned from Massachusetts Correctional Institution at Framingham to Boston for causing trouble. Framingham is a pioneer prison and has been called a 'cross between a college campus and a country club'. There every effort is made to please and cushion the offender; little work is done, and much time is spent in the open-air swimming pool and watching television. This inmate was to 'serve' (a misnomer) for a year at Charles Street before being freed, presumably unrepentant and resentful.

There may be a lesson here for Scottish and English prisons for the Framingham experiment has boldly advanced far along the road which we are now treading with increasing rapidity. Since my visit in 1973 authorities at Framingham have gone even further towards 'correction reform' It has become 'the nation's first co-ed prison'. Some inmates work outside in the community, others not so eligible may work inside, sewing American flags or similar tasks. No uniform is worn, the inmates may wear as bizarre clothes as they please. Men and women eat, swim and associate together. About the time of my visit several couples who met there were married on trips away from the prison, without permission from the authorities. Framingham is to date (1980) 'the only State Prison in the US where men and women are allowed to mingle', although several more are planned. The woman clinical psychologist who is superintendent, believes this to be a more realistic approach to prison life, and hopes Framingham 'will become a model for all other institutions in the nation, a model for people learning to get along together and developing mutual respect'.[3]

However, the Director at Charles Street may have the last word. To the question 'Does Framingham cut down convictions?' he replied 'No, not at all. The numbers are just as great as ever'.

The whole enormous problem facing our penal authorities may be thus expressed. There is always a conflict between the custodial and treatment policies of an institution; that is, to protect society from the criminal activities of the prisoner, and to rehabilitate him. The aims may seem incompatible but both are vital.

Bibliography and References

SELECT BIBLIOGRAPHY

This list does not include every source mentioned in the notes. It is intended as a convenient reference for the general reader who might wish to make a further study of the subject.

PRIMARY SOURCES
M.S.S.
Bloody Roll of Perth (S.R.O.)
Minute Book of the Prisons 1839-40, 53-54
The Bridewell Commitment Book 1798-1804
Governors' Journals of Perth Prison 1845-55 and 1862-65
Governors' Journals of Glasgow, Duke Street Prison 1848-51
Governors' Journals of Greenock Prison 1848-72

Pamphlets and Booklets
Willox, Rev. Henry, *Her Majesty's Pleasure in Scotland* and other matters concerning criminal lunatics and mental defectives of violent tendencies and criminal propensities. (Carnwath 1967)
State Hospital, Carstairs – *The Scottish Special Hospital* (Paper prepared by State Hospital, Feb., 1974)

Printed Records
The Register of the Privy Council of Scotland edited by Hume Brown. 3rd series, vols. I and II (Edinburgh 1909)
Pitcairn's Ancient Criminal Trials in Scotland 3 vols. (Bannatyne Club 1833)

Law Publications
Arnot, H., *Collected Celebrated Criminal Trials in Scotland 1536-1784* (Edin. 1785)
Hume, D., *Commentaries on the Law of Scotland respecting Crimes*. Vols. I and II (1829)
MacKenzie, Sir G., *The Laws and Customs of Scotland in Matters Criminal* (1699)

H.M.S.O. Publications
Prisons in Scotland. Reports for 1968-80
Parole Board for Scotland. Reports for 1968-80
Report on The Reduction of Pressure on the Prison System Vol. I 1977-78
Reparation by the Offender to the Victim in Scotland 1977
Committee of Inquiry into the U.K. Prison Services. (The May Report 1979)

SECONDARY SOURCES

Aikin, J., *A view of the character and public services of the late John Howard* (London 1792)

Badello, J., and Haynes, M., *A Bill of No Rights: Attica and the American Prison System* (New York 1972)

Barrow, G. W. S., *Robert Bruce*. (Eyre and Spottiswoode 1965)

Burt, E., *Letters from a Gentleman in the North of Scotland, 1726*. (London 1818)

Casse, G. R., *A Prisoner of France, 1809-14*. (London Edition, Howard Baker 1976)

Chambers, R., *Domestic Annals of Scotland from the Reformation to the Revolution*. (Edinburgh 1859)

Chambers, W., *Memoir of W. and R. Chambers*. (2nd edition Edinburgh 1893)

Clarke, M., *His Natural Life*. (Edited by S. Murray-Smith, Penguin Books 1970)

Cockburn, H., *Memorials of his Time*. (Edinburgh 1909)

Cowan, I., *The Scottish Covenanters 1660-88*. (Gollancz 1976)

Cross, R., *Punishment, Prison and the Public*. (Stevens & Sons 1971)

Dickinson, W. C., *Scotland from the earliest times to 1603*. (Oliver and Boyd 1930)

Dickinson, W. C., and Donaldson, G., *A Source Book of Scottish History*. 3 vols. (2nd edition, 1958-61)

Dickinson, W. C., and G. S. Pryde. *The New History of Scotland*. 2 vols. (Nelson 1961-2)

Donaldson, G., *The Scottish Reformation*. (C.U.P. 1960)

— *The Scots Overseas*. (London 1966)

— *Scottish Kings*. (Batsford 1967)

— *Scotland: James V to James VII*, vol III in the Edinburgh History of Scotland. (Oliver and Boyd 1971)

— *Scotland: Church and Nation through sixteen centuries*. (2nd edition, Scottish Academic Press 1972)

— *Scotland: The Shaping of a Nation*. (David and Charles 1974)

Dunbar, J., *The Historic Architecture of Scotland*. (Batsford 1966)

Early Travellers in Scotland. edit. Hume Brown. (Edinburgh 1891)

Fitzgerald, P. J., *Criminal Law and Punishment*. (Oxford 1962)

Garneray, L., *The French Prisoner*. Translated by L. Wood. (London 1957)

Grant, I. F., *Social and Economic Development of Scotland before 1603*. (Oliver and Boyd 1930)

Grant, J., *Old and New Edinburgh*. 3 vols. (Cassell)

Gurney, J. J., *Notes on a visit made to some of the Prisons in Scotland and the North of England 1818*. (London 1819)

Hibbert, C., *The Roots of Evil. A Social History of Crime and Punishment*. (Penguin 1966)

Howard, D. L., *John Howard, Prison Reformer*. (London 1958)

Howard, J., *The State of the Prisons in England and Wales with an account of some foreign prisons 1777/1780 and 1784*. (Everyman edition 1929)

Johnson, W., *The English Prison Hulks*. (Johnson 1957)

Klare, H., *People in Prison*. (Pitman's Eye on Society Series 1973)

Knox, J., *The History of the Reformation in Scotland*. (2 vols. ed. D. Laing, 1846-8, and W. C. Dickinson 1949)

Mayhew, H., and Binny, J., *The Criminal Prisons of London and Scenes of Prison Life*. (1895)

Neild, J., *The State of the Prisons in England, Scotland and Wales 1812*. (London, John Nichols & Son)

Nicholson, R. G., *The Later Middle Ages*. Edinburgh History of Scotland. (Oliver and Boyd 1974)

Peacock, D., *Perth: Its Annals and its Archives*. (Perth 1849)

Penny, G., *Traditions of Perth*. (Perth 1836)

Radzinowicz, Sir Leon, *The Growth of Crime*. (Hamish Hamilton 1977)

Rae, J., *Conscience and Politics. The British Government and the C.O. to Military Service 1916-19* (O.U.P. 1970)

Ruck, S., *Paterson on Prisons. Collected Papers of Sir A. Paterson*. (1951)

Sievwright, W., *Historical Sketch of the Old Depot or Prison for French prisoners of war at Perth*. (1894)

— *Historical Sketch of the General Prison for Scotland at Perth*. (1894)

Smout, T. C., *A History of the Scottish People 1560-1830*. (Collins 1969)

Thomas, J. E., *The English Prison Officer since 1850*. (Routledge and Kegan Paul 1972)

Tobias, J., *Nineteenth Century Crime, Prevention and Punishment*. (David and Charles 1972)

Walker, N., *Crime and Punishment in Britain*. (E.U.P. 1965)

Whitney, J., *Elizabeth Fry*. (Guild Books 1947)

Wilde, O., *The Ballad of Reading Gaol*. (Complete Works, Collins 1969)

Wildeblood, P., *Against the Law*. (Harmondsworth, Penguin Books 1955)

Youngson, A. J., *The Highlands after the Forty-Five*. (E.U.P.)

Zeno. *Life*. (Macmillan 1963)

REFERENCES

Chapter 1: Medieval Scotland

★ See note 45.

† See note 13.

1. Ralph Pugh: *Imprisonment in Mediaeval England* (C.U.P. 1970) p. 2.

2. W. C. Dickinson: *Scotland from the earliest times to 1603* (Nelson 1961) p. 59.

3. John Macintosh: *The History of Civilisation in Scotland*, Vol. I (Edinburgh 1878) p. 241.

4. *The Court Book of the Barony of Urie in Kincardineshire, 1604–1747*, edited and introduced by D. G. Barron (Scottish History Society 1892, Vol. XII) Introduction p. VI.

    Cosmo Innes points out that when the King gave the Four Pleas of the Crown to religious houses, the abbots were given 'the direct appeal to heaven by ordeal. The abbots of all our great monasteries had this higher jurisdiction. The Abbot of Scone had a specific grant of the island in the Tay for the trial of accused persons by water, by hot iron, by duel.' *Lectures on Scotch Legal Antiquities* (Edinburgh 1872) p. 61.

5. *Acts of the Parliaments of Scotland*, Ass. Dav. C.17.I.320.

6. *A.P.S.* Leg. Mal. Mak. C.9. I.711.

7. *The Court Book of the Barony of Carnwath, 1528–42*, edited and with an introduction by W. C. Dickinson. (Scottish History Society 3rd series Vol. XXIX 1937) p. XLIII.

8. *Court Book of Urie*, op. cit., p. XVII.

9. ibid.

10. *Court Book of Carnwath*, op. cit., p. LXXX.

11. ibid., pp. CIII, CVIII.

12. T. C. Smout: *A History of the Scottish People, 1560–1830* (Collins 1969) p. 102.

13. *Early Travellers in Scotland*, edited by Hume Brown (Edinburgh 1891) p. 43.

14. C. A. Malcolm: *Old Scottish Prisons*, Scots Magazine 1932, Vol. 17, p. 55.

15. W. Douglas Simpson: *Dunvegan Castle, Isle of Skye, Official Guide* (Aberdeen University Press 1957) p. 11.

16. Carnwath, op. cit., p. XXVII.

17. W. Mackay Mackenzie: *The Mediaeval Castle in Scotland* (Methuen 1927) pp. 106–7.

18. Robert Pitcairn: *Ancient Criminal Trials in Scotland, 1488-1542*, Vol. I, Part I (Bannatyne Club 1833) p. 52.

19. Robert Chambers: *Domestic Annals of Scotland from the Reformation to the Revolution*, Vol. I (Edinburgh 1859) p. 52.

20. W. C. Dickinson, op. cit., p. 95.

21. *Court Book of Balnakeilly 1699-1745*, owned by Mrs Stewart Stevens of Balnakeilly, Pitlochry.

22. George Hay: *Architecture of Scotland* (Oriel Press 1969) p. 72.

23. *Extracts from the Records of the Burgh of Edinburgh*, 1403-1528, p. 39.

24. *A.P.S.* C.7.II.9.

25. *A.P.S.* C.6.II.177.

26. *The Book of the Old Edinburgh Club*, Vol. IV (Edinburgh 1912) p. 76.

27. Malcolm, op. cit., p. 50.

28. *The Book of the Old Edinburgh Club*, op. cit., Vol. IV, p. 80.

29. ibid., pp. 86, 88.
    ibid., p. 88. 'About the middle of the seventeenth century the word "tolbooth" became synonymous with prison, and prisoners were sentenced to detention in the "tolbooth" for many years after the Old Tolbooth had disappeared and the Calton Prison had taken its place.'

30. A. H. Millar: *Haunted Dundee* (Dundee 1923) p. 244.

31. George Penny: *Traditions of Perth* (Perth 1836) p. 10.

32. David Peacock: *Perth: Its Annals and its Archives* (Perth 1849) p. 598.

33. W. C. Dickinson, op. cit., p. 248.

34. James Grant: *Old and New Edinburgh*, Vol. I (Cassell) p. 134.

35. *Court Book of Urie*, op. cit., p. XVI.

36. *New Statistical Account of Scotland*, Vol. XV (Perthshire) (Edinburgh 1845) p. 31.

37 and 38. ibid., Cant quoted, p. 31.

39. James Grant, op. cit., Vol. I, p. 84.

40. I. F. Grant: *Social and Economic Development of Scotland before 1603* (Edinburgh 1930) p. 191. It seems clear that the State appeared to be more concerned with indemnifying the victim, than in enforcing public order; if a man was rich enough he could slay many men of no substance and the only consequence to him would be the need to pay a fairly nominal sum to the next-of-kin.

41. W. C. Dickinson, op. cit., p. 250.

42 & 43. Pitcairn, op. cit., pp. 71, 69.

44. ibid., pp. 92, 63, 64, 'Merk': the old Scots mark, or 13s 4d Scots, 13½d Sterling.

45. Jean Froissart: *Chronicles of England, France, Spain, and the adjoining Countries*, Vol. II. Translated by Thomas Johnes (London 1849) p. 36.

46. *Early Travellers in Scotland*, op. cit., p. 26.

47. Gordon Donaldson: *Scotland: The Shaping of a Nation* (David and Charles 1974) p. 207.

48. W. Croft Dickinson and Gordon Donaldson: *A Source Book of Scottish History*, Vol. II, 1424–1567 (Nelson 1963) p. 1.

49. *A.P.S.* J.I 1425, C.20.II.11.

50. *A.P.S.* J.II 1455, C.8.II.43.

51. *A.P.S.* J.II 1457, C.17.II.49.

52. *A.P.S.* J.IV 1503, C.14.II.251.

53. *A.P.S.* J.V. 1535, C.29.II.347.

54. Gordon Donaldson: *Scotland: James V to James VII*, Vol. III in *Edinburgh History of Scotland* (Oliver and Boyd 1971) p. 138.

Chapter 2: Crimes or Sins? 1560–1747

* J. G. Lockhart: *The Life of Sir Walter Scott, 1771–1832*, Scott's Journal entry for 8th October 1827 (London 1896) p. 671.

1. Robert Chambers: *Domestic Annals of Scotland from the Reformation to the Revolution*, 2nd edition, Vol. I (Edinburgh 1859) p. 5.

2. *The Historie & Life of King James the Sext from 1566–1596*, author unknown, for year 1569–70 (Bannatyne Club 1825) p. 52.

3. Jhone Leslie, Bishop of Rosse: *The Historie of Scotland*, Vol. II, p. 210 (translated from the Latin by Father James Dalyrymple, 1596) (Scottish Text Society 1890). Leslie speaks of 'deidlie feid ful feirse' (p. 209).

4. I. F. Grant: *Social and Economic Development of Scotland before 1603* (Edinburgh 1930) p. 188.

5. W. Croft Dickinson: *Scotland from the earliest times to 1603*, Vol. I of *A New History of Scotland* (Nelson 1961) p. 374.

6. James VI: *Basilikon Doron or His Majesty's instructions to his dearest sonne Henry*, 1599 (Roxburghe Club 1887) p. 54.

7. *An Introductory Survey of the Sources & Literature of Scots Law* (Stair Society, Edinburgh 1936) p. 374.

8. *The Quarterly Review*, 1831, Vol. 44, p. 470.

9. *Bloody Roll of Perth*: B59/1457/2 Scottish Record Office (West Register House, Edinburgh).

10. *Letter* on behalf of Duke of Atbole: B 59/1774 (West Register House).

11. Edwin Muir: *Scottish Journey* (Heinemann & Gollancz 1935) p. 227.

12. Gordon Donaldson: *Scotland: James V to James VII*, Vol. III in *Edinburgh History of Scotland* (Oliver & Boyd 1971) p. 225.

13. *Extracts from the Kirk-Session Records of Perth, The Chronicle of Perth 1210–1668. A Register of Remarkable Occurences chiefly connected with that city.* (Maitland Club 1831) pp. 54, 55.

14. *Register of the Privy Council of Scotland*, Series I, Vol. III p. 224.

15. *Perth Kirk Session Records*, op. cit., pp. 79–80.

16. Hugo Arnot: *A collection & abridgement of celebrated Criminal Trials in Scotland 1536–1784* (Edinburgh 1785) pp. 312–13.

17. ibid., p. 313.

18–20. *Perth Kirk Session Records*, op. cit., pp. 56, 71–2.

21. Excerpts from *St Andrews Kirk Session Records*, 7th June 1638–21st June 1725, C.H.2/316 App.R.1/453 (West Register House).

22. Gordon Donaldson: *Knox the Man* (St Andrew Press 1975) p. 13.

23. *An Old Session Book: Being studies in Alyth's 2nd Session Book by James Meikle, Minister of Alyth, 1918* – Minutes of the Session, 1669–88, pp. 99, 101.

24. *Perth Kirk Session Records*, op. cit., p. 68.

25. Arnot, op. cit., p. 324.

26. R. L. Stevenson: *Edinburgh Picturesque Notes* (Tusitala Edition, Heinemann 1924) p. 140.

27. *Chronicle of Perth*, op. cit., p. 20.

28. *The Spottiswoode Miscellany*, op. cit., pp. 256–74.

29. David Hume: *Commentaries on the Law of Scotland respecting crimes*, Vol. I (Edinburgh 1829) pp. 469, 470, 451.

30. Arnot, op. cit., pp. 306–7.

31. *The Justiciary Records of Argyll & the Isles 1664–1705*, Vol. I (Stair Society 1949) pp. 67, 68.

32. ibid., pp. 111–12, 196–7.

33. Hume, op. cit., p. 588.

34. Chambers, op. cit., Vol. I, p. 273.

35. Arnot, op. cit., pp. 350–51.

36. Chambers, op. cit., Vol. II, p. 279.

37. *Scots Peerage*, Vol. VI, p. 363.

38. Arnot, op. cit., p. 129.

39. 'In March 1684 was given to James Campbell ... supplicant who has been prisoner in Perth these nine years by-gone – 56 shillings.' *Alyth's 2nd Session Book*, op. cit., p. 166. Note too the case of Neville Payne, an English Catholic who in 1690, because of suspected complicity in a plot to restore James VII, was tortured severely in Edinburgh, and kept in the various state prisons of Scotland for ten years (Chambers, op. cit., Vol. III, pp. 40–41).

40. Gordon Donaldson: *The Scots Overseas* (London 1966) p. 39.

41. *Transactions of the Literary & Antiquarian Society of Perth*, Vol. I (Perth 1827). (Pages unnumbered.)

42. *Extracts from the Records of the Burgh of Edinburgh, 1626–41* (edited by M. Wood, Edinburgh 1936) p. 190.

43. *Register of the Privy Council*, 1st series, Vol. IV, p. 550.

44. William Mackay: *Prison Life in Inverness 1700–20*, in *Transactions of the Inverness Scientific Society & Field Club 1883–88*, Vol. III, pp. 98–100.

45. Pitcairn: *Ancient Criminal Trials in Scotland*, Vol. III 1609–24, p. 219.

46. J. G. Dunbar: *The Historic Architecture of Scotland* (Batsford 1966) pp. 200, 201, 202.

47. & 48. *Chambers' Journal*, 6th series, Vol. 8, Dec. 1904–Nov. 1905, *An Island Prison on the Forth* (May 20th 1905) (W. & R. Chambers 1905) pp. 386–7.

49. *A London Broadside of 1694*, being 'A true & Faithful Relation of the Particulars of the Surrender of the Island of the Bass in Scotland, together with the

Articles of Surrender'. (Printed for R. Allen at the George in Fleet Street 1694.)

50. Ian B. Cowan: *The Scottish Covenanters 1660–88* (Gollancz 1976).

51. Donaldson: *Scotland: James V to James VII*, op. cit., p. 373.

52. Cowan, op. cit., pp. 92, 101, 102.

54. Chambers: *Domestic Annals*, op. cit., Vol. II, p. 480.

55. *The Court Book of Balnakeilly 1699–1745*, owned by Mrs Stewart Stevens of Balnakeilly, Pitlochry.

56. W. C. Dickinson and G. Donaldson: *A Source Book of Scottish History*, Vol. III (Nelson 1954) p. 359.

57. Edward Burt: *Letters from a Gentleman in the North of Scotland, 1726* (London 1818) Vol. II p. 252, Vol. I pp. 48, 49.

58. Donaldson: *The Scots Overseas*, op. cit., p. 57.

59. *The Prisoners of the '45, edited from the State Papers*, by Sir Bruce Seton and Jean Gordon Arnot, Vol. I, 3rd series (Scottish History Society 1928) p. 66.

60. & 61. ibid., pp. 166, 158.

62. Donaldson: *The Scots Overseas*, op. cit., p. 58.

63. Gordon Donaldson: *Scotland: The Shaping of a Nation* (David & Charles 1975) p. 81.

Chapter 3: The Humanitarian Reformers 1747–1835

Part I

* See note 10 Part I.

† See note 2 Part II.

1. & 2. Christopher Hibbert: *The Roots of Evil* (Penguin 1966) p. 158.

3. Patrick Medd: *Romilly* (Collins 1968) p. 233.

4. Howard 'well knew, from manifold observation, that human nature could not endure, for a long time, confinement in perfect solitude, without sinking under the burden ... he never thought of its being made the sentence of offenders during the *whole term* of their imprisonment; such being not only extreme and scarcely justifiable severity, but inconsistent with the design of reclaiming them to habits of industry by hard labour.' John Aiken, M.D.: *A view of the character and public services of the late John Howard* (London 1792) pp. 171, 172.

5. Garnish was entrance money paid to fellow-prisoners on entering prison. Chummage meant quartering two or more in one room and was the fee demanded from a new 'chum'. The cruel custom of jailers demanding garnish of newcomers, 'Pay or strip,' was too often the rule in English prisons and new arrivals sometimes died of cold.

6. Alexander Wedderburn; *Observations on the State of Prisons* (1794) p. 24.

7. Adam's plan had not allowed for separate confinement. Bentham himself disapproved of it. The fact that the Edinburgh Bridewell was the closest approximation to Bentham's theory ever built has never been adequately recognised. Lecture on *Scottish Prisons and Hanoverian Forts in the 18th Century* to the Scottish Georgian Society by Ian McIver (now Chief Inspector of Ancient Monuments of Scotland) March 1972.

8. J. J. Gurney, writing in 1818, says: 'Howard, indeed, drew much of the public attention to our prisons, which before his time were generally the sinks of extreme misery and terrible disease. But his efforts, and the efforts which he excited in others, were directed more to the alleviation of distress than to the diminution of crime; more to the maintenance of the prisoner's health than to the reformation of his morals.' *Notes on a Visit made to some of the Prisons in Scotland and the North of England in company with Elizabeth Fry* (London 1819) p. 98. But Howard 'extremely lamented that the plan of reformation seemed, of all parts of his system of improvement, least entered into or understood in this country ... Merely to *get rid* of convicts by execution or perpetual banishment, he regarded as a piece of barbarous policy, equally denoting want of feeling, and deficiency of resource.' Aiken, op. cit., pp. 81, 82.

9. & 10. Janet Whitney: *Elizabeth Fry* (Guild Books 1947) pp. 155, 177.

11. J. J. Gurney: *A brief Memoir of Elizabeth Fry* in Vol. *Law of Kindness* by Rev. G. W. Montgomery, p. 242.

12. Hibbert, op. cit., p. 176.

13. Thomas Fowell Buxton: *An Inquiry whether Crime and Misery are produced or prevented by our present system of prison discipline*, p. 5 of Preface (Edinburgh 1818). Buxton was an M.P., the Quaker brother-in-law of Mrs Fry, and a member of the New Society for the Improvement of Prison Discipline.

Part II

1. *Memoir of the Life of Elizabeth Fry*, edited by two of her daughters, K. Fry and R. Cresswell, Vol. II (London 1848, 2nd edition) p. 79.

2 & 3. *Works of the Rev. Sidney Smith* 2nd edition, Vol. I (London 1840) pp. 462, 442, 443, 462.

4. J. G. Lockhart: *Life of Sir Walter Scott 1771-1832*. Scott's Journal entry for 20th February 1828. (London 1896) p. 680.

5-8. John Howard: *State of the Prisons in England and Wales with an account of some foreign prisons 1777/1780 and 1784* (Everyman edition 1929) pp. 149, 148.

9. & 10. John Aiken, M.D.: *A View of the character and public services of the late John Howard* (London 1792) pp. 123, 160-61.

11 & 12. Howard, op. cit., pp. 148, 147.

13. Christopher Hibbert: *The Roots of Evil, A Social History of Crime and Punishment* (Penguin 1966) p. 154. See also Dickens: *The Pickwick Papers*, p. 628, 'the just and wholesome law which declares that the sturdy felon shall be fed and clothed, and that the penniless debtor shall be left to die of starvation and nakedness.' (Nelson 1912.)

14 & 15. Howard, op. cit., pp. 2, 148.

16. David Hume: *Commentaries on the Law of Scotland respecting Crimes*, Vol. I (Edinburgh 1849) p. 10.

17. Howard, op. cit., p. 6.

18. Hume, op. cit., p. II.

19 & 20. Howard, op. cit., pp. 147, 148.

21. James Neild: *State of the Prisons in England, Scotland and Wales, 1812*, p. 2. See

also p. 617 where Neild declares himself to be, 'Animated with the hope of giving permanency and improvement to that reform in our Prisons which was so ably begun by my excellent Predecessor, Mr Howard.'

22. J. J. Gurney: *Notes on a visit made to some of the Prisons in Scotland and Northern England* (London 1819) p. 105. See also Rev. Thomas Timpson: *Memoirs of Mrs. Elizabeth Fry* (London 1847) pp. 87, 88. 'Though prisons were not so numerous in that country as in England, Mrs. Fry found many, and those in a very deplorable condition.'

23. Gurney, op. cit., pp. 19, 35. Neild, op. cit., pp. 3, 11, 21, 24.

24. Sir Walter Scott: *The Heart of Midlothian* (London 1893) p. 8.

25. *The Heart of Midlothian* notes p. 544.

26. Henry Cockburn: *Memorials of his Time* (Edinburgh 1909) p. 229.

27 & 28. William Chambers: *Memoir of William and Robert Chambers* (13th edition, Edinburgh 1893) pp. 99, 100.

29. Cockburn, op. cit., p. 228.

30 & 31. Gurney, op. cit., pp. 39, 42.

32 & 33. Neild, op. cit., pp. 238, 239.

34. Neild, op. cit., p. 22; and for other examples see Neild pp. 3, 176, 193 and Gurney, op. cit., pp. 19, 25.

35. Gurney, op. cit., p. 46.

36. Neild, op. cit., p. 254.

37–40. Gurney, op. cit., pp. 24, 25, 26, 111.

41. Robert Southey: *Letters from England, 1807* (edited by J. Simmons, Cresset Press 1951) p. 218.

42. Neild, op. cit., pp. 187, 200, 238, 242, 1.

43. Gurney, op. cit., pp. 52–3.

44. Letters from Professor Garscombe of New York: *The Contrast: or Scotland as it was in the year 1745, and Scotland in the year 1819* (London 1825) p. 299. Garscombe says of Calton Bridewell, 'It is too cheerful for the purpose of salutary discipline and penitentiary confinement. Each prisoner is provided with a straw matress, a pillow, a clean sheet and two double blankets; their food is wholesome and good. In short there are too much comfortable living and hilarity in this prison, to answer the main purpose of deterring the poor and vicious from the commission of crime.' (p. 241) At Glasgow Bridewell, Garscombe found the 'chief employment of the prisoners, male and female is spinning linen yarn, weaving, tambouring, ... cutting corks, clipping muslin ... and picking oakum.' (p. 299.)

45 & 46. Gurney, op. cit., pp. 47, 34.

47. Southey, op. cit., p. 208.

48. *Memoir of the Life of Elizabeth Fry*, op. cit., Vol. I, p. 255.

49 & 50. Neild, op. cit., pp. 189, 399.

51 & 52. Gurney, op. cit., pp. 43, 44, 51. See also Timpson, op. cit., p. 98. Although 'Scotland needed far less the example of Mrs. Fry and her devoted colleagues in seeking the reformation of female prisoners', yet, 'She found our prison very badly managed; the women crowding by night, four or five into one cell, without any work, without a matron, no chaplain and locked

up by the common turnkey.' *Letter from a Scotch lady who was with Mrs. Fry in Glasgow*, quoted by Timpson pp. 87, 88. As a result of Mrs Fry's visits to Scottish prisons, Ladies' Visiting Committees were started and later shelters for liberated prisoners appeared in Edinburgh, Glasgow, Perth, and Greenock (p. 100).

53. Neild, op. cit., p. 475.

54. *New Statistical Account of Scotland*, Vol. XV (Edinburgh 1845) p. 135.

55. ibid., p. 135. 'Occasionally they enact what they call a "Hell scene".' In the day-room 'amidst shouts and yells ... and uttering revolting exclamations, they pull the fire to pieces, and fling the live coals round in every direction; others, at the same time, dashing water about, and in every way creating uproar and confusion.'

56. Ibid., pp. 136, 137.

57. Neild, op. cit., p. 201.

58. Gurney, op. cit., p. 46.

59-68. Neild, op. cit., pp. 201, 243, 202, 239, 238, 239, 253, 300, 189, 240, 25.

69. *Act of Council of Lord Provost and Magistrates and Council of Edinburgh*, 5th September 1810, quoted by Neild, op. cit., p. 190.

70-73. Neild, op. cit., pp. 238, 239, 174, 239, 241.

74. Bell's *Principles of the Law of Scotland*, 5th Edition (1860) Sect. 2315.

75. William Bell: *Dictionary and Digest of the Law of Scotland* (1838) under title *Sanctuary*.

76. Bell's *Principles*, sect. 2316.

77. Chambers, op. cit., p. 97.

78. Neild, op. cit., p. 199.

79. ibid.

80. Act of Session, 14th June 1771, quoted in Erskine's *Principles*, 21st Edition, pp. 703, 704.

81 & 82. Neild, op. cit., pp. 523, 405.

83 & 84. Gurney, op. cit., pp. 107-8, 21-2.

85. *Edinburgh: a satirical novel by the author of London, or a month at Steven's*, Vol. III (London 1820) p. 45.

86. Neild, op. cit., p. 474.

87. Gurney, op. cit., p. 39.

88. Neild, op. cit., p. 21.

89 & 90. Gurney, op. cit., pp. 53, 75.

91 & 92. Neild, op. cit., pp. 188, 201.

93. *The Contrast*, op. cit., pp. 297, 299.

94 & 95. H. H. Millar; *Haunted Dundee* (Dundee 1923) pp. 247, 249.

96. *H.M. Prison and Borstal Institution at Greenock*, S.H.H.D. File No. P. 12295/1.

97. John G. Dunbar: *The Historic Architecture of Scotland* (Batsford 1966) p. 207.

Chapter 4: Prisoners of War 1756–1815

* See note 20.

1. Francis Abell: *Prisoners of War in Britain, 1756–1815* (London 1914) pp. 449–50.

2. Sir Walter Scott: *Waverley* (Dryburgh Edition, Edinburgh 1892) pp. 249–50.

3. Abell, op. cit., p. 118.

4. George Penny: *Traditions of Perth* (Perth 1836) p. 91.

5. ibid., p. 92.

6. William Sievwright: *Historical Sketch of the Old Depot or Prison for French Prisoners-of-War at Perth* (Perth 1894) p. 35.

7. Abell, op. cit., pp. 197, 198.

8. Quoted by Abell, op. cit., p. 270.

9. Louis Garneray: *The French Prisoner*. Translated by Lawrence Wood (London 1957) p. 175. In France the Government 'allowed one Louis d'or to every person that should detain or bring back a prisoner of war.' Casse infra p. 59.

10. *The Letters of Sir Walter Scott 1811–1814*, edited by H. J. C. Grierson (London 1932) p. 111.

11. D. L. Howard: *John Howard, Prison Reformer* (London 1958) p. 82.

12. George Richard Casse: *A Prisoner of France, 1809–14; A Narrative of the Napoleonic Wars* (1st Edition 1828, London Edition, Howard Baker 1976) pp. 42, 48, 85, 92, 98.

13. *Locks, Bolts and Bars; Stories of Prisoners in the French Wars, 1759–1814.* Collected by Mrs Oliver Elton (London 1945). Foreword, p. 8.

14. Abell, op. cit., p. 8.

15. Garneray, op. cit., pp. 16, 17.

16. ibid, p. 8.

17. Letters in Scottish United Services Museum, Edinburgh Castle. S.U.S.M. documents, French Forces 808.1. These letters are copies – originals unknown.

18. George Borrow: *Lavengro*, in 3 vols. (London 1926) Vol. I, p. 23.

19. Quoted by Abell, op. cit., p. 18.

20. Elton, op. cit., p. 18. From a 1779 play performed in Theatre Royal, Covent Garden.

21. Garneray, op. cit., p. 11.

22. Penny, op. cit., p. 93.

23. Garneray, op. cit., p. 55.

24. Abell, op. cit., p. 254.

25 & 26. *The Yarn of a Yankee Privateer*, edited by Nathaniel Hawthorne (New York & London 1926, Lexington, Mass., public library) pp. 167, 173, 219, 230. Identity of author is unknown.

27. R. L. Stevenson: *St. Ives* (Tusitala Edition, Heinemann 1924) p. 4.

28 & 29. Quoted by Abell, op. cit., pp. 258, 91.

30. Stevenson, op. cit., p. 5 'the prison was daily visited at certain hours by a concourse of people'.

31. Penny, op. cit., p. 94.

32. Casse, op. cit., pp. 99, 51.

33. Abell, op. cit., p. 288.

34. William Chambers: *Memoir of William and Robert Chambers* (Edinburgh 1893) pp. 68, 69.

35. Elton, op. cit., p. 255.

36. Henrietta Keddie (Sarah Tytler): *The Story of a Middle-Class Scottish Family* (London 1911) pp. 36, 37.

37. *Rutherford's Southern Counties Register & Directory of 1866*, extracts enclosed in letter from J. Rutherford to Sir G. Douglas, S.U.S.M. documents, French Forces 814.1.

38. Fullarton's *Imperial Gazeteer of Scotland*.

39. Abell, op. cit., p. 340.

40. Chambers, op. cit., pp. 67, 71.

41 & 42. James Grant: *Old & New Edinburgh*, Vol. I, pp. 248, 71.

43. Stevenson, op. cit., p. 47.

44. Sievwright, op. cit., p. 48.

45. Garneray, op. cit., p. 174.

46. Chambers, op. cit., pp. 71, 72.

47. Sievwright, op. cit., pp. 46, 47.

48. Penny, op. cit., p. 94.

Chapter 5: Repression and the Separate System 1835-77

* See note 16 Part I.

† See note 21 Part I.

‡ See note 23 Part I.

Introduction

1. P. J. Fitzgerald: *Criminal Law and Punishment* (Oxford 1962) p. 208.

2 & 3. *Latter Day Pamphlets*, edited by Thomas Carlyle, *Model Prisons 1850* (London 1872) p. 50.

4-10. ibid., pp. 49, 45, 47, 52, 53, 57.

11 and 12. Hugh Miller: *Essays, Historical & Biographical, The Felons of the Country* (Edinburgh 1875) pp. 269, 271.

Part I

1. 5 & 6 Will. IV. C. 38.

2. Henry Mayhew: *London's Underworld*. Selections from Vol. IV of London Labour and the London Poor, p. 26 of Introduction by Peter Quennell (London 1966).

3. Quennell, op. cit., p. 26.

4. Christopher Hibbert: *The Roots of Evil* (Penguin 1966) p. 184.

5-7. ibid pp. 181, 182, 183.

8. 'So that the discipline pursued at the prison [Pentonville] yields upwards of ten times more lunatics than should be the case according to the normal rate'. Henry Mayhew and John Binney: *The Criminal Prisons of London and scenes of Prison Life* (London 1862) p. 104.

9. *Memoir of William Ellery Channing*, Vol. III, edited by W. J. C. (London 1848) pp. 26, 27.

10 & 11. *Memoir of William Ellery Channing*, Vol III p. 27.

12. Dickens: *American Notes*, (Nelson 1912) pp. 107, 108.

13-18. ibid., pp. 109, 115, 117, 118, 119. Dickens did not however approve of pampering prisoners. When describing a visit to incorrigibles awaiting transportation in solitary confinement at Millbank penitentiary, he says, 'there was a striking contrast between these plentiful repasts of choice quality, and the dinners ... of ... the great bulk of the honest working community - of whom not one man in five hundred ever dined half so well'. David Copperfield (Nelson 1912) p. 892.

19 & 20. *Memoir of the life of Elizabeth Fry*, with extracts from her journal and letters edited by two of her daughters, 2nd edition, Vol. II (London 1848) pp. 159, 253.

21. Janet Whitney: *Elizabeth Fry* (Guild Books 1947) p. 235.

22. Emil Frankel: *Crime Treatment in New Jersey, 1668-1934 Journal of Criminal Law and Criminology*, Vol. XXVIII, No. I (May-June 1937) pp. 98, 99, quoted by Gresham Sykes: *The Society of Captives, A Study of a Maximum Security Prison* (Princeton U.P. 1971) pp. 6, 7.

23. On the other hand Dostoevsky describing his life in a Russian penal settlement in *The House of the Dead, or Prison Life in Siberia* in 1849, says, 'could I ever have imagined the poignant and terrible suffering of never being alone even for one minute during ten years?' (p. 11); but he nevertheless maintains 'I am convinced that the celebrated cellular system gives results which are specious and deceitful. It deprives a criminal of his force, of his energy ... and at last exhibits a dried up mummy as a model of repentance and amendment.' (Everyman 1916) p. 17.

24. Sykes, op. cit. (see note 22) p. 6.

25. By Section 6 of the 1839 Act, certain rules were laid down. Among them were; Prisoners certified fit by the doctor and already sentenced to transportation could be sent to Millbank; those sentenced to 7-10 years transportation, to Millbank first for $3\frac{1}{2}$ years; 10-15 years transportation, to Millbank for 4 years. (2 & 3 Vict. C 56.)

26. *S.H.D. File No. P 12295/8* p. 22.

27. *The Prison System. Classification of Prisoners and Institutes*, Dumfries Prison.

Part II

1. Minute Book of the Prisons, 1839-40. H.H.6/1 (West Register House). The information was gathered from 1) Reports of 1830 in obedience to the Act, 6 Geo. IV c. 54; 2) Reports of Burgh Commission 1835; 3) Report of Inspectors of Prisons, 1835, -36, -37, and -38; 4) Returns obtained from the sheriffs, 1840.

2. *Report 1830*, p. 3.

3. *Sheriffs' Report 1840.*

4. *Report of the Burgh Commission Local Report*, Part I, p. 235.

5. *Inspectors' Report*, 4.75.

6. *Report of the Burgh Commission Local Report*, Part II, p. 117.

7. *Report 1830*, p. 238.

8. *Report of the Burgh Commission*, Part II, p. 117. From the *New Statistical Account of Scotland Vol. XV, 1845*: When the new Perth jail was built in 1819, the old one was abandoned but later fitted up as a small bridewell. The prisoners were well disciplined and worked separately at teasing hair or picking oakum. 'For aliment, they are allowed two diets during the day – in the morning they have oatmeal porridge and milk; and at three o'clock afternoon, they have broth and bread. Thus fed, they enjoy excellent health.' (p. 136)

9. *Inspectors' Report*, 4.81.

10. *Reports of the Burgh Commission Social Report*, Part I, p. 306.

11 & 12. *Inspectors' Reports*, 2.119, 2.123.

13 & 14. *Report 1830* pp. 199, 3, 4.

15. *Inspectors' Report*, I.25.

16. *Reports of the Burgh Commission*, Part II, p. 31.

17 & 18. *Inspectors' Report* 3.102, 149.

19. *Reports of the Burgh Commission*, Part II, p. 31.

20 & 21. *Inspectors' Reports*, 2.109, I.69.

22. *Reports of the Burgh Commission Local Report*, Part II, p. 117.

23. *Inspectors' Report* 4.75.

24. *Reports of the Burgh Commission Local Report*, Part II, p. 117.

25 & 26. ibid., Part I, p. 306.

27 & 28. *Inspectors' Report* 2.126, 153.

29. ibid., no. 25.

30. *Inspectors' Report* I.53.

31. ibid., no. 24, p. 31.

32. *Inspectors' Report* 3.86.

33. ibid., no. 31, p. 325.

34–44. *Inspectors' Report* 3.22, 3.23, 4.166, 2.62, 3.99, 3.26, 3.21, 2.85, 3.61, 3.26, 2.68.

45. *Report 1830*, p. 260.

46 & 47. *Inspectors' Report* 2.48.

48. *Report 1830*, p. 273.

49 & 50. *Inspectors' Report* 3.12, 4.166.

Part III

Governors' Journals of the General Prison at Perth

1845–47 H.H.12/63/1.
1847–49 H.H.12/63/2.

1849–51 H.H.12/63/3.
1851–55 H.H.12/63/4.

1. *Journals* 1849–51.
2. ibid., 1847–9.
3. *ibid., 1845–7*.
4. ibid., 1847–9.
5. August 1850: James Murray, aged 11, died of 'worn out constitution resulting from neglect and starvation prior to admission'.
   August 1852: 'On the opening of the prison this morning a 19-year-old man, a transportation prisoner, was found dead in his bed; he had been falling off for some time, but had no specific complaint.'
6. November 1847: a 13-year-old got 24 hours in handcuffs 'for communicating with another prisoner by talking to him in the airing yard'.
   January 1849: a 13-year-old got two days in handcuffs in a dark punishment cell for 'breaking two holes through the wall of the cell with intent to communicate'.
7. December 1848: a 10-year-old was put in handcuffs in his own cell for 31 hours for being 'noisy in his cell and being disrespectful towards the teacher'.
   February 1851: a 12-year-old spent three hours in irons in the Epileptic Ward for 'being noisy on the Sabbath'.
8. May 1847: 'John Baillie, aged 10 years, has of late become very mischievous, tearing his clothes and destroying his cell furniture; the surgeon does not consider him a fit subject for punishment in the usual way as his mind might give way. And on the 12th he was doubled up with another prisoner.'
   January 1849: a 12-year-old got three days in a dark punishment cell, the last 24 hours in irons, for 'destroying the mask of his bonnet, his bed-rug, and breaking a hole through the wall of his cell.'
   November 1849, a sad entry: a 16-year-old imbecile prisoner spent two days in irons in the imbecile prison for 'disorderly conduct and breaking his cell door with his crutch'.
9. November 1847: 'a 15-year-old was handcuffed in his cell for two days for refusing to put down his mask in coming from the airing yard and making use of improper language.'
10. December 1853: a 12-year-old was punished in handcuffs for 'talking at exercise and throwing his porridge in a warder's face'.
11. August 1847: John Darling, aged 17, was punished by 'being put in irons in his cell for having (apparently) made an attempt to commit suicide'.
12. October 1849: The Governor going on his rounds found the inside night watchman asleep on duty. He was immediately dismissed.
13. January 1850: The Superintendent of the Juvenile and Imbecile Prisons was suspended by the Governor for 'repeated acts of intoxication', and a few days later his 'services were dispensed with by direction of the General Board in consequence of severe acts of intemperance'.
14. December 1846: a female warder had 'contrary to express orders taken out a prisoner to assist her to extinguish the gas' and on returning her to her cell she forgot to lock it. Next morning the prisoner emerged from her cell and proceeded to lock the female wardresses in their room. The offending wardress was dismissed the same day.

15. June 1848: The assistant matron was sacked by the matron 'for general inefficiency', but her successor, appointed on the 13th, was 'dismissed by the matron on the 25th as being a very unsuitable person for the office'.

16. August 1851: The weaver warder resigned his situation on the ground that his duties were too arduous for him.

17. August 1851: 'The furnace warder resigned ... he assigned as a reason that the head Warder was in the practice of making use of unnecessarily severe language towards him.'

18. May 1847: A female warder resigned, departing for Dundee 'to commence business as a milliner'.
April 1854: The assistant shoemaker warder resigned: he 'ceased his duties at the prison with the intention of emigrating to America'.

19. November 1853: A warder in the Juvenile Wing 'ceased his duties without assigning any reason for so doing'.

20. *Visitors to the General Prison of Scotland, 1842-98.* (West Register House H.H.12/62.)

21-23. *Report of the Commissioners appointed by the Lords Commissioners of H.M. Treasury to inquire into certain civil departments in Scotland* (Edinburgh 1870) pp. 152, 154, 155.

24. *Minute Book of the Prisons, 1853-54.* Scottish Record Office (West Register House) H.H./6/12 pp. 13, 14.

25-29. ibid., pp. 53, 51, 60, 52, 54.

30. *Governors' Journals at Perth 1862-65*, West Register House H.H.12/63/5.

31-33. S.H.H.D. File no. P12295/I.

Part IV.   Transportation

1. West Register House A.D./58/97.

2. Take the terrible example of one James Williams who was transported aged 19 and died in 1849 having spent 20 years in irons, and suffered more than 2,000 lashes. Marcus Clarke: *His Natural Life* (edited by S. Murray-Smith, Penguin Books 1970) p. 237.

3. Thus Abel Magwitch in Dickens' *Great Expectations*: 'I was sent for life. It's death to come back. There's been overmuch coming back of late years, and I should of a certainty be hanged if took.' (Nelson 1912) p. 327. By an Act for abolishing Capital Punishment in case of returning from Transportation, 1834, punishment of transportation for life was substituted for the death sentence in such cases.

4. December 1851: 'This day forty three convicts under sentence of transportation were removed with a view to transmission to the 'Stirling Castle' hulk at Portsmouth by order of Secretary, Sir George Grey.' *Governors' Journals, Perth 1851-55.*

Part V   Towards Centralisation

1. Charles Reade: *It's Never Too Late To Mend* (1856).

2. S.H.D. File no. P12295/8.

3. 23 & 24 Vict. C. 105, S LXIII and S LXIV.

Chapter 6:   Centralisation and Reform 1877–1908
Part I

* See note 17 Part I.

1. 'It was not an easy task to obtain his acquiescence' over the matter of the 1779 Penitentiary Houses, and Howard resigned from the office of supervisor in January 1781. John Aiken, M.D.: *A View of the character and public services of the late John Howard* (London 1792) p. 107.

2. D. L. Howard: *John Howard, Prison Reformer* (London 1958) p. 169.

3. The appalling condition of some US county jails today, where no central authority is in control, emphasises this fact. At the Cummins Prison Farm, Arkansas, 'convicts stoop in the vast cotton fields twelve hours a day, 5½ days a week – for zero pay ... A virtual slave plantation in the 20th century'. *Time* 18 January 1971.

4. *Report of the Commissioners appointed by the Lords Commissioners of H.M. Treasury to inquire into certain civil departments in Scotland, 1870,* p. 156.

5–9. ibid., pp. 3, 4.

10. *Penal Servitude Act 1853.* 'An Act to substitute, in certain cases, other Punishment in lieu of Transportation.' 16 & 17 Vict. C. 99.

11. Christopher Hibbert: *The Roots of Evil. A Social History of Crime and Punishment.* (Penguin 1966) p. 188.

12. The Gladstone Report: *Report from the Departmental Committee on Prisons 1895.* Para. 25 Command 7702.

13. ibid., Para. 47. The Report's recommendation that crank and treadmill be abolished (para. 40) contrasted with the 1863 House of Lords Committee's recommendations of hard labour, hard fare and hard bed. The Report recognised that 'recidivism is the most important of all prison questions and it is the most complicated and difficult.' (para. 18)

14–16. Rupert Cross: *Punishment, Prison and the Public.* (London 1971) pp. 19, 20.

17–18. Oscar Wilde: *The Ballad of Reading Gaol,* in *Complete Works of Oscar Wilde* (Collins 1969) pp. 848, 858, 857.

19. ibid., *The case of warder Martin: some cruelties of Prison Life:* in a letter to the *Daily Chronicle.* Ibid., p. 962. Written ten days after Wilde's release from prison, May 1897.

20–24. 'Prison Reform', a letter to the *Daily Chronicle,* March 1898, Wilde, op. cit., pp. 965, 966, 967, 968, 969.

25. W. B. Neville: *Penal Servitude* (London 1903) p. 81.

26–27. ibid., pp. 76, 77, 104.

28. *The Rules for Prisons in Scotland 1888* gives the rules for prison diet:
    Rule 395 'In one day –
        Table VII 2 pints barley broth.
             1½ oz. cheese.
             12 oz. wheaten bread.'
    And 'In one day –
        1 lb. suet pudding.
        1 pint barley broth.
        12 ozs. wheaten bread.

Rule 395

        Table X 'For females same diet, except that the allowance of meat
           shall not exceed 6 ozs.'
        And 'on one day of the week –
        Bread.
        16 oz. of fresh fish.
        11 lb. of potatoes.
        Broth.
        Pudding might be added.'

Rule 402 '¾ oz. molasses or sugar and seasoned with salt'.

Rule 409 'Fish soup to be made with the head and trimmings of the fish, with ½ oz. flour added for every ½ pint of soup, and 1 gallon of skimmed milk and ¾ oz. pepper added for every 50 pints of soup.'

Rule 419 'Fish to be weighed after being cleaned and trimmed, but before being cooked.'

Board of Agriculture Report 1889 Prisons (S) includes Rules for Prisons in Scotland, settled and approved 1888 by Secretary for Scotland under Prisons (S) Act 1877 and Secretary for Scotland Acts 1885 and 1887.

29. Neville, op. cit., p. 290.

30-31. William Sievwright: *Historical Sketch of the General Prison for Scotland at Perth* (1894) pp. 48, 49-51.

32-35. Neville, op. cit., pp. 128, 129; 136, 137; 255; 295, 296.

36. William Sievwright, op. cit., pp. 88-90.

Part II

1. See Part I.

2. The corresponding numbers for 1840 had been 1,362 males, 686 females, total 2,048, but the population then was only 2,600,692. *Report of the Prison Commissioners (S) 1898-1904* App. II, p. 13.

3. Ibid. *1898 Report*, App. I, p. 12. These were, for both civil and criminal prisoners, Aberdeen, Ayr, Dumfries, Dundee, Edinburgh, Glasgow (Barlinnie General), Glasgow (Duke Street), Greenock, Inverness, Kirkwall, Lerwick, Perth General, Stornoway. Peterhead was for male convicts only. There were also many police cells legalised under Section 30 of Prisons (S) Act 1877 for imprisonment of not more than 14 days.

4. *1904 Report*, App. IX, p. 21.

5. *1904* Report, App. II, p. 13. The Reports pointed out that sometimes the numbers differ from those corresponding in previous reports, the reason being given that errors made were subsequently discovered.

6. *1898 Report*, Apps. XVIII and XIX p. 28.

7. *1878-79 Report*, p. 72.

8. *1898 Report*, Preface, p. 8.

9. *1904 Report*, Preface, p. 6.

10. *1904 Report*, App. XX, pp. 28, 29.

11. *1898 Report*, Preface, p. 9.

12-15. ibid., p. 6. 'Our attention has been drawn to the last Reports of the Chief Constables of the Cities of Glasgow and Liverpool, which are in many respects similarly situated as regards population. In Glasgow, with a population of about 725,000, about 19,000 persons were taken into custody for drunkenness and 21,000 for breach of the peace and petty assaults, while in Liverpool, which has a population of about 630,000, the cases of drunkenness and disorder were only 4,339 and common assaults about 800.' *Report of the Prison Commissioners 1898-1904. 1898 Report*, Preface, p. 7.

16-19. *1904 Report*, Preface, pp. 5, 6, 5, 6.

20. *1898 Report*, App. XXII, p. 32.

21. *1884 Report* in vol. 1878-84, App. V, p. 29.

22. *1904 Report*, App. XVII, p. 26.

23. *1878 Report*, in vol. 1878-84, Preface, p. 7.

24. *1898 Report*, Preface, p. 10.

25. *1884 Report*, App. XI, pp. 38, 39.

26. ibid., App. XII, pp. 40, 41.

27. See Part I note 28 on Scottish prison diet.

28. App. no. VII, p. 24. *Rules issued by the Secretary of State under Prisons (S) Act 1877, 1878 Report* being First Annual Report of the Commissioners under Prisons (S) Act 1877.

29 & 30. ibid., pp. 24, 25, 25.

31. *1878 Report*, pp. 82, 83.

32. *Report of Medical Advisers to the Prison Commissioners for the year 1898* vol. 1898-1904, App. XXIX, p. 40.

33. *Report of Medical Advisers for 1904*, ibid., App. XXIV, p. 34.

34. ibid., App. XXVII, pp. 38-41.

35. *1878 Report* in vol. 1878-84, p. 84.

36 & 37. *1882-83 Report*, App. XXVI, p. 99.

38. *1879 Report*, Preface, p. 8.

39. *1898 Report*, Preface, p. 8.

40. *1904 Report*, Preface, p. 7.

41 & 42. *1883-4 Report*, Preface, p. 9.

43. *1898 Report*, Preface, pp. 7, 8.

44. *1904 Report*, Preface, pp. 7, 8.

45. *1880 Report*, App. VI, p. 22.

46. *1898 Report*, App. XIV, p. 23.

47. *1904 Report*, App. XIV, p. 23.

48. *1883 Report*, App. XIX, p. 82.

49. *1882-83 Report*, App. XXXI, p. 103.

50. *1883 Report*, App. XXXIV, p. 106.

51. *1898 Report*, App. XXXIX, p. 74.

Part III

1. S.H.D. File No. P.12295/6.
2. S.H.D. File No. P.12295/1.
3. S.H.D. File No. P.12295/8.
4 & 5. S.H.D. File No. P.12295/9.
6. S.H.D. File No. P.12295/4.

Chapter 7: Lunatics in Prison

* Dr Clouston, Craig House Hospital, 1894. *Focus on Change* (Pamphlet of the Royal Edinburgh Hospital) (1965) p. 17.

1. Christopher Hibbert: *The Roots of Evil: A Social History of Crime and Punishment* (Penguin 1966) p. 226.

2. John Howard: *State of the Prisons in England and Wales* with an account of some foreign prisons 1777, 1780 and 1784 (Everyman edition 1929) p. 6.

3. J. J. Gurney: *Notes on a visit made to some of the Prisons in Scotland and Northern England* (London 1819) pp. 109, 110; 19, 20; 39, 40.

4. James Neild: *State of the Prisons in England, Scotland and Wales, 1812*, pp. 401, 402.

5. *Second Report of the Directors of the Dundee Lunatic Asylum*, 1822, pp. 3, 4.

6. Printed statement *The Charity Workhouse and the City Bedlam* (in possession of Royal Edinburgh Hospital). The Charity Workhouse was opened in 1743, built by voluntary contributions and maintained by the Kirk Sessions from their collections and by the Town Council by their power of assessment under the Poor Law Act 1579.

7. *Focus on Change*, op. cit., p. 16.

8. ibid., p. 17.

9. David Peacock: *Perth: Its Annals and its Archives* (Perth 1849) p. 498.

10. George Penny: *Traditions of Perth* (Perth 1836) p. 269.

11. Hibbert, op. cit., p. 62.

12. *Report of Commissioners on Lunacy 1857*, Vol. II, p. 34.

13. *Memorandum of the General Board of Prisons, June 1859*, pp. 4, 8, 13, 18, 19, 20. (Lord Advocate's Papers on Lunacy, Letters & Reports, Box 89, West Register House.)

14. Letter to the Lord Advocate, April 1874. (Lord Advocate's Papers, Box 88.)

15. Memorandum on the Criminal Lunatics Bill 1884 by Dr Mill, ibid.

16. Rev. Henry Willox: *Her Majesty's Pleasure in Scotland and other matters concerning criminal lunatics and mental defectives of violent tendencies and criminal propensities* (Carnwath 1967) p. 64.

17. *State Hospital, Carstairs – The Scottish Special Hospital* (Paper prepared by State Hospital, February 1974) p. 1.

18. Willox, op. cit., p. 136.

19. *State Hospital paper*, op. cit., p. 2.

20. *Sunday Times* 4 March 1973.

21. *Evening Telegraph* 17 December 1970.

22. *Scotsman* 2 December 1976.

Chapter 8: The Twentieth Century

* Buxton, Sir T. Fowell: *Inquiry whether Crime and Misery are produced or prevented by our Present System of Prison Discipline* (London 1818) p. 22.

† See note 4.

1. Quoted by R. S. E. Hinde: *The British Penal System 1773-1950* (London 1951) p. 44.

2. J. Devon: *The Criminal and the Community* (1912).

3. J. E. Thomas: *The English Prison Officer since 1850; A study in conflict,* (London 1972) p. 157.

4-7. *Paterson on Prisons: collected papers of Sir Alexander Paterson* (London 1951) pp. 23, 96, 22.

8. J. Rae: *Conscience and Politics: The British Government and the C.O. to Military Service, 1916-1919* (London 1970) pp. 226, 103.

9. The famous Cat and Mouse Act of the suffragettes.

10. R. K. Middlemas: *The Clydesiders: A Left Wing Struggle for Parliamentary Power* (Hutchinson 1965) p. 68.

11. John McNair: *James Maxton: The Beloved Rebel* (Allen & Unwin 1955) p. 65.

12. David Kirkwood: *My Life of Revolt* (1935) p. 149.

13. *English Prisons Today: Being the Report of the Prison System Inquiry Committee.* Edited by S. Hobhouse and F. Brockway. (London 1922)

14 & 15. Paterson, op. cit., pp. 102, 105, 106.

16. Peter Wildeblood: *Against the Law* (London 1955) p. 154. The author was sentenced to eighteen months for homosexual offences.

17-19. Zeno: *Life* (Macmillan 1968) pp. 180, 19, 63. The author served nine years for murder.

20. *Life in the Scottish Prison Service.* (Foreword in pamphlet 1973.)

21-24. *Application for Appointment to Situation of Officer in Scottish Prison Service.* Enclosed notice to candidates No. 319 paras. 1, 15, 9. RE1673TBL.

25. ibid., and enclosed tests. No. 319 RE 20301 TBL. Test A asks the candidate to select the correct word or phrase and underline it:
   1) He { flewed
        { flew to America as this was more convenient
        { flied
        { in going by sea
        { than going by sea
        { from going by sea
   2) The { garbidge   litterring the street
         { garbage   was littering the street
         { garibage

26. *Sunday Times* 17 May 1970.

27-28. *Committee of Inquiry into the UK Prison Services,* October 1979 (*The May Report*), pp. 188, 215.

29. *Prison Service Journal* No. 12, new series (October 1973) p. 22.

30. Hugh Klare: *People in Prison* (Pitman's *Eye on Society* Series) p. 39.

31. *Programme on Prisons* Part I, 'The Screws', BBC 2, 10.10 pm, 20 February 1974.

32. *Scotsman* 5 May 1980.

33. Jessica Mitford: *Kind and Usual Punishment* (New York 1973) pp. 8, 9, 10.

34. *The Tasks of Penology: A Symposium on Prisons and Correctional Law*. Edited by H. S. Perlman and T. B. Allington. Chap. II, Nathan Leopold: 'What is wrong with the Prison System?' (University of Nebraska Press 1969) p. 36.

35. *Programme on Prisons*, op. cit.,

36. Wildeblood, op. cit., p. 159.

37. Zeno, op. cit., p. 55.

38. *The Organisation of Work for Prisoners* (H.M.S.O. 1964) p. 10, para. 35.

39. *Penal Practice in a Changing Society 1959* (reprinted 1966 H.M.S.O.) p. 14, para. 56.

40 & 41. ibid., p. 15 para. 65 and p. 17 para. 71.

42. *The Scottish Prison System* (H.M.S.O. 1949) p. 8.

43. *The Tasks of Penology*, op. cit., p. 31.

44. *The Scottish Prison System*: Report by the Scottish Advisory Council on the Treatment and Rehabilitation of Offenders. (H.M.S.O. 1949) p. 43.

45. *Prisons in Scotland, Report for 1980*, p. 20.

46. *Prisons in Scotland, Report for 1978*, p. 19, and *Report for 1980*, p. 22.

47. *People in Prison*, op. cit., p. 34, para. 70.

48. *The Scottish Prison System* (H.M.S.O. 1949) App. C, p. 40.

49. *People in Prison*, op. cit., p. 33, para. 67.

50. *Scotsman*, 11 April 1980.

51. *The May Report*, op. cit., pp. 30, 31.

52. *The Scottish Prison System* 1949, p. 32, para. 155.

53. R. Cross: *Punishment, Prison & the Public* (1971) p. 167.

54. *Prisons in Scotland, Report for 1972*, p. 1.

55. *Penal Practice in a Changing Society*, pp. 13, 14, para. 54.

56 & 57. Allan K. Taylor: *From a Glasgow Slum to Fleet Street* (London 1949) pp. 82, 136, 137.

58 & 59. Wildeblood, op. cit., pp. 142, 187.

60 & 61. Zeno, op. cit., pp. 190, 187.

62. *Sunday Times*, Colour Supplement, 'Portrait of a Criminal', Part II, 4 November 1973.

63. J. Boyle: *A Sense of Freedom* (Canongate 1977) pp. 128, 107, 246.

64. Nigel Walker: *Crime & Punishment in Britain* (E.U.P. 1965) p. 124.

65. *European Committee on Crime Problems: Collected Studies in Criminological Research*, Vol. 1, 'Research on the Prison Community'. Report presented by T. Morris, Reader in Sociology at the London School of Economics. (Council of Europe, Strasbourg 1967.)

66. Buxton, op. cit., p. 40.

67. *The Life of David Haggart*; 'a true account ... partly written by myself and partly taken down from my own lips while under Sentence of Death'. (1822) pp. 134, 135.

68. *Prison Service Journal*, No. 14, April 1974, p. 8.

69. *Programme on Prisons*, op. cit.

70. *Scotsman*, 7 April 1972.

71. Buxton, op. cit., pp. 15, 16.

72. *Prison Service Journal*, No. 14, op. cit., p. 7.

73. *Prison Service Journal*, Vol. X, No. 36, July 1970, p. 19.

74. Paterson, op. cit., p. 66.

75. Radzinowicz, *Sunday Times* 9 March 1969.

76. *Penalties for Homicide* (H.M.S.O. 1972) p. 19, para. 42.

77. *Journal of the Law Society of Scotland*, Vol. 15, No. 4 (April 1970) p. 81.

78. C. H. Rolph: *Homeless from Prison*. A Report on five hostels set up by the Special After-care Trust (London 1970) p. 5.

79. *Prisons in Scotland, Report for 1972*, p. 7, para. 27.

80. ibid., App. 18, p. 66.

81. *Prison Service Journal*, No. 14, April 1974, p. 11.

82. *Scotland, the Violent Nation. Scotsman* 9 March 1974.

83. *Scotsman* 1 May 1979.

84 & 85. ibid. 22 February 1977.

86. *Scotland, the Violent Nation*, op. cit.; and Chief Constable of Aberdeen quoted in *Sunday Telegraph* 31 March 1974.

87. *Prisons in Scotland, Report for 1978*, p. 67.

88. *Scotsman* 12 November 1979.

89. George Jackson: *Soledad Brother. The Prison Letters of George Jackson* (Penguin 1971) pp. 49, 35.

90. *A Bill of No Rights. Attica & the American Prison System* (New York 1972) p. 9. At Attica Prison, N.Y. State, in 1971, 26 prisoners and 9 hostages died in a four-day prison riot, and 83 prisoners were wounded in the bloodiest prison rebellion ever seen in the U.S.A. Most of the prisoners were black or Puerto Rican.

91. *Reparation by the Offender to the Victim in Scotland* (the Dunpark Committee 1977).

92. ibid., p. 6, para. 2.06.

93. *The Dangerous Offender: A Consultative document* prepared by the Floud Committee, and issued by the Institute of Criminology, University of Cambridge (March 1977).

94. *Fifteenth Report from the Expenditure Committee: Session 1977–78: The Reduction of Pressure on the Prison System*. (H.M.S.O. 662–I) Vol. I, p. xxiii.

95. For attempting to escape from Gartree Prison, Sewell (who is serving a life sentence, recommended 30 years, for killing a policeman) was punished by losing privileges for 760 days, was given 392 days of non-associated labour

and 56 days loss of earnings. This means that for 760 days Sewell was locked in his cell every evening after work, and for 392 days worked alone in his cell; the loss of earnings meant that for 56 days he was unable to buy anything. *Scotsman* 19 December 1972. There are no figures available on the number of British prisoners in solitary confinement and how long they have been there.

96. Bread-and-water prison punishment was abolished in British prisons in May 1974.

97. *The May Report* op. cit., p. 125.

98. ibid., p. 261.

Conclusion

1. *Committee of Inquiry into the United Kingdom Prison Services, October 1979.* (The May Report) p. 7.

2. J. E. Thomas: *The English prison officer since 1850. A study in conflict.* (London 1972) p. 1.

3. Rupert Cross: *Punishment, Prison and the Public* (London 1971) p. 169.

4. Karl Menninger: *The Crime of Punishment* (New York 1971) p. 223.

5. *Programme on Prisons* Part I 'The Screws', BBC 2, 10.10 pm, 20 February 1974.

6. 'I am personally in no doubt that the value and virtue of any penalty imposed upon a person convicted of such a crime' (violence and vicious crimes against the person) 'must be judged primarily by the extent to which it can be expected to achieve the purposes of deterrence and prevention ... the judges will not hesitate to continue to use their ample powers to discourage the criminal and to protect society against him and his kind to the maximum extent possible.' Lord Emslie's address to the Law Society of Scotland, 'The Role of Judges in Society in Scotland', *Journal of the Law Society of Scotland* July 1974, vol. 19, no. 7, p. 208.

7. Attempted suicide was not a crime in Scotland whereas in England, until recently, it was.

8. Hugh Klare: *People in Prison* (Pitman 1973) p. 137.

9. *Journal of the Law Society of Scotland* April 1970, vol. 15, no. 4, p. 81.

Postscript

1. Radzinowicz: *Spectator* 23 July 1977.

2. *Inmate Guide. Suffolk County Jail, Boston, Massachusetts.* pp. 2, 3.

3. *The Boston Globe* 3 September 1973.

Index

Perth General Prison—*cont.*
  Criminal Lunatic Department, 176,
    178
  death rates, 146
  diet, 103–5, 137–8
  diseases, 105–6, 146
  established as central prison, 99, 122
  health of prisoners, 111
  Lunatic Department, 103, 104, 112,
    153, 166–7, 174, 175, 176
    accommodation, 153
    staffing, 110
  numbers of prisoners, 111, 174–5
  punishments, 107–8, 112–13
  riot at, 113–4
  salary bills (1868), 109–10
             (1884), 144
  staffing, 108, 109–10, 144
  suicides at, 103, 104
  visitors to, 108–9
  see also Governors' *Journals of the*
    General Prison at Perth
Perth Kirk Session Records, 26
Perth Museum, 80, 159
Perth Old Jail, 9–10, 50, 64
Perth Spey Tower Prison, 10
Perth Steeple Prison, 33
Peterhead Prison, 149, 194, 202, 203
  employment at, 230
  establishment of, 153–4
  present-day conditions, 228
  recommended redevelopment, 218
Philadelphia Penitentiaries, 95–8
pit prisons
  medieval Scotland, 6–7
Pitcairn, Robert
  Criminal trials in Scotland (*1484–*
    1624), 12–13, 33
Pittsburg, 95
Plymouth Prison, 70
political prisoners
  medieval Scotland, 11
  seventeenth-century, 34
  see also Covenanters; Jacobites
Poor Law Commission Enquiry for
    Scotland, 168
Portsmouth Prison
  and penal servitude, 126
poverty
  in medieval Scotland, 13
pre-release courses, 204
Prison Acts, *see* Acts of Parliament
prison buildings, 151–6
  Aberdeen, 152–3
  Dumfries, 31, 155
  Glasgow, 155

Inverness, 32–3, 151–2
medieval, 7
'Panopticon', 47
Perth General Prison, 99, 153
Peterhead, 153–4
recent recommendations, 218
sixteenth-century, 31–5
Prison Commission for England, 126–7
Prison Commission for Scotland, 126–
  7
Prison Commissioners for Scotland,
  128
  reports (1878–1904), 141–9
prison conditions
  and penal servitude, 130–3
  at turn of century, 140–50
  eighteenth-century England, 44
  eighteenth-century Scotland, 49–67
  for conscientious objectors, 187–8
  Greenock Prison (1834–64), 114–17
  in Glasgow Prison (1912), 185
  in Scotland (1840), 100–3
  Oscar Wilde on, 134–5
  Perth General Prison (1845–65),
    103–14
  present-day, 226–34
  seventeenth-century Scotland, 29–
    30
  W. B. Neville on, 135–7, 138–9
  see also bedding; clothing; diet in
    prison
prison officers, 191–6
  motivation, 195
  qualities required, 192–3
  training, 193
  working conditions, 191–2, 193, 219
  views quoted, 208, 225–6
  see also jailers; warders
Prison Service College Museum, Polmont, 112, 202
Prison System Inquiry Committee
  (1919), 190
prisoners
  characteristics, 144, 226
  classification of, 99, 204
  views quoted
    on prison officers, 191–2
    on rehabilitation, 206–7
prisoners of war in Britain, 70–89
  accommodation for, 70–3
  amusements of, 83–5
  as craftsmen, 79
  attitudes to, 87
  behaviour of, 78–9
  conditions of, 77
  clothing for, 73, 77, 82